Cicero's Social
and Political Thought

Cicero's Social and Political Thought

Neal Wood

University of California Press

Berkeley · Los Angeles · Oxford

University of California Press
Berkeley and Los Angeles, California
University of California Press, Ltd.
Oxford, England
© 1988 by
The Regents of the University of California

Printed in the United States of America

1 2 3 4 5 6 7 8 9

First Paperback Printing 1991

Library of Congress Cataloging in Publication Data
Wood, Neal.
  Cicero's social and political thought.

  Bibliography: p.
  Includes index.
  1. Cicero, Marcus Tullius—Political and social views.
  2. Cicero, Marcus Tullius—Contemporary Rome.
  3. Rome—Politics and government—265–30 B.C.
  4. Rome—Social conditions. I. Title.
PA6320.W66 1988   937′.05′0924   87-5968
ISBN 0-520-07427-0 (pbk.)
ISBN 0-520-06042-3 (cloth)

For Ellen again

To be ignorant of what occurred before you were born is to remain always a child. For what is the worth of human life, unless it is woven into the life of our ancestors by the records of history?

Cicero, *Orator*, 120

Contents

Preface

I have written this study—to my knowledge the first if its kind in English—out of a conviction that Cicero the social and political thinker deserves far more attention than he has received in recent years, when few any longer read him. Long-standing concerns with the history of political theory and classical antiquity and my previous work on John Locke led me quite naturally to Cicero. My interpretation of his ideas rests on a reading of his voluminous writings in their historical setting. Lengthy references to secondary sources and discussion of them have been kept to a minimum. Much remains to be assayed. So, for example, little in the following has been done to relate in detail Cicero's thought to the contexts of Roman law and rhetoric or to his own legal and rhetorical views; and the intellectual origins of his conceptions have been touched upon only briefly. I shall be content if students, social scientists, and the general public are further encouraged to think about Cicero, a process of enlightenment already begun by the stimulating scholarship of W. K. Lacey, T. N. Mitchell, Elizabeth Rawson, and D. R. Shackleton Bailey.

The research and writing of the book were virtually completed during a sabbatical leave in 1979–1980 and a leave of absence in 1983–1984, for which free periods I am obligated to York University. Various commitments and circumstances, however, delayed immediate preparation for publication. Some of my opinions on Cicero have already circulated. Two papers were read: "Cicero and the Modern Concept of the State," at the annual meeting, organized by Bernard Crick, of the British Conference for the Study of Political Thought, New College, Oxford, January, 1980;

and "Cicero on Violence in Politics," at the Department of Political Science Colloquium of York University, arranged by Douglas V. Verney, in the autumn of 1980. The friendly and construc-
tive criticisms of both papers at these meetings have been of
considerable value. Passages from the book have been taken from
my article "The Economic Dimension of Cicero's Political
Thought: Property and State," *Canadian Journal of Political Science* 16 (1983): 739–56. In addition, I have pursued some of my
thoughts in "*Populares* and *Circumcelliones*: The Vocabulary of
'Fallen Man' in Cicero and St. Augustine," *History of Political
Thought* 7 (1986): 33–51, the issue of the journal being a *Fest-
schrift* in honor of Herbert A. Deane, edited by Maurice M. Goldsmith and Thomas A. Horne.

A book of this kind is in no small part a collective effort resting
on the selfless labor of others, who of course are in no way responsible for the deficiencies of the outcome. For the very helpful
suggestions and comments on various drafts I am immensely indebted to Herbert A. Deane of Columbia University; Cary J.
Nederman of the University of Canterbury, Christchurch, New
Zealand; and the two anonymous readers of the University of
California Press. As usual my debt to Ellen Meiksins Wood—this
is my second book dedicated to her—is unrepayable. Cheerfully
accepting the burden of a critical reading at a most busy time, her
unfailing interest throughout the tedium of gestation and composition, acute and perceptive suggestions, and constant encouragement rendered the project possible. Once again I have been
fortunate to benefit from the skillful copyediting of Jane-Ellen
Long of the University of California Press, who saved me from
numerous errors and tidied up my prose. Several years ago George
Comninel did some research for me on a matter related to this
book for which I am most grateful. For the irksome chores in
preparing a manuscript for press I wish to thank Joanne Boucher
and Thom Workman of York University. Mrs. Sybil Rang of
Hampstead, London, good-naturedly typed an early draft. A special thank-you is due Mrs. Florence Knight of Toronto for her
invariably accurate and speedy typing. The final draft was done
on short notice with her customary efficiency and amiable support
by Ruth Griffin of Glendon College. The secretarial staff of York

University's Department of Political Science came to my rescue as always at the most awkward times for them and for me. Over the years my undergraduate and graduate students at York have subjected many of my views on Cicero to rigorous scrutiny, for which I owe them more than they can imagine.

Neal Wood
Toronto
March, 1987

Note on the Sources

Latin texts of Cicero's works and letters (with the exception of the ones to Atticus) are those of the Loeb Classical Library, as are all translations, with occasional changes. For the correspondence with Atticus, D. R. Shackleton Bailey's *Cicero's Letters to Atticus* (Cambridge, England: Cambridge University Press, 1965–1970), 7 vols., has been used. His notational system has been employed in the relevant footnotes. Both his *Letters to Atticus* and *Letters to His Friends* are in convenient single-volume paperback editions published by Penguin in 1978. All titles of Cicero's works have been rendered into English in the text. Latin abbreviations, usually of a conventional nature, appear in the notes. Some abbreviations have been adopted for the sake of convenience: *Att., Letters to Atticus; Q.F., Letters to His Brother Quintus; M.B., Letters to Marcus Brutus; Fam., Letters to His Friends.*

CHAPTER ONE

Introduction:
Cicero's Significance

Why should anyone today be concerned with the social and political ideas of the late Roman republican thinker and statesman
Marcus Tullius Cicero? Is it not flailing a dead horse? Cicero's
merit as philosopher has been so deflated and his popularity as
sage and stylist has so declined that the endeavor would appear
to be without intellectual or practical merit. Who today troubles
to read Cicero, save a handful of Latinists and ancient historians,
and an ever-diminishing number of students? Yet despite the many
alterations in mentality and literary taste over the last two centuries, there are several good reasons for examining his social and
political views and introducing them to an English-speaking audience. He is, after all, the only Roman republican social and political thinker of supreme importance, and if we are to recapture
something of the experience of the Roman state, structure of rule,
and cast of mind, his many works are a rich source and an indispensable guide. Ancient social and political thought is Roman
as well as Greek, including Cicero and St. Augustine in addition
to Plato and Aristotle; and from the standpoint of a fuller understanding of modern political culture, the Roman element is of
crucial significance. Whatever Cicero's reputation today, he was
deeply admired by eminent social and political thinkers of early
modern Europe. He was to that epoch what Aristotle had been
to the late medieval world of ideas: an inspiring, informative, and
illuminating preceptor. Cicero may be all but forgotten, but in the
period of our past that gave rise to distinctly modern institutions
and attitudes, he of all ancients was possibly the most esteemed

and influential. Apart from these considerations, however, some of Cicero's ideas, because of their originality and insight, deserve more attention than they have hitherto been accorded.

A brief summary of Cicero's rise and fall in modern Europe can for our purposes commence with the Renaissance.[1] Once the *Letters to Atticus* were uncovered by Petrarch in 1345, to be followed by the discoveries of the *Familiar Letters* by Salutati and the legal speeches by Bracciolini, Cicero began to be seen in a new light. He was no longer solely the moderate and self-disciplined savant whom he had been to his many medieval readers, but a genuine human being and statesman. For the humanists he became a venerated teacher of civic virtue, the staunch republican apostle of liberty and relentless foe of tyranny; and until the early Cinquecento, a stylistic model affecting in form and content works of the stature of Castiglione's *Il Cortegiano*. In sixteenth-century schools of Italy, France, and England, Cicero's writings were read and studied: the letters, the orations, *On Friendship, On Old Age,* and *On Duties*. While his style was increasingly to be criticized, most notably at the beginning of the sixteenth century by Erasmus, and a preference was shown for Seneca and Tacitus, Cicero continued to be a highly respected thinker. Like other humanists, Machiavelli had closely studied Cicero.[2] Given the Florentine's dedication to republicanism and liberty, his love for ancient Rome, emphasis on civic virtue, and recommendation of the mixed constitution, he undoubtedly recognized the authority of the Roman, although rejecting him as a literary mentor and on numerous substantial issues.[3] Cicero was also a cherished figure in Renaissance France. That he was the "patron saint" of French civic humanism should be obvious not only from the theorizing of Jean Bodin but also from the writings of lesser intellects.[4]

Cicero's prose style declined in reputation in the seventeenth century; nevertheless, he continued to be widely read and honored. The father of international law, Hugo Grotius, was a self-acknowledged disciple of the ancient. Hobbes objected to Cicero's republicanism and doctrines of the mixed constitution and tyrannicide but owed much to his views on ideal imitation and imagination and referred in his 1629 translation of Thucydides to the *Orator* as an authority for the writing of history.[5] A contemporary of Hobbes, James Harrington, whose *Commonwealth of Oceana* appeared five years after the publication of *Leviathan*, thought highly of Cicero for the very reasons that he was either explicitly or implicitly criticized by Hobbes. The English "classical republicans" like Harrington and his disciples, John Neville and Algernon Sidney, spawned a "commonwealth" tradition of "real whigs" extending well into the next century, a time in which, as we shall see, Cicero's popularity reached its zenith. Perhaps no seventeenth-century English political thinker was more indebted to Cicero than John Locke. Seldom generous in his praise of others, Locke included Cicero among the "truly great men," possibly treasuring him above all authors. The judgment of the distinguished French scholar Raymond Polin is that Cicero was an important influence on Locke's thought. Significant differences between the ideas of the two thinkers certainly exist, but Cicero undoubtedly proved to be an illuminating teacher on a number of subjects.[6]

The peak of Cicero's authority and prestige came during the eighteenth-century Enlightenment. In terms of the enthusiastic revival of interest in classical antiquity, it was a Ciceronian century. Unquestionably Cicero was a leading culture-hero of the age: revered as a great philosopher and superb stylist, hailed as a distinguished popularizer, and praised as a humanistic skeptic who scourged superstition; a courageous statesman and dedicated patriot, the ardent defender of liberty against tyranny. Voltaire, Montesquieu, and Diderot were effusive in their compliments, and even Rousseau, who could be critical, dubbed him the "Prince of Eloquence."[7] The esteem for Cicero was widely shared by French revolutionaries, of all shades of opinion from Mirabeau to Robespierre, who relished his skepticism, republicanism, and libertarianism. The British during the Enlightenment were no less captivated by Cicero than the French. It was a period of accomplished Ciceronian stylists and orators: Gibbon, Burke, Johnson, Pitt, Fox, Sheridan. Conyers Middleton's best-selling two-volume work, *The History of the Life of Marcus Tullius Cicero,* appeared in 1741, and several translations of Cicero's writings were issued.[8] David Hume and Adam Smith were particular admirers, but perhaps there was no more devoted Ciceronian, as to both literary style and ideas, than Edmund Burke, whose thought has been called "a Cicero filtered through the Christian scholastic tradition."[9] Just as the Enlightenment was not confined to Europe, so Cicero's high status among French and British thinkers was at least equalled by the regard of the American founding fathers. As in Europe recognition of Cicero cut across political divisions, so it was in America: for example, both John Adams and Thomas Jefferson were inspired by him. All evidence seems to validate a recent verdict that "among the numerous classical rôle models in America . . . pride of place was given above all to Cicero."[10] American constitutionalists, no less than French revolutionaries a decade later, thought of themselves as heirs to the Roman republicans and most appropriately looked to their greatest political thinker, the cultured statesman and *pater patriae,* for tutelage in the colossal task of founding a new order.

What, then, is the explanation for the spectacular popularity and influence of Cicero throughout the early modern era? He profoundly affected thinkers of different, even contrary social and political persuasion, some "conservative" and others "radical," with all tinctures of view in between. They seem to have taken from him what they wished to underpin their own differing positions, ignoring the more uncongenial aspects of his thought. Among the most obvious social/political and related elements that they selectively exploited in manifold ways were the principles of natural law and justice and of universal moral equality; a patriotic and dedicated republicanism; a vigorous advocacy of liberty, impassioned rejection of tyranny, and persuasive justification of tyrannicide; a firm belief in constitutionalism, the rule of law, and the mixed constitution; a strong faith in the sanctity of private property, in the importance of its accumulation, and the opinion that the primary purpose of state and law was the preservation of property and property differentials; a conception of proportionate social and political equality, entailing a hierarchy of differential rights and duties; a vague ideal of rule by a "natural aristocracy"; and a moderate and enlightened religious and epistemological skepticism.

Far from being new, some of these ideas had been voiced by other ancient seers. Yet the particular conjunction of such ideas in Cicero's works, often presented with greater clarity and precision than they were elsewhere, and always in an elegant and persuasive rhetorical style, must have been especially seductive to early modern readers. Perhaps it was his very eclecticism that drew so many to his writings; perhaps it was his rationalism, his constant appeal to reason, his reliance on argumentation, canvassing opposing points of view, and weighing one against the other. Whatever the reasons, he had several advantages over other ancient thinkers. His writings, with some exceptions, had physically survived the vicissitudes of time and fortune, more so than was true of any other single Roman republican thinker; and he managed to combine social and political ingredients drawn from many sources into some kind of detailed and not entirely inconsistent whole, articulated in unsurpassed prose. Many of the ideas of important Greek thinkers are known solely through his works. Of the Greek philosophers, of course, only the works of Plato and Aristotle rival if they do not surpass his own for survival value. But even here, Cicero can be seen to have an edge in respect to a potential for popularity among the early moderns. For unlike the surviving works of the two Greek philosophers, Cicero's voluminous corpus of extant correspondence could and did reveal to modern readers many of the most intimate thoughts, feelings, and actions of a private life—an all too human philosopher and statesman—at a time when the educated were bent on self-discovery, when biographies, autobiographies, memoirs, and novels began to express a new individuality. While Europeans were increasingly reflecting on themselves and their society and natural setting, Cicero was perhaps just the type of *uomo universale* who might be most attractive. To the polymath of early modernity, from Bodin to Hume and Jefferson, striving for orientation and self-realization on a new frontier, who could be more enticing than Cicero: youthful poet, consummate literary artist, versatile man of letters, philosophic educator, eloquent orator, brilliant advocate, witty and urbane cosmopolite, perceptive statesman, possible acquaintance of Lucretius, friend of Varro, and enemy of Caesar?

Cicero's acclaim was aided no doubt by his writing in Latin, which had become the *lingua franca* of educated European gentlemen. The fact that he was an eminent Roman lawyer perhaps added to his luster with the revival of Roman law and its spread as the basis of most European legal systems, and the increasing prominence of jurists. Moreover, the vernacular of government and politics was basically derived from Latin, and given the emergence of the modern state, the rise of absolutism, the notion of sovereignty, and the development of international law, Cicero's works must have been avidly read, for they were encyclopedic in political and legal terms, definitions, and concepts. When nebulous republican sentiments were crystallizing in reaction to the despotism of kingly rule and attaining fruition in an earth-shattering way, who could be turned to for instruction if not the most famous republican and foe of tyranny in all of antiquity? Conversely, traditionalists like Montesquieu and Burke, who yearned for a return to the ancestral constitution, could find solid comfort in the conservatism of the Roman. The fact that he offered something for everyone, however, should not blind us to his true social and political outlook.

This may go some way in accounting for Cicero's fame and authority among early moderns, but then the further question of the reasons for his downfall and discredit in the nineteenth century arises. If, as Kant wrote in his well-known essay, the Enlightenment was the attainment of the age of reason, a coming of age of Europeans previously in bondage to superstition and traditional authority, much of the enchantment and novelty of this "youthful" questioning and self-examination had worn away by the next century. Educated Europeans had to some extent freed themselves from the past without, however, losing their optimism and faith in human progress. Moreover, the gentlemanly values of Cicero, so much a part of precapitalist agrarian society and landed class, were rendered anachronistic by the rapid economic and demographic changes in Western Europe. The rise of capitalism, the abuses and deprivations brought about by a growing industrialism and urbanization, the mobilization of a massive factory work force laboring and living under the most onerous physical conditions led to demands for social justice and democracy. Socialism and the labor movement were born. Under such circumstances, Cicero, the sworn enemy of popular rule, the implacable foe of social amelioration and economic reform, a leader of the Roman landed oligarchy who decried any drift toward arithmetical equality or social parity, could hardly have attracted the intellectual spokesmen of the new impetus for fundamental change. The reaction of the young Marx in 1839 was perhaps typical of the altering evaluation of the Roman. Although using the *Republic,* the *Laws,* and *On Duties* for anthropological data, young Marx wrote that Cicero "knew as little about philosophy as about the president of the United States of North America."[11]

But in the very circles that feared the mounting pressures from below for basic social reform, other forces helped to deflate Cicero's former reputation. During a time of unprecedented practical inventiveness and great artistic and intellectual genius, the century of Goethe and Hegel, Balzac and Dickens, Darwin and Faraday, Beethoven and Wagner, and Marx and Nietzsche, prized originality far beyond the popularization of time-honored ideas. When positivism and agnosticism were spreading among the intellectuals, the pompous, pretentious, and long-winded moralizing of Cicero was simply alienating, out of harmony with the prevailing zeitgeist. In England ancient Greece was rediscovered, and Hellenism was being forwarded by the historical efforts of William Mitford, Connop Thirlwall, and George Grote. All this prodigious work on Greece left little room for Cicero and Rome. Moreover, Plato was resurrected by Grote, and Benjamin Jowett continued the work at Balliol, translating the dialogues of the philosopher and molding the minds of a generation of distinguished political figures.

German scholars, on the other hand, after the earlier Hellenism of Fichte, Lessing, Schelling, Hegel, Boeckh, and Winckelmann, became entranced with Rome and less concerned with the particularism of Greece, largely in response to the persisting political fragmentation of their own nation. The landmark of the tendency was Theodor Mommsen's *Roman History* (1854–1856), a detailed and sweeping analysis inaugurating modern Roman studies and dealing a final blow to the prestige of Cicero. A dedicated liberal, Mommsen saw his hopes for German unity dashed in the failure of 1848. He discovered in Julius Caesar the charismatic hero who had brought order into the chaos of the last days of the Republic by checking the divisive activities of the Roman mob and the oligarchic reactionaries. Thus Caesar founded what Mommsen took to be a strong and enlightened regime of moderation. Just such a figure, he believed, was needed to unify Germany by curbing the masses and the Junkers. As viewed by Mommsen, Cicero was a second-rate, indecisive, disruptive politician and muddled thinker who paled beside the clear-minded, purposeful, and magnetic Caesar, a brilliant and cultured leader in war and peace. Cicero's reputation has never recovered from the stresses and shifts in fashion of the nineteenth century, despite such attempts to rehabilitate him as Zielinski's classic reply in 1912 to both Mommsen and his equally anti-Ciceronian predecessor, Wilhelm Drumann.

Today Cicero is seldom taken very seriously except by classicists. As one might expect, he is praised by them for being one of the most indispensable and richest mines of knowledge about the late Roman Republic; for having popularized ancient political and philosophic ideas that might otherwise have been lost, thus preserving them for posterity; and perhaps above all for his literary style and culture. So Gilbert Highet writes that he was "the greatest master of prose who ever lived."[12] For R. G. M. Nisbet, he also "was the greatest prose stylist who ever lived . . . with the single exception of Plato"; and J. P. V. D. Balsdon labels him "perhaps the most civilized man who has ever lived."[13] Many, however, while not disputing these estimates, are inclined to agree with Sir Frederick Pollock's verdict in the popular *Introduction to the History of the Science of Politics* (1890): "Nobody that I know of has yet succeeded in discovering a new idea in the whole of Cicero's philosophical and semi-philosophical writings."[14] This evaluation in one form or another is reproduced ad nauseam in later widely read commentaries on European political thought, one of the more recent being that of Mulford Q. Sibley: "Cicero was neither an original nor a particularly profound social and political thinker."[15] Apparently the last book-length study in any language on his political ideas was published over eighty years ago in Berlin.[16] No book on his social and political thought has appeared in English. The nearest thing to it is the lengthy introduction by G. H. Sabine and S. B. Smith to their translation of the *Republic*, entitled *On the Commonwealth*, originally issued half a century ago and reprinted in 1976.[17] Their essay discusses his political thought in general, although concentrating on the *Laws* and especially the *Republic*. Reference is made to a broad range of the other works including *On Duties*, but little effort is made to discuss their most important ideas. In regard to the *Republic* and *Laws*, they conclude: "their noble insistence that it is the duty of all men to serve their country, in their inculcation of the principles of justice and fair-dealing, in their recognition of the universal society, founded upon reason and including all rational beings within its ambit . . . denotes an advance in political thinking."[18]

Sabine and Smith's stress on Cicero's views on natural law, justice, and equality is repeated in most subsequent popular commentaries, where these subjects are treated in highly abbreviated form to the exclusion of other aspects of his social and political thought so greatly admired in the past. Such works are ample testimony to a depressing aspect of intellectual life: the sterile repetition from generation to generation of a stereotyped interpretation of a specific thinker without deviation or spirit of critical inquiry. Perhaps another reason for the cool reception given to Cicero's social and political ideas has been that the relevant commentators are either philosophers or imbued primarily with a philosophic instead of an historical approach. Since Cicero is not much of a philosopher, philosophers who study him are customarily dismissive, neglecting his non-philosophic ideas. Yet his crucial social and political ideas basically fall outside the strictly philosophic sphere.

Of nearly two dozen commentaries and anthologies of source materials widely used at various times in this century by English-speaking students of social and political thought, two omit any consideration of Cicero whatsoever.[19] Only one adequately discusses Cicero on private property and its relationship to the state, a mere three take *On Duties* seriously, and one deals with the question of tyranny and tyrannicide.[20] Little if any attention is devoted to his conception of the state. The doctrine of the mixed constitution, if it is mentioned, receives no rigorous examination, nor is the reader ever given an adequate impression of Cicero's conception of the activity of politics.[21] In the main, the many analyses have been cast in the Sabine-Smith mold. Suggestive of the almost total lack of interest among social scientists in Cicero's thought is the absence of an article on him in the *International Encyclopedia of the Social Sciences,* published in 1965 to replace the *Encyclopedia of the Social Sciences* of 1930.[22] For the earlier work, Sabine wrote the essay (slightly longer than one column) on Cicero, with a conclusion similar to the one he and Smith had reached the previous year.[23] We can only surmise that for the social sciences today, Cicero is of little or no significance.

A matter of further interest in regard to Cicero's dismissal by contemporary social science deserves attention. At the beginning of the century, in the first volume of the Carlyles' valuable study, A. J. Carlyle remarked that Cicero was the dividing line between the ancient Greek political ideas of Plato and Aristotle and modern political thought.[24] Thirty years later, Charles H. McIlwain stated his agreement with Carlyle, for, in the case of Cicero, "we are plainly in the presence of the beginnings of 'modern' political thought," an opinion apparently shared by Sabine in 1937 in his widely read and exceedingly influential *History of Political Theory*.[25] The reasons originally given by Carlyle for his estimate, approved by McIlwain and Sabine, were Cicero's doctrine of natural law and justice, his stress on moral equality, and his conception of the state. On this latter subject little or nothing is said by way of explanation. More recently, Cumming in a brilliant but frequently overlooked two-volume examination of the intellectual roots of John Stuart Mill's liberalism, *Human Nature and History* (1969), also accepts the pronouncement of Carlyle, while rejecting his reasons. Cumming interestingly argues that Polybius and Cicero can rightly be called the co-founders of modern political thought. Polybius made history the context for treating social and political problems, thereby influencing the Continental tradition of political thought that included Machiavelli, Bodin, and Montesquieu. In contrast, Cumming maintains, Cicero's postulation of human nature as the basis for considering social and political matters shaped the British tradition of Hobbes, Locke, and Hume. The historical and psychological modes of analysis were joined in the liberal outlook of Mill.

It is not my purpose either to discuss or challenge the Carlyle-McIlwain-Sabine and Cumming theses, but instead to learn from them and to use them as perceptive points of departure. What can be accepted from both positions is that Cicero, for whatever reasons, represents a new direction for social and political thought. Perhaps "transition to modern political thought" is preferable to "beginnings of modern political thought." Cicero is obviously ancient in values and viewpoint. A republican anti-monarchist with no notion of political representation, he upheld the traditional virtues of a warrior class (glory, magnanimity, nobility, courage, and liberality), condemned manual labor and accepted slavery as a matter of course, and reflected an agrarian precapitalist mentality on economic concerns. At the same time, however, he began to fashion and articulate certain ideas that were to be much more fully developed in the early modern period and in many ways to become the focus of social and political speculation.

Cicero may have been a mediocre philosopher, unoriginal and eclectic, but to say this is not to suggest an absence of anything new and valuable in his thought. Can it be that such a brilliant advocate and learned student of philosophy, who alone of all major social and political thinkers attained the summit of political power as consul of the Roman Republic in 63 B.C., and who influenced so many illustrious minds—among them, Bodin, Grotius, Harrington, Locke, Montesquieu, Hume, Adam Smith, and Burke—should have had so little of significance to say about society and politics as to warrant neglect by most social scientists at the end of the twentieth century? There can be no question of the importance of his transmission to the early modern era of the Stoic conceptions of natural law and justice and of universal moral equality. But his claim to distinction would seem to rest on more than simply being a middleman or broker of such influential ideas.

More than any other ancient thinker he foreshadowed some of the views that were to be basic to the early modern conception of the state whose principal architects were Machiavelli, Bodin, Grotius, Hobbes, and Locke. Cicero was the first major social and political thinker of antiquity to offer a concise formal definition of the state. He was also the first to stress private property, its crucial role in society, and the importance of the state for its protection. In other words he gave to the state, with reservations, a central non-moral purpose. For Cicero the state exists primarily to safeguard private property and the accumulation of property, not to shape human souls according to some ethical ideal of the virtuous. He was the first major social and political thinker to distinguish clearly state from government, and to begin in a very rudimentary fashion to separate conceptually state from society, ideas that were to become hallmarks of the early modern conception of the state. He was the first thinker, as one might expect of an adroit master of the political art, to be concerned with the mechanics of politics, with political tactics and strategy, and with the serious problem of the role of violence in political life. He was the first thinker to devote considerable attention to the details of governmental economic policy: to public credit, taxation, the cancellation of debts, distribution of corn to the urban poor, land reform, and agrarian colonization. After him Bodin was the first to deal comprehensively with problems of economic policy, to be followed by the even greater concern of John Locke. Cicero was really the first major thinker who can be called a thoroughgoing and systematic constitutionalist, a dedicated upholder of the rule of law, conceiving of government as a trust with a sacred responsibility to the governed, and advocating civil resistance to tyranny. Although he was definitely not the first proponent of proportionate equality or theorist of the mixed constitution, he related the two in a fairly precise way; and perhaps more clearly than most ancient thinkers, including Polybius, he expounded the doctrine of a governmental mixture and the basic assumptions on which it rested. Permeating his reflections on all these subjects was a marked moral, economic, and political individualism—possibly in part reflective of the social atomism of his age—that was so uncharacteristic of the thought of Plato and Aristotle and was to be such a pronounced trait of much of the early modern social and political outlook. No wonder that his writings were so carefully studied by the leading theorists of that time.

In light of these reasons for calling Cicero a social and political thinker of significance, a grave injustice seems to have been committed in our own century by relegating him to the obscurity of unoriginal popularizer and philosopher hardly worthy of the name. He is decidedly not one of the greatest social and political thinkers of our culture, if by "greatest" we have in mind Plato, Aristotle, Hobbes, Locke, Rousseau, Hegel, and Marx. On the basis of his accomplishments, however, he is certainly entitled to a place with major political thinkers of the second rank: Machiavelli, Hume, Bodin, Montesquieu, Burke, and J. S. Mill.

To whatever status Cicero is assigned, the intention of this book is to stimulate an awareness among inquiring social scientists of his social and political thought. Political scientists, sociologists, non-classical historians, and specialists on social and political theory can ill afford to overlook his ideas, their relationship to his age, or their profound influence throughout the centuries. Classicists and historians of ancient Rome have perhaps little to learn in detail about Cicero, yet no single work published by them treats the range of questions addressed below. No claim in what follows is made to being particularly original, exhaustive, or erudite. Much of it is a synthesis of Cicero's views, neither breaking new scholarly ground in respect to the origins of his thought nor investigating those origins. Nevertheless, these pages will be justified if a curiosity about Cicero's social and political ideas is aroused in those who have never taken him intellectually very seriously or even troubled to read him.

Ciceronian Society

1. *The Changing Social Structure*

Polybius, who witnessed the destruction of Carthage in 146 B.C. in the company of his friend the Roman commander Scipio Aemilianus Africanus Minor, begins his great history of the Republic by stating his purpose: "For who is so worthless or indolent as not to wish to know by what means and under what system of polity the Romans in less than fifty-three years have succeeded in subjecting nearly the whole inhabited world to their sole government—a thing unique in history?"[1] He apparently was thinking of the period from just before the outbreak of the Second Punic or Hannibalic War (218–202 B.C.) to the victory of the Romans over Macedonia and Greece at the Battle of Pydna in 167 B.C. Polybius might well be astonished at the spectacular Roman achievement of world conquest since at the onset of the third century, in which these events unfolded—that is, on the eve of the First Punic War (262–242 B.C.)—the Roman territorial state was scarcely more than a rural backwater.[2] It was small in area, about the size of ancient Sparta, some three times larger than classical Attica, and culturally undistinguished. Rome's remarkable military prowess had slowly pushed forward its frontiers in perpetual strife with predatory neighbors from the time of the legendary foundation by Romulus and Remus nearly five hundred years before. It was a densely populated state of probably fewer than several hundred thousand male adult citizens, the overwhelming proportion of whom were impoverished and underemployed peasants eking out a living in an agrarian subsistence economy without adequate coinage. Landed holdings were extremely modest in extent. The majority of the primitive peasantry were probably freeholders, cultivating their own acreage. The best land seems to have been divided into relatively small estates held by a few aristocratic war leaders. At the bottom of the scale was a large minority of dependent peasants, tenants of the notables or better-off farmers. Such a comparatively small area, simple agrarian economy, and primitive social structure contrasts sharply with the later Rome, master of the Mediterranean world.

Initial attention must be given to the far-reaching social changes occurring in such a remarkably short period of time, before turning to a brief discussion of the state and the troubles afflicting the late Republic. Throughout, the reader should keep in mind the two critical actors on the historical stage, aristocratic landlord and laboring peasant, and their relationship. At the end of the first century B.C. the total population of Roman Italy (excluding Cisalpine Gaul) was about six million of whom possibly two million were slaves.[3] Citizens—men, women, and children—numbered about four million, with approximately a further million in the Empire, which had a total population in the neighborhood of fifty million, one-fifth to one-sixth of the estimated world population. Two centuries before, at the outbreak of the Second Punic War, Italy's population was roughly five million, including a half-million slaves. Between the two chronological poles, the demographic rise was due mainly to a marked increase in slaves and freedmen and the decline of the freeborn and their families resulting from emigration and war losses. The fivefold increase in the number of citizens had been primarily the consequence of gradual enfranchisement and then its complete extension in Italy following the Social War (91–89 B.C.). The City of Rome had burgeoned from an urban center of some 150,000 free men, women, and children and a purely conjectural figure of 100,000 or more slaves, to a colossal metropolis of little under a million, two-thirds freeborn and freedmen and their families and one-third slaves; in other words, a threefold increase in proportion to the Italian population as a whole, from 5 to 17 percent. Even with the tremendous growth of the capital, Italy remained predominantly a rural society, with just under 70 percent of the population living in the countryside as compared to the previous 90 percent.

Nearly three-quarters of the free population (or about one-half of the total) were rural, to whom must be added over one-half of the two million slaves. The overwhelming majority of free Italians, therefore, were peasants, who also outnumbered rural slaves—many of whom were not agricultural workers—by over two to one. Outside Italy, 90 percent of the Empire's nearly fifty million subjects were also peasants. If Italy is joined with the provinces, probably more than 80 percent of the total population were engaged in food production. Rome was by far the largest city, to be followed at later dates by Alexandria and Carthage. Towns in Italy of over 75,000 were rare; there were perhaps only about six. Pompeii's 20,000 was possibly the urban norm for Italy and Empire. Italy's 434 "municipalities," contrary to the implication of the name, were not necessarily populous urban units, since many of them were rural.

What, then, were the chief characteristics of the social structure of Italy in Cicero's day, still predominantly a peasant society, although dominated by the enormous city on the Tiber? Agricultural land remained the foundation of the economy, and agricultural wealth derived from the exertions of independent and dependent peasants and agrarian slaves was the foundation of power and prestige. A very small, leisured, aristocratic class, whose members were of varying degrees of wealth and influence, owned or controlled the productive land of Roman Italy and had succeeded in dominating state and society.[4] The aristocracy consisted of three groups in a descending hierarchy of legally defined orders or estates: senators, equestrians, decurions. At the apex were the six hundred senators (and their families). Their enormous collective wealth came from inheritance, rents, the exploitation of slave labor on large landed estates, commercial investment at home and abroad, and the enormous profits reaped from holding posts in the provinces. Below the senators were a lesser nobility, approaching two thousand gentlemen (and their families) of the equestrian order, whose income likewise was based on landed property, with a minimal qualification of 400,000 H.S. Most equestrians were country squires, living on their estates and perhaps owning a townhouse in Rome. Although equestrians cannot be compared to a "middle class" of businessmen, the richest were the *publicani* who made large fortunes by being public contractors, engaging for private profit in numerous state enterprises and services: provisioning, building, mining, banking, operating the postal system; and collecting taxes, customs duties, and rents from public land. Yet their wealth was firmly rooted in landed property, since they had to put up their holdings as security for their state projects. Some equestrians were also *negotiatores,* specializing in private banking, trading, and moneylending, particularly outside Italy, although freedmen and even slaves engaged in similar business. The third and by far the most numerous group of the aristocracy (after the Social War) of Italy were the decurions, the one hundred leading proprietors in each of the 434 municipalities who sat in the local councils. The decurial landed qualification was nominally 100,000 H.S., the actual figure probably considerably less. The 40,000 or so decurions headed by the 2,600 senators and equestrians formed a ruling class (including families) of about 3 percent of the entire Italian population, controlling the destinies of nearly fifty million souls in the Empire.

Traditionally the major human resource at the disposal of these aristrocratic estate owners and warlords had been the class of innumerable peasants, determined toilers of the soil and valiant legionnaires, who were largely responsible for the leisure of their superiors; their food, drink, clothing, and shelter; and their far-flung Empire. The proportion of free Italian peasants and their families had declined between the Second Punic War and the foundation of the Principate (27 B.C.) by about 25 percent, from just over four million to under three million. Nevertheless they remained by far the most numerous single class and a sizable majority of the whole. Even with agrarian slavery at its peak in Italy, Hopkins informs us, "free peasants probably constituted a majority of the Italian population outside the city of Rome," perhaps as much as 60 percent, and he adds, "The Roman economy in Italy and the provinces in all periods rested upon the backs of peasants."[5] This view is confirmed by Finley: in the Empire at a later date the peasantry comprised "the vast majority of the population of the ancient world."[6] Most Italian peasants led an impoverished and backbreaking existence on ten acres or more. Some were freeholders; many more were tenants, who might also hire out for seasonal farm labor. Freeholders were also often tenants, working leaseholds in order to better their condition. Perhaps as much as one-fifth of the surplus labor of the average peasant was appropriated by the ruling class in the form of rents, taxes, and market exchange. This does not include one of the primary means of peasant exploitation by the aristocracy: military conscription. Until the important reforms of Marius in 107 B.C., conscription was restricted—restrictions gradually reduced over the years—to those with sufficient property qualifications, the *assidui*, which at least in the early years meant that conscription was confined to the freeholders. The nobility always feared to give arms to the very poor, who were consequently called up only in emergency war situations, for the first time in 381–380 B.C. During the Punic Wars, especially when Italy was invaded by Hannibal, every male citizen of military age was conscripted, even the *proletarii*, the propertyless poor. Property qualifications were abolished by the reforms of Marius, and the urban poor as well as landless peasants slowly replaced the freeholders in the ranks until by the end of the first century B.C. the army had become essentially professionalized. For all his labors in the service of the ruling class, the peasant, in our period of two centuries, was rewarded with displacement by the increasing use of agrarian slaves; dispossession of his land, often through forcible seizure and confiscation, and of his rights to common land; indebtedness; and ever greater hardship and poverty.

After the peasants, a third large class, no less subject than the peasants to the control and exploitation of the aristocracy, were the 600,000 citizens and freedmen confined to the frightful living conditions of the city of Rome and the somewhat smaller element (500,000) in other Italian towns, of whom practically nothing is known. For want of a better name, this class can be called *urban plebeians*. Consisting of free laborers, craftsmen, tradesmen, and professionals, they coexisted in the appalling slums of metropolitan Rome with perhaps 300,000 to 350,000 slaves, many of whom were engaged in identical occupations. The freeborn, as distinct from the freedmen and their families—those in servitude and subsequently freed—were a definite minority of the urban plebeians, less than twenty percent. Of them by far the biggest number were the fifty thousand poor freeborn male adults, many of them displaced peasants, forced (along with slaves and freedmen) to do the menial and unskilled tasks in the city: building, carting, and seasonal work on the docks and adjacent farmland. Probably the largest segment of the urban plebeians, approaching 60 percent of the total, were the freedmen and their families, many from Greece and the Near East, who with slaves performed most of the skilled and professional functions. A sizable number, also like the freeborn and slaves, were hired for particularly unsafe and arduous jobs. Possibly fewer than ten percent of the artisans were freeborn, as was apparently also the case in other Italian towns. The many small enterprises combining crafts and shopkeeping were primarily in the hands of freedmen: the butchers, bakers, dyers, cloth makers, metal workers, jewelers, and goldsmiths. Mass production in the modern sense was nonexistent; but such commodities as bricks, lead pipes, glass, and lamps were made on a scale larger than in the normal small shops, in establishments owned by freeborn and sometimes freedmen, usually supervised by freedmen, and employing slaves. Teaching, medicine, architecture, sculpture, and painting were typically occupations of freedmen and sometimes slaves. Freedmen and slaves served as confidential secretaries and occasionally were men of letters. Frequently freedmen were household stewards and civil servants. Regardless of vocation, slaves, freeborn, and freedmen, except for a very few comparatively affluent and enterprising individuals among the latter, comprised the vast numbers of the urban poor subject to the ruling class, and there was no distinct middle class of moderately well-off businessmen or professionals.

A final, absolutely crucial component of Roman social structure was the huge slave force, aspects of which have been mentioned previously. After the turn of the third century B.C., Roman Italy began to develop into what has been called a slave society—one of five historical instances, the others being classical Athens, Brazil, the West Indies, and the American South.[7] Fundamental to the notion of a slave society is not so much the proportion of chattel slaves to the free population, although those of servile status have generally exceeded twenty percent of the population in such social formations, but the importance of slaves in production. After the defeat of Hannibal ending the Second Punic War in 202 B.C., prisoners of war enslaved by the Romans increasingly replaced peas-

ants in agriculture and free artisans in workshops producing con-
sumer goods, constituting a seemingly bottomless reservoir of
labor power for all kinds of menial and skilled work.

Prior to the First Punic War the Romans used slaves, human
booty captured in the military operations against other Italian peoples. Slaves, nevertheless, were probably employed far less extensively in a basic productive capacity before than after hostilities
with Carthage. No evidence exists for slavery during the period
of the early kings (753–510 B.C.), although the lack of evidence
does not confirm the absence of slaves, who undoubtedly served
in the households and workshops of better-off citizens. An auction
of slaves took place as early as 396 B.C., and the first slave market
in Rome was established in 259 B.C., just after the outbreak of
the First Punic War. The struggle with Carthage was by far the
most serious and lasting armed conflict waged by the Romans up
to that point, probably involving at one time or another something approaching 100,000 troops. The capture and enslavement
of war prisoners were proportional to the vast dimensions of the
life-and-death contest between the two implacable foes: 20,000 in
256 B.C. in Africa, 25,000 in 261 in Sicily, 30,000 in 209 in southern Italy, and later 150,000 at the Battle of Pydna in 167. As Rome
advanced along the road of world conquest and empire, the enslavement of captive peoples continued. Caesar is supposed to
have enslaved a million inhabitants of Gaul. More than two million enslaved alien peasants were transported to Italy between 80
and 8 B.C., according to Hopkins's estimate.[8] By the end of Cicero's life about one-third of Italy's six million people were slaves,
working in households, fields, and workshops, in contrast to the
approximately ten percent of the five million before the Second
Punic War.

Great care must be exercised to avoid unwarranted generalizations about the role of slavery in ancient Rome, which became a
slave society about 200 B.C. When *Rome* is employed in this context, the time span and geographical area must be specified. Rome
was a slave society for less than half its lengthy history—although
probably the most important half, that is, roughly from 200 B.C.
to earlier than A.D. 300. In addition we should always recognize
that if by *Rome* is meant Italy and the Empire, the whole was
never a slave society at any time. Slavery apparently dominated

agrarian production only in Italy and Sicily and the western provinces of Gaul and Spain. In the most populous regions of the Empire at its greatest extent—North Africa, Egypt, the Near East, Greece, and Macedonia—slavery evidently was never so vital to agriculture. Even in Italy during the critical five-hundred-year period the significant role of the peasant in farming must not be overlooked or underestimated. So Rodney Hilton's observation should be a warning: "there seems little doubt that peasantries were the basis of the ancient civilizations . . . and that the class of slaves, though economically and culturally of great significance at certain times and in certain sectors of the ancient world, was numerically inferior and of less permanent importance than the peasant producers."[9]

The role of slaves in the social structure and the nature of their relationships to free productive workers exploited by the ruling aristocracy raise difficult questions still unresolved by scholars. Since slavery was not the only important form of exploitation in classical antiquity, how, given the paucity of evidence, do we accurately compare the exploitation of peasants in terms of the appropriation of surplus labor, or the exploitation of free provincial subjects, against that of slaves; or precisely measure their respective contributions to the total system of production? Furthermore, the constant strife within the ruling class of landlords and between landlords and peasants may be more fundamental to the dynamics of Roman history, to the basic process of social change, than the conflict between masters and slaves. This, of course, is a contentious matter to which we must return later in the chapter. Finally, how are slaves to be fitted into a conception of class structure? Did slaves in Roman Italy of the first century B.C. comprise a class distinct from aristocrats, peasants, and urban plebeians? Slaves were a legally defined status group clearly distinct from freeborn and freedmen, but in terms of their position in the social division of labor and the productive system, they performed every function carried out by free peasants and urban plebeians. If slaves are categorized together as a single class, should not freedmen be similarly treated? Or should slaves and freedmen be distributed according to their economic functions among the classes of freeborn and allotted special statuses within those classes? These problems are still the subject of scholarly debate and cannot be dis-

cussed further here, but they should not deflect from the social
and economic significance of slaves in the Ciceronian age.

2. *Some Characteristics of Roman Government*

In an effort to explain why Rome in such a short time had conquered the Mediterranean world, Polybius offered his largely
Greek audience a masterful analysis of the Roman constitution
within the framework of Greek political thought.[10] He "looked at
Rome with Greek presuppositions," according to one recent assessment; "he foisted an Hellenic face upon her government, describing it in terms of the tripolitical structure so commonly ap-
pealed to by his fellow countrymen."[11] The specific reference is
to the Greek conception of the mixed constitution, a mixture of
elements of the three traditional simple constitutions: monarchy,
aristocracy, democracy. After Polybius, the Roman state was often
viewed in these terms by commentators throughout the ages, not
the least being Cicero himself.[12] How applicable the Greek notion
was to the Roman structure of government depends to an important extent on the meaning given to *mixture*. A keen observer
and capable military tactician with little sympathy for democracy
in the pure Greek form, the aristocratic Polybius, whatever the
other shortcomings of his analysis, never maintained that the victorious Roman state was a composite of *equal* royal, noble, and
popular proportions. Mixture for him, as it did for his two mentors on the subject, Plato and Aristotle, signified fundamentally
aristocratic rule with limited popular participation. Nor did Polybius, at least in one passage, apparently identify the Roman
"people" in the mixture with all citizens, but only with the equestrians, the *publicani* involved in public contracts. Rome, he believed, attained the zenith of its constitutional development during
the Second Punic War, when the warrior aristocracy represented
by the senate dominated the mixture.[13] Rome's spectacular success
over Carthage, therefore, was in effect explained by senatorial supremacy.[14]

   We know what Polybius strongly implied, that senatorial supremacy was not simply a matter of the leading role in government, but a major factor in Rome's unprecedented military accomplishments. The Roman state was a superb military machine
commanded by the senate, basically a gathering of warlords.

While Sparta, a warrior aristocracy, was organized primarily for preservation, Polybius claimed, Rome was the expansionist state par excellence, far superior to Carthage in the conduct of land warfare, to which Roman citizens were fully dedicated.[15] It seems clear to us that Roman civil and military offices, if not always identical, were often little more than two sides of the same coin. Most senior and junior magistrates at the highest level were also military commanders. The two oldest popular assemblies, the *comitia curiata* and *comitia centuriata,* seem to have had their historical roots in military arrangements. The latter, even in the Ciceronian age, was formally a convocation of armed citizens on the field dedicated to Mars, the god of war.

What, then, were the nature and power of the senate, the actual governing institution of the Roman military state, no less in the Ciceronian age than during the Second Punic War? The senate, whose size had been doubled from 300 to 600 by Sulla at the end of the second decade of the first century B.C., was not an hereditary assembly, nor did members receive payment. Membership was replenished annually by the principal magistrates of the year, who were entitled to seats for life. Since only those of senatorial family or of equestrian rank were entitled to stand for election to the higher magistracy, the senate was the citadel of the wealthy and propertied. Within the senate, business was customarily dominated by former consuls, *consulares,* and an exclusive elite, *nobiles,* those who had a consul or possibly another curule magistrate among their ancestors.[16]

From a strictly legal standpoint, the senate was solely an advisory body without legislative powers and could only be convened by a consul, both characteristics reflecting its distant origins in the king's council. Unlike the popular assemblies, the senate could not pass laws, *leges,* only motions or resolutions, *senatus consulta.* By constitutional convention, however, the senate was consulted by magistrates on important questions. Before introducing a bill to one of the popular assemblies, a magistrate was expected to lay it before the senate for debate. Indeed, the senate was the only genuinely deliberative body in the Roman system of government. In the name of the people, a tribune could veto *senatus consulta* and acts of other magistrates, but as custodian of the constitution and hence the ultimate judge of religious matters, the senate was usually able to find an excuse of a religious nature to prevent unilateral action by a popular assembly or official. In addition to its grip on legislation, the senate in practice possessed the power of the purse, supervising the state treasury or *aerarium* and all expenditures and holding magistrates accountable for their outlays. Except for a formal declaration of war—which traditionally was the right of the assembled people, although the tradition may have lapsed by Cicero's day—the conduct of foreign affairs was an exclusive power of the senate. Not all wars were formally declared, and military operations were in the hands of senate and magistracy. In addition, the senate defined the sphere of activity of magistrates and had the dispensing power which enabled ex-magistrates to spend what amounted to a second term of office as provincial administrators.

Elected independently for one-year terms by the people were the major magistrates: two consuls and eight praetors, all with the *imperium,* or what amounted to the royal power; two curule aediles and two plebeian aediles, ten tribunes, and twenty quaestors, all wielding *potestas,* or magistral power.[17] As was previously noted, the overwhelming majority of citizens could not seek public office, a prohibition concisely formulated by Gelzer: "The principle that not every citizen should be allowed to take part in government was to the Romans so self-evident that there was no law on the subject and they never enunciated it."[18] The two consuls who replaced the king, once the monarchy was abolished, and who had large civil and military powers, legally undefined, but limited by convention, were by the mid-first century B.C. little more than chief executives in the capital and in Italy.[19] Their junior associates, the eight praetors, were given essential judicial duties, presiding over civil and criminal courts. The two curule aediles, chosen by the *comitia tributa,* and the two plebeian aediles, selected by the *concilium plebis,* were basically municipal officers charged with the cleanliness of the city, the maintenance of roads and public works, the water and grain supply, some police and market supervisory functions, and the staging of certain public entertainments. The ten tribunes, elected by the *concilium plebis,* convened, chaired, and introduced bills into that assembly. The twenty quaestors had financial responsibilities, both in Rome and the provinces, assisting consuls and proconsuls, and a few were given specially assigned offices for other functions in Italy. None of the leading magistral posts was salaried, some of them entailed considerable expense, and the costs of electoral campaigns could be very high. Curule magistrates, of course, could look forward to a second year in the provinces as a means of recovering their heavy financial losses in public service. Ambitious young gentlemen who aimed at the power and glory of the *vita activa* were expected to pass in a highly competitive race with their peers over successive electoral hurdles, with some variation as to the number and sequence. This *cursus honorum,* or career of office, began with the quaestorship, followed customarily by the post of aedile or tribune, and then praetor and consul, at the respective minimal ages of 30, 36, 39, and 42.

The four assemblies were the various forms taken by the meetings en masse of the *populus Romanus* in that "partnership" of senate and people designated by the initials *S.P.Q.R. (senatus populusque Romanus)*, which were affixed to authorized state documents such as treaties. The "people" with the right to attend assemblies consisted of all freeborn male adult citizens as well as freedmen, former slaves possessing the status of citizens but not, however, entitled to bear arms or hold political office. Roman assemblies were in marked contrast to the *ecclesia* of democratic Athens. Voting in Rome always took place by groups instead of by individuals, a majority within each group determining the vote of that group, one vote per group. Consequently, a majority decision, although identical with the majority vote by group, was not necessarily reflective of the majority opinion of the individuals composing the assembly. While groups might vary enormously in size, each group had only one vote. As we shall see, these arrangements worked to the advantage of the wealthy minority of citizens and to the detriment of the poor majority. No stipulations existed about the number of assembly meetings, which could only be convened by the appropriate magistrate, who likewise was the presiding officer. An assembly as such was never a deliberative body, only a voting mechanism for electing magistrates or passing legislation. The convening and presiding magistrate had the sole right to introduce legislation, which could neither be discussed nor amended. Not only were relatively few laws actually passed by the popular assemblies throughout their history, but also, at least since the Second Punic War, the proportion of the total of qualified citizens actually able to vote was minute. Roman expansion throughout Italy and the Mediterranean world meant that attendance was confined mainly to those living in the metropolis or the nearby countryside. The wealthy, of course, could afford to travel long distances to cast their vote, depending on the election or issue at stake. The vast majority of eligible male citizens, increasing from 270,000 in 218 B.C. to over one million in 69 B.C., was thus disfranchised. Moreover, in the capital only a comparatively small convocation of eligible citizens could be accommodated physically, for even in the late Republic, when the site of meetings had been enlarged, no more than 70,000 could be present.

The four conclaves of citizens in the mid-first century B.C. were the curial assembly (*comitia curiata*), the centuriate assembly (*comitia centuriata*), the tribal assembly (*comitia tributa*), and the plebeian council (*concilium plebis*). The last three were of equal legislative competence and their enactments had the status of laws (*leges*). By this time the oldest assembly, the curial, performed only certain religious and public and private law functions. Next to it in age was the centuriate assembly, with the primary political task of electing consuls, praetors, and censors, convened and chaired by a consul or praetor. It also traditionally exercised the exclusive powers of declaring war and ratifying treaties. The voting group of the centuriate assembly to which citizens were assigned was the century. Voting centuries were unequal in size, a small minority of well-to-do cavalrymen and citizens of the highest property class having a far larger number of them—98 (with 98 votes) of a total of 193—than the citizen majority of the lower property classes. Because the 98 upper-class centuries voted first, elections could sometimes be concluded without the need of summoning the lower-class centuries.

The tribal assembly was the one most commonly employed for legislative and judicial purposes. Convoked and chaired by consuls, praetors, or curule aediles, it was also responsible for electing curule aediles, quaestors, and lesser magistrates. An appropriate magistrate who wished the assembly to enact a law would by convention present a drafted bill to the senate for discussion. Then the bill had to be promulgated for at least twenty-four days before convening the assembly, during which period the magistrate might call informal public meetings (*contiones*) for debate by speakers of his selection. The tribal assembly was closely linked with the plebeian council; indeed, for all practical purposes they were virtually identical. Originating in the early struggle between patricians and plebeians, the council was exclusively plebeian, electing its own officers: tribunes and plebeian aediles. After the mid-fifth century the tribunes numbered ten and remained at that figure. In the Ciceronian age the only differences between the two assemblies were that the very few remaining citizens of patrician family were ineligible for the plebeian council and that it could only be convened by its own elected officers, the tribunes and two plebeian aediles. Voting in both bodies was by tribe, a geographical unit to which each citizen belonged. Because the city of Rome was allotted only four of the thirty-five tribes, others being apportioned to the countryside surrounding the capital, the heavy concentration of urban poor was easily outvoted by affluent rural propertyholders.

From this brief and simplified resumé of the tortuous complexities of Roman governmental institutions, one can only concur with Syme's terse judgment that the "constitution was a screen and a sham."[20] Behind the facade of the traditionally held conception of the Roman state—initially postulated by Polybius—as a mixture of monarchical, aristocratic, and democratic components, each checking the other, lay the stark reality of political power: the rule of an oligarchy of wealthy landed proprietors. The senate was the supreme governing council of the oligarchy, their instrument of state control consisting of the most influential magnates and constantly renewing its membership from magistrates elected from the upper propertied classes. Traditionally, the senate had been able to manage the magistracy, and by the Ciceronian age it was still decisive in the spheres of religion, legislation, finance, and in the conduct of war and foreign affairs. Democracy in any very meaningful sense seems to have had little authentic part in the political system. Elections and the relatively few laws passed were the responsibility of the popular assemblies, so arranged, however, as to exclude the bulk of the eligible citizens and to forward the domination of the propertied, thus perpetuating the hierarchical structure of power under the senate. In the absence

of any organized legal means of expression, the sentiments, grievances, and needs of the Roman masses could only be registered
in extralegal ways, in the violence of riot and mob action. Oligarchical hegemony was furthered by the fact that the rules of
classical Roman law favored wealthy landed proprietors as against
small peasants and the propertyless. In addition, prior to the Gracchi only senators were entitled to jury service, and afterward the
right was extended to equestrians, who possibly shared it with
senators. Nor should it be forgotten that priests of the civic religion, which played such a central political role in Roman affairs,
were chosen solely from the upper classes.

Polybius, therefore, was correct as far as he went in giving to
the senate the leading role during the Second Punic War, but his
analysis, encumbered by the Greek conception of mixture, ob-
scured many aspects of supreme oligarchical power. Also, perhaps
because of his primary concern with the formal legal characteristics of the constitution, he failed to consider the informal levers
and transmission belts of senatorial command. Two networks of
interpersonal relationships, the *amicitia* and *clientela,* were vital
in consolidating and strengthening senatorial control, at least prior
to the first century, and undoubtedly contributed to Roman unity,
vigor, and success.[21] *Amicitia* referred to the nexus of friendship,
loyalty, and cooperation cultivated by a worthy, for example a
consular, with other notables of senatorial and equestrian rank. At
an exalted social level, it was comparable to the patron–client connection, the *clientela* or reciprocity of protection and service between a dignitary and members of the lower orders. Both sets of
relationships were critical in mobilizing support for elections, the
passage of legislation, and the policies and actions of government.
Once, however, the ruling class was increasingly fractured by the
individualistic pursuit of wealth and power developing from the
end of the second century with the growth of imperialism and the
exploitation of the provinces, these ganglia were gradually transformed from being agents of integration and harmony into warring factions, cliques, and private armies. Another possible factor
in accounting for the order and achievements of the state, overlooked by Polybius, was the prudent way the Roman victors
treated their newly conquered peoples in Italy, granting them a
measured autonomy under their own potentates, so that the pen-

insula resembled a confederation of local aristocracies under the Roman aegis.

Even after the Gracchi, Rome—divided internally and plagued by ever mounting factional strife and violence—can with some justification be called a classic example of the conception of the state as an instrument of the ruling classes to promote and protect their interests. Of relevance to this thought are the words of Gelzer: "Roman magistrates regarded themselves much less as administrators than as possessors. . . . The crushing of the revolution by Sulla is therefore regarded as a recovery of the state by the nobility."[22]

3. *The Late Republican Time of Troubles*

For the purposes of chronology and general orientation, a discussion of the difficulties besetting the late Republic can perhaps best be prefaced by a brief catalogue of some of the main political events of the century. The Ciceronian age was fraught with turmoil and upheaval, culminating in the dictatorship of Caesar, his assassination on the fifteenth of March in 44 B.C., the establishment of the Second Triumvirate, and Cicero's proscription and murder in the autumn of 43. The century opened in 91 with a full-scale, ferocious struggle, the Social War between Rome and the Italian allies, the latter demanding citizenship and its attendant privileges. More than a quarter of a million soldiers were engaged in the conflict that brought about economic devastation probably exceeding that of the Punic Wars. Although hostilities were all but over after two years of intense fighting, not until 81 was Italy completely enfranchised. No sooner did this struggle terminate than Rome plunged into another, the First Civil War, which filled the rest of the decade of the eighties. L. Cornelius Sulla, a prominent conservative Roman commander during the Social War, had been sent to Greece to resist the invasion of King Mithridates VI of Pontus. Relieved of his command in favor of the popular Marius, Sulla marched on Rome in 88. His appointment restored, he returned overseas to pursue the war against Mithridates. L. Cornelius Cinna, elected consul in 87, was deprived of his office by his senatorial opponents and, to regain it, allied himself with the aged Marius and eliminated his enemies. After a relatively peaceful interlude, Sulla returned victorious in 84 to seize power and launch a reign of terror by proscribing 2,000 notables who had supported Marius and Cinna. Sulla introduced a conservative program of reform aimed at strengthening senatorial power and curtailing the popular political role. In order to secure replacements in the ruling class for the dignitaries who had been so violently eliminated, he doubled the membership of the senate to 600. Few of Sulla's other reforms—the abolition of the grain dole, limiting tribunal powers—were lasting or had such a profound impact on Roman state and society.

Difficulties and disorders continued, although they did not for some time match the tumultuous age of Marius and Sulla. The senatorial conservatives were soon busied with mounting popular agitation against the Sullan reforms, the third slave war led by Spartacus, the new aggression of Mithridates, and the defection of Quintus Sertorius in Spain. Sulla gave up his dictatorship to be elected consul in 80, and after his death in 78, M. Aemilius Lepidus, consul in that year, attempted to abolish the innovations of his predecessor, only to be put down by the young, ambitious general Gnaeus Pompeius (106–48 B.C.), who afterward was dispatched to pacify Spain. Returning triumphant from Spain, he and Marcus Licinius Crassus, who had vanquished Spartacus, were elected consuls in 70. They proceeded to undo some of the less popular Sullan reforms and to hold the first census since 90. The conservative notables, strengthened by Sulla, were willing to make concessions, and any tensions between equestrians and senators that had held over from the days of the Gracchi soon disappeared. Pompey became preoccupied in 67 with eliminating the pirates in the eastern Mediterranean, and then after the conquest of Mithridates in 66 he stayed on as virtual ruler of the Empire in the East until 62. Cicero was elected in 64 for the consulship in 63, with the ruling oligarchy's blessing and support, for they were fearful of the popular agitation of Catiline, whose conspiracy was suppressed by Cicero. Sometime earlier the young senator, Julius Caesar, had gained a reputation as a popular leader who in alliance with Crassus had supported the agrarian legislation defeated by Cicero. Caesar was elected consul for 59; his informal power-sharing arrangement, known as the First Triumvirate, had been sealed with Pompey and Crassus the previous year. Following his term of office, Caesar was sent as proconsul to the province of Cisalpine Gaul and Illyricum, where between 58 and 50 he conquered Transalpine Gaul. The Triumvirate was revitalized at a meeting of the three generals in Lucca in 55, and Caesar's proconsulship in Gaul was renewed for five years. When Clodius, the popular urban aristocratic leader and tribune in 58 who had exiled Cicero, was murdered in 52 by one of the orator's friends, Milo, such rioting ensued that Pompey was appointed sole consul to restore public order and his governorship in Spain was extended for five years. By this time, with Crassus dead, Pompey was moving closer to the conservative magnates led by the young Marcus Cato, great-grandson of the famous censor of the previous century.

Pompey and the conservatives, however, seemed no longer able to control Caesar. The break between them became irrevocable when the latter, on the expiration of his proconsulship in 50 and knowing that he faced prosecution on his return to Rome, threw down the gauntlet by crossing the river Rubicon in 49, invading Italy with his faithful veterans of the Gallic Wars. Such was the beginning of the Second Civil War. Unlike the struggle in the eighties, it embraced the whole of the Empire, ending with the defeat of Pompey at Pharsalus in Greece in 48 and his subsequent assassination in Egypt. War, however, continued between Caesar and the partisans of Pompey until 45. Caesar, ruling as dictator from 49 until his assassination in 44, avoided behaving as Sulla had done in the eighties. He showed extraordinary generosity and moderation toward his enemies and minimized popular reforms, adopting a policy designed to win friends among the ruling class. On his death, power passed to the Second Triumvirate of his nephew Octavian, his master of horse Lepidus, and Marc Antony. Many of their foes, including Cicero, were proscribed. A state of civil war effectively continued, however, terminating with Octavian's crushing of Marc Antony and the latter's death in Egypt in 30. The surviving Octavian became the ruler of Rome, founding the principate in 27 B.C. as Augustus Caesar.

Most historians agree that the Ciceronian age was marked by decay and disintegration leading to the final collapse.[23] Even more than before, senators and equestrians had embarked on a frenzied course of self-aggrandizement, each for himself in an insatiable quest for property and riches, and a bloody lust of power after power.[24] Nothing so nearly resembled the Hobbesian *bellum om-*

nium contra omnes in which everyone must be the eventual loser. Sources of income and business interests of senators and equestrians seem to have become identical in the first century B.C.: rents from landed properties and urban slum tenements, buying and selling real estate for profit, the mass production of grain and cattle, investing and trading in the enterprises of the *publicani,* and money-lending at high rates of interest. The biggest plum of all was the Empire. Notables embarked on their looting of the provinces with arrogant disdain for the common interest: living in a most lavish and luxurious style, buying strings of palaces, country mansions, and way stations and furnishing them with shiploads of art treasures plundered from conquered subjects. Badian's conclusion is apt: "No administration in history has ever devoted itself so whole-heartedly to fleecing its subjects for the private benefit of its ruling class as Rome of the last age of the Republic."[25] The powerful proconsular forces—now recruited from impoverished townsmen and landless poor—in Gaul, Spain, and the East were in fact the private armies of such great commanders as Caesar, Pompey, and Crassus, who increasingly flouted senatorial authority and conducted themselves as independent overlords. Much of the cutthroat conflict among the notables was in the name of their esteem and honor, their *dignitas* or personal standing in the eyes of their peers and lesser mortals.[26] They strove with prodigious effort to maintain their *dignitas,* to enhance it or recover it after some blow to their prestige or slight from a rival. Such motives may partially explain the struggle during the Second Civil War between Caesar and Pompey, and the animosity of Clodius for Cicero. Something of the unfettered individualism that was leaving the aristocracy in disarray is reflected by the upsurge of portrait sculpture commissioned by the fierce antagonists to immortalize themselves in stone: stern, strong, unbending, cruelly ambitious faces—formidable foes; certainly ones to be remembered and reckoned with.[27] The century began in an orgy of violence, the strife between Marius and Sulla and the bloody proscriptions of the latter, and ended similarly with the Second Civil War, the dictatorship and assassination of Caesar, and the ruthlessness of the Second Triumvirate. Between these two extremes violence erupted with ever-growing frequency in both town and country. Gangs of bullyboys serving the oligarchs, rioting urban mobs manipulated by unscrupulous politicians, and marauding bands of avaricious landlords and their henchmen all converted republican order into the law of the jungle.

The hapless victims of this intensely individualistic and violent strife over power and riches were the vast exploited majority: urban plebeians and peasants. An ever-widening gulf that was to last to the time of St. Augustine separated the wealthy minority of warring grandees from the laboring masses. The income differential between rich and poor approximated a minimum of 1,200 to 1 and a maximum of 20,000 to 1, in contrast to a probable ratio of several hundred to 1 of ancient Athens after the Peloponnesian War.[28] The social and economic history of Rome during the centuries following Cicero's birth has been summarized by MacMullen in the words "fewer have more."[29] In glaring contrast to the sumptuous splendor to which these ever-striving combatants had grown accustomed were the hovels, the disease, the filth, the hunger and daily insecurity in which the urban masses of the city of Rome lived. In Cicero's day the capital had grown to a gargantuan size, a total of just short of a million inhabitants crammed into an area no larger than a small town of less than 4,000 acres, or 200 per acre as compared to a density of 250 per acre in the worst slums of modern industrial cities. Living conditions for the wretched population were simply shocking. Probably one in three was destitute. The poor lived in tenements sixty to seventy feet in height. No fire-fighting units had been organized to put out the numerous conflagrations to which these squalid slums were susceptible. No police force existed for the maintenance of public order and safety and the prevention of crime. No health service or sanitation department combatted disease and filth or ministered to the needs of the poor. Employment was insecure, and there was no unemployment insurance, no pension plan, no means of appealing or redressing grievances unless one was lucky enough to have the ear of a powerful patron. Courts existed, but they were largely the preserve of wealthy litigants. The average slum-dweller had little or no opportunity to participate in government or make his voice heard in the system of power dominated by the wealthy. One result of the dreadful living conditions and the daily struggle for survival among the poor was perpetual violence and crime and, with the lack of institutionalized safety valves, constant agitation, rioting, and civil disturbances of major proportions.

The peasants, who even in Cicero's age probably constituted the majority of the total Italian population and who had been the real authors of the wealth and world power of their social superiors, never succeeded as did their Athenian counterparts from the time of the reforms of Solon and Kleisthenes in becoming first-class citizens, real actors in a direct democracy. One crucial factor in the anarchism of the aristocracy and the calamitous events of the late Republic appears to be the failure of the peasantry to become active participants in governing their state. Fragmented, exploited, and excluded from any meaningful political role, they had become the instruments of the oligarchs in their internecine warfare. Constantly fighting with neighboring peoples for survival and lebensraum, the Roman state developed into a mighty war machine commanded by aristocratic landlords and manned by peasants. Rome, unlike Athens, was never a democracy, although severely limited popular participation perhaps helped maintain morale and strengthen social solidarity. As previously noted, notwithstanding popular elections and citizen assemblies, the Republic had always been and continued to be managed by a narrow if changing oligarchy of landed wealth and noble privilege.

The more the militarized peasants triumphed in war, the more likely they were to suffer in peace, losing their holdings and being replaced by agrarian slaves. Peasants under arms—as high as 10 percent of the eligible men during and following the Punic Wars—for lengthy campaigns of up to two years were compelled to neglect their farms. In their absence rapacious landlords might seize their holdings or occupy the *ager publicus,* the public land, on which most of the poorer peasants depended. Returning veterans might have to abandon their farms, if they had not already been appropriated; to sell them at serious losses; or to mortgage and in the long run lose them. In one way or another, peasants were being dispossessed and thus deprived of the means of livelihood, forced to be tenants if they had been freeholders, or to become agrarian laborers, to migrate to other parts of Italy and to the provinces, or to the towns and the city of Rome, whose population swelled to an incredible density. In the capital, without the skills demanded by an urban population, they faced the bleak prospect of eking out a bare survival by performing thankless menial tasks including seasonal labor of several kinds.

For greedy landlords, the military accomplishments of the peasant soldiers they were dispossessing proved to be a bonanza. The endless supply of enslaved war captives was used for agrarian labor in exchange for the costs of their purchase and upkeep, and without being subject to conscription. The new expropriated holdings were amalgamated with the old ones by avaricious proprietors from the beginning of the third century to create huge estates of thousands of acres, the *latifundia* in southern Italy and Sicily, devoted to grain and cattle, manned by slave gangs domiciled in barracks. But the replacement of free peasant labor by the exploitation of slaves on a colossal scale in such concentrated form on the *latifundia* and in such a relatively short period of time had grave results for the ruling class of great landlords. Slave uprisings occurred in Italy in 198, 196, and 185 B.C., but were ruthlessly suppressed. Much more serious, once the *latifundia* had been firmly established, were the slave wars of 134–132, 104–101, and 73–71. In each case the aims of the slaves seem to have been limited to the desires of freedom and returning to their homelands. During the second war, slaves succeeded in occupying most of the Sicilian countryside and were only quelled by a large military force. The most famous of the three slave wars was led by Spartacus in Italy, whose followers may have been as many as 150,000, requiring ten legions under M. Crassus for their defeat.

As Rome expanded in Italy the question of land distribution and the peasant was possibly the most pressing political problem. A proportion of all newly captured territory was set aside as *ager publicus* or state land, either to be colonized by citizens or divided into leaseholds at nominal rents for their use.[30] Numerous agrarian laws, championed by the tribunes, sought to regulate *ager publicus* in the interests of the peasants. Affluent landlords of the dominant nobility constantly attempted to sabotage the implementation of these enactments in order to exploit the state lands for their own profit. Following the Punic Wars, once free peasant farmers began to be displaced by slave labor on *latifundia* often created by the expropriation of state land, the agrarian problem came to a head. By the time of Tiberius Gracchus, tribune in 132, veterans were in a rebellious mood, and the land question seriously threatened

civic peace. Assassinated by less enlightened aristocrats who opposed his efforts on behalf of the peasants, his cause was resumed
by his brother Gaius, tribune in 124. Gaius instituted a grain dole
to alleviate the conditions of the urban poor—to be a regular feature of future state policy—reenacted his brother's reform measures, and devised a plan for resettling landless veterans overseas,
which subsequently became an accepted way of attempting to de-
fuse the peasant problem. Again the oligarchy proved to be less
than fully compliant, and agitation for land reform continued to
be the platform of such popular leaders as Marius, Saturninus,
Caesar, and Catiline in his unsuccessful bid in 63 B.C. for the
consulship of 62. About one-half of the peasant families of Italy,
or one and a half million people, were probably resettled between
80 and 8 B.C. either to other lands in the peninsula or overseas,
or they voluntarily migrated to the towns and the capital. Such
mass transplantation was necessitated by the influx during the
same period of some two million enslaved peasants and their families from abroad. As dictator, Caesar sought to relieve the plight
of landless Italian peasants by resettlement, but he was careful not
to harm the interests of the aristocracy. The acuteness of the problem was probably eased by the gradual professionalization of the
army, thereby reducing the number of returning veterans, and was
ultimately resolved by the massive resettlement projects of Augustus and the early emperors.

Despite the many trials and tribulations of urban plebeians and
peasants and the waves of mass unrest and violence, the late Republic does not seem to have been on the brink of a popular overthrow of government or social revolution.[31] Urban plebeian violence was not so much of a radical revolutionary nature as it was
the only available mode of protest, of ventilating accumulated
grievances and expressing demands for sorely needed reforms of
the existing system. Whether plebeians as a whole had attained a
collective awareness of themselves and their own interests as distinct from and in conflict with the ruling class and its aims is open
to question. It seems certain, nevertheless, that anything approaching a revolutionary class-consciousness organized politically
for the achievement of basic changes in the system had yet to
materialize. The exploited peasantry, aroused at the end of the
second century by the Gracchi, Marius, and Saturninus, and re-

sorting to arms in support of Catiline's brief, abortive insurrection, apparently longed for little more than land and a livelihood. Peasant dispersal by constant resettlement, the absence of a physical concentration and close ties so characteristic of an urban populace, and, after the Gracchi, the lack of an enlightened leadership were all obstacles to the generation of a revolutionary consciousness. A possible reason for the failure of peasants and urban workers to unite against the aristocracy was their conflict over the emphasis to be given in social reform: the former demanding land distribution; the latter, grain doles.[32] There is no evidence at this early date of an alliance on any scale between peasants and plebeians or of both with protesting slaves, who after the defeat of Spartacus showed little inclination to repeat their ill-fated struggle for freedom. Contrary to what one might expect, there were no signs of slave protests and uprisings in the urban centers. The only conclusion to be drawn is that the aspirations of peasants and urban plebeians, alienated as they undoubtedly were from the regime, probably never transcended the immediate goal of improving their living conditions. Members of both classes were pawns manipulated by the oligarchs in their internecine strife. Catiline and Clodius seem to have been motivated more by honor, ambition, and vengeance than by social idealism. Caesar, backed from the first in the Civil War by Cicero's old adherents, the *publicani,* and once in power rapidly gaining the support of other equestrians, the municipal aristocracy, and lesser senators, soft-pedaled the promises of social reform that had originally wooed the masses. Aside from the missing progressive leadership, the rural and urban populace were not mobilized and fired by an ideology as was true at a later date of the Donatists and Circumcellions of North Africa. Consequently, because of these various factors, the motive force of late Republican history must be sought not in conflict between the laboring poor and the aristocracy or between masters and slaves, but, rather, in the struggle within the ruling class.[33] The crisis of the Ciceronian age was essentially a crisis of the aristocracy.

Critical to the conflict within the late Republican aristocracy, however, was its changing relationship to the peasantry. Always the source of aristocratic wealth and power by means of the appropriation of its surplus labor, largely in the form of rents and military conscription, the peasantry had been further subjected by the failure of the development of authentic democratic institutions. The domination of the aristocracy had also been enhanced by their blockage of agrarian reform, use of *latifundia* and agrarian slave labor, and suppression of slave uprisings. Thus exploited and politically powerless, the peasantry had also been dislocated and dispersed by resettlement programs. Conflict within a ruling class tends to be a function of interclass conflict. As struggle between the ruling class and its chief class enemies wanes, when their threat diminishes, members of the dominant class can afford to quarrel among themselves, especially if the stakes are very high. The increasing strife within the Roman aristocracy seems, then, to have been proportionate to the decline of the peasant danger to their interests and security.

In a word, the peasantry was no longer a powerful enough countervailing social and political force to prevent the dissolution of aristocratic solidarity. The situation was further complicated by the existence of the Empire. Once the world had been conquered, so to speak; once its peoples had been successfully subjected, at least temporarily; and once the peasantry was no longer a constant threat, the unity of the aristocracy began to crumble in competition over access to the sources of wealth. Classes, especially ruling classes, are seldom phalanxes. A class is nothing so much as a flux of altering relationships, of constantly varying groups, alliances, factions, and cliques. Fluctuating intraclass relationships not only depend on changes in interclass relationships, however, but also on changes in the composition, sources of income, and economic interests of the particular class under consideration. From the latter standpoint, three overlapping phases of the internal history of the Republican aristocracy after the Punic Wars can be identified in a somewhat schematic fashion. The three phases are those of *heterogeneity, homogeneity,* and *fragmentation.* They must be considered always in the context of the changing situation of the peasantry vis-à-vis the aristocracy.

At the beginning of the second century, the Roman ruling class was characterized by heterogeneous groupings: senators, country gentry, *publicani, negotiatores.* Each of these major groups was divided into different statuses, factions, and personal followings.

The class as a whole, however, in spite of the growth of differing and conflicting group and factional interests, was still under the domination of the senatorial order, especially their elite, the *nobiles,* who exercised their hegemony over an internal hierarchy of power, prestige, and wealth. Banned from taking on state contracts and from owning ships of large capacity, senators left business ventures to equestrian *publicani* and *negotiatores,* who turned progressively to the new provinces for profit. In forwarding their social goals the Gracchi sought the support of the equestrians against the entrenched senatorial oligarchy. The consequence was that equestrians achieved a new consciousness of themselves, an awareness of the divergence of their interests from those of the senatorial order.[34]

The enfranchisement of the Italians following the Social War (91–89 B.C.) and the doubling of the size of the senate from 300 to 600 members by Sulla slowly ended the phase of heterogeneity and launched a developing homogeneity, indeed, what amounted to a basic change in the nature of the ruling class.[35] By his proscription of 2,000 notables in 84 B.C., Sulla was forced to turn to equestrians to fill the 300 additional seats in the senate. Many of the recently enfranchised Italian decurions who qualified for equestrian rank, thereby being entitled to hold magistral office, were among Sulla's new senatorial recruits. Thus began—at first gradually, but steadily accelerating—the penetration of the senate by Roman equestrians, and increasingly those of Italy. Moreover, the growing divergence in interests of the two orders, given an impetus by the politics of the Gracchi, diminished because senators old and new, no longer now refraining from business activity, began to assume a leading role in the economic exploitation of the Empire. The ruling class exhibited a growing homogeneity and egalitarianism that weakened the previous hierarchy under senatorial domination. Relying fundamentally on landed wealth, all groups of the ruling class—senators, equestrian gentry, *publicani, negotiatores,* decurions—increasingly invested in commercial enterprises and reaped the gains of colonial exploitation. Separate interests and identities, in fact if not in name, tended to fuse in the shift from heterogeneity to homogeneity, from hierarchy to equality. Equestrians infiltrated the senate, although still seldom reaching consular office, and senators turned to business. In a special sense, the ruling class was being transformed into an undifferentiated mass.

The movement in the direction of homogeneity and equality at the level of social background and economic interest, however, rapidly produced a fragmentation at another level: a fracturing of the ruling class into a melee of fiercely contending individuals and factions. Aristocratic unity was no longer necessitated by the threat of the peasantry. The new fragmentation differed appreciably from the old heterogeneity in at least three major respects. The old *nobilitas* was no longer able to maintain its sovereignty or traditional identity. By the time of the principate the traditional ruling families had all but disappeared.[36] The new factions could not now be equated with the old orders and groupings, but instead cut across them. Finally, the stakes to be won were infinitely higher than ever before since the wealth and power of a great empire would go to the victor. No longer, for example, was the conflict between senators and equestrians, but fluctuating cliques of senators and equestrians were pitted against other cliques of a similarly mixed composition. Members of the ruling class were embroiled in a Hobbesian war of all against all, each shifting set of aristocratic allies seeking an ever larger share of the spoils, a greater proportion of the surplus that was being pumped out of the exploited classes at home and the subjected peoples abroad. Obviously, not all the factions and cliques were engaged in the frenzied pursuit of power and riches, but all were sucked into the fray, if only for self-protection. Classes or class groups, exploited as well as exploiters, were engulfed by the struggle, instruments of the noble exploiters to be used for their own advantage. So the whole of society, rulers and ruled, fueled the conflagration. This atomization and warfare, first within the ruling class and then involving other classes, seems to have been the historical motor of the Ciceronian age and perhaps affords an explanation of the collapse of the Republic, a generalization that leans toward Badian's provocative assessment: "The study of the Roman Republic—and that of the Empire to a considerable extent—is basically the study, not of its economic development, or of its masses, or even of great individuals: it is chiefly the study of its ruling class."[37] The conflict and disintegration of the last years of the

Republic are possibly best understood as a crisis of the ruling aristocracy, one freed from the constraints of a peasantry that lacked unity, militancy, and an institutionalized role of political opposition. Cicero's social and political thought can perhaps be most appropriately appreciated as a theoretical expression of this aristocratic crisis.

CHAPTER THREE

Cicero's Life and Works

1. *Biographical Milestones and Intellectual Influences*

The extraordinary intellectual ferment and literary creativity of the last years of the Republic were possibly in direct response to these chaotic conditions and the attendant anxieties about the future instilled among the upper echelons of society.[1] Roman culture bloomed in a spectacular way. It was the age of Varro, Lucretius, Catullus, Sallust, Caesar, and a host of minor men of letters. At the center of this flowering was a *literatus* of genius who encouraged his talented contemporaries in their inventive endeavors and called for enlightenment, the figure of Marcus Tullius Cicero, to whose life and works we must now turn.[2] The fact that he was socially a *novus homo* does not imply that he struggled on his own to the top against insuperable odds or that he was handicapped by poverty, inferior education, and the lack of well-placed friends. The chief obstacle in Cicero's path was the social snobbery of the noble elite toward a gentlemanly outsider. He came from an old, affluent family of country gentry, intimately associated with prominent members of the inner circle of power. He received the best education in literature, philosophy, and law that could be given a young Roman gentleman, from some of the leading teachers of the main philosophical schools and from the legal luminaries of the age. Financial independence, family connections, and schooling paved the way for the talented and urbane youth with a taste for letters and scholarly pursuits and a skill in human relations. Instead of rusticating in the country, he chose the only alternative to a military career available to an ambitious person of his rank: law and politics. Fortunately for us, his rapid ascent to power was followed by a swift descent, which gave him ample leisure for study and reflection and for writing the many works for which he is famous.

Cicero was born January 3, 106 B.C., on his grandfather's estate about sixty miles southeast of Rome in Arpinum, which had been enfranchised in 188. The Tullii Cicerones were a well-established landed family of equestrian rank. By marriage the grandfather was related to two other local families of gentry, the Gratidii and Marii. Gaius Marius of the latter family, famous general, consul, and popular hero, had too been born in Arpinum and was by marriage an uncle of Julius Caesar's. Involved in local politics, in opposition to the Gratidii and Marii, the grandfather of Cicero seems to have had a powerful friend in Rome, the distinguished consul Aemilius Scaurus. Bookish and ailing in health, Cicero's father married Helvia, who also had important connections in the capital. His brother was an intimate of the great orator Marcus Antonius, grandfather of Marc Antony. Cicero's father was closely associated with the son of Marcus Cato the Censor, also the brother-in-law of Livius Drusus, tribune in 91; and Helvia's sister was the wife of a friend of Lucius Licinius Crassus's, who in turn was the son-in-law of Scaevola the Augur, the cousin of Scaevola Pontifex. These worthies—Scaurus, Antonius, L. Crassus, and the Scaevolae—formed the intricate web of influential relationships helping to pave the way for Cicero's career and to shape his political outlook.

When he was about ten the family moved into a town house in a stylish quarter on the Esquiline Hill in Rome to begin his education and that of his younger brother, Quintus. The early schooling of the boys and their cousins was supervised by L. Crassus, the owner of a mansion on the Palatine Hill. Among their first teachers was Aulus Licinius Archias, a Greek poet from Antioch. Plutarch records that poetry was Cicero's first love. His boyhood verses have been lost, as has much of a later epic, *Marius,* but a fragment of one of two autobiographical poems survives, together with passages from a translation, in hexameters, of Aratus.[3] Possibly later Cicero read a draft of *On the Nature of Things,* the finest Latin poem to date, making some suggestions to its author, Lucretius.[4]

At the age of sixteen Cicero commenced the study of law under Quintus Mucius Scaevola the Augur, a renowned lawyer and consul in 117, father-in-law of L. Crassus and son-in-law of Gaius Laelius, who was the intimate of Scipio Aemilianus Africanus Minor. Scaevola, Laelius, and Scipio were to figure in varying degrees as speakers in the *Republic*. The Augur had also been a colleague of Scaurus's, who would be the model *optimate* for Cicero. On the death of the Augur in 87, legal studies continued with his cousin, Q. Scaevola Pontifex, consul with L. Crassus in 95, distinguished author of the first systematic treatise on Roman civil law, and a Stoic. No doubt during his legal apprenticeship Cicero was influenced by an old family friend, Antonius, eminent orator and consul in 99 and grandfather of Marc Antony. Also studying under Pontifex with Cicero was Titus Pomponius, known as Atticus, who became an intimate friend, fellow philo-Hellene, prolific correspondent, and who served him in various capacities as business agent, publisher, and adviser. Atticus, like Cicero, was of an affluent equestrian family with important social connections. Far wealthier than Cicero, interested but never involved in politics, nominally an Epicurean, he survived his friend by many years. He became the father-in-law of Agrippa, who was a colleague of Augustus Caesar's, and a granddaughter of his was engaged to Tiberius.

Any effort to understand the nature of Cicero's social and political values cannot ignore his exposure at an impressionable age to statesmen of the caliber of L. Crassus, Antonius, and the Scaevolae, all associates of Scaurus. Cicero was to shower them with compliments.[5] He honors Crassus by making him the chief speaker in *On Oratory*, referring to "the wellnigh infinite extent of his own talent," and elsewhere to the "foresight" of Scaevola the Augur.[6] Scaurus, consul in 115 and *princeps senatus* from 115 to 89, the author of an autobiography, is singled out for most fulsome praise.[7] The ideal *optimate* for Cicero, he is "one of the highest authorities on statesmanship," unique for his "steadfastness," one "who resisted all revolutionaries from Gaius Gracchus to Quintus Varius, whom no violence, no threats, no unpopularity ever caused to waver."[8] These dignitaries, Mitchell emphasizes, "emerge as leading spokesmen of the conservative *nobilitas* in the nineties and the dominating influence in the formulation of senatorial policy."[9] One might argue, indeed, that Cicero's mature social and political thought is substantially the forceful and eloquent expression of their point of view. Central to it is a strict conservatism, which Cicero made his own, one that upholds the ancestral constitution narrowly construed as the only proper guide for current policy. Domination of the senatorial aristocracy tightly controlling the state, suppression of popular leaders and movements, and adamant opposition to any economic, governmental, or cultural reforms are the basic ingredients of their conservative ideology. Not the least impassioned of Roman worshippers of the past, to Cicero these stern and ruthless worthies and their rigid policies must have epitomized the *mos maiorum* or ancestral custom, which could best serve as the standard of political and social values in the troubled flux of his age.[10] In fact, their powerful political and intellectual influence could have been a major impediment to the much-needed reform that might have saved the Republic.

Cicero's early education was by no means confined to legal studies and literature. A common opinion is that his first exposure to philosophy was in the company of Atticus in the establishment of L. Crassus, at the hands of the Epicurean Phaedrus (140–70 B.C.). In the light of the most recent scholarship, this seems a mistaken view, since there is no evidence that Phaedrus was in Rome at the time.[11] Both youths, however, later attended Phaedrus's lectures in Athens where he headed the school. While Cicero rejected the creed, he expressed a genuine fondness for Phaedrus, "an honest, amiable, and obliging man."[12] Hence the blind Stoic, Diodotus, perhaps has the honor of being Cicero's first philosophic mentor. He came to Rome in 88, resided in Cicero's villa, becoming his dear friend and tutor, and died in 59, leaving 100,000 H.S. to his admiring pupil.[13] Diodotus imbued Cicero with the tenets of Stoic philosophy, taught him music and geometry, and gave him a "thorough training in dialectic."[14] The most profound impact on young Cicero, however, was made by Philo of Larissa, head of the New Academy, a refugee in Rome from the Mithridatic wars, where he died not later than 79. Under him Cicero was probably exposed to a modified version of the radical skepticism of Carneades, which stressed the uncertainty of all knowledge and recognized the crucial nature of social and political matters. Other teachers contributed to Cicero's youthful intellectual regimen, if not as significantly as Diodotus and Philo. He may have gleaned some knowledge of Aristotelianism from Staseas of Naples, the first Perapatetic to reside in Rome. Cicero came to prize Aristotle, owning *Topics* and the *Rhetoric,* although he apparently attributed the *Politics* to Theophrastus and the *Ethics* to Nicomachus.[15] Cicero may also have conversed with Aelius Stilo, a friend of the Scaevolae, the first Roman scholar of note, Stoic literary critic, antiquarian, and author of a commentary on the Twelve Tables of the Law. A final mentor seems to have been Apollonius of Alabanda, known as Molo of Rhodes, who visited Rome as an envoy from his island where he taught rhetoric. Cicero later studied with him in Rhodes, valuing his stylistic corrections and criticisms and the discipline he thereby gained over his verbal excesses.

Little is known about Cicero's personal life at the time. In the Social War he did his stint in the army, his only real experience with military service. He was attached first to the staff of Pompeius Strabo, where he made the acquaintance of his son the future opponent of Caesar, and his later enemy Catiline; he then served with the forces of Sulla in Campania. During the struggle between Marius and Sulla, and under the regime of Cinna, Cicero prudently refrained from politics and pursued his studies. Once normality had been restored under the dictatorship of Sulla—Cicero always found his ruthless exercise of power distasteful—the practice of law was the order of the day. He probably took his maiden case in 81; at least the *Defence of Publius Quinctius* is his first extant forensic speech, although possibly there were earlier ones. With a subsequent brilliant defense of Roscius, he gained the reputation of being an up-and-coming advocate. Either just before he left for Athens in 79 or sometime after his return in 77, he married the wealthy Terentia, possibly of the consular family of the Varrones. If this is true, then Marcus Terentius Varro (116–27 B.C.), the foremost scholar of the age and author of the famous *On the Latin Language* (43 B.C.) and *On Farming* (37 B.C.), and many other books, may have become a distant relative by marriage. The two authors were acquainted and corresponded. Varro dedicated a portion of his great treatise on the Latin language to Cicero, who reciprocated with the second edition of his

Academics. Terentia bore Cicero two children: first a daughter, Tullia, and then a son, Marcus. They were divorced in 46, and Tullia's untimely death the following year was a heartfelt loss to the father. After the divorce Cicero married Pubilia, forty-five years his junior, a relationship lasting only a few weeks and ending in divorce after the tragic demise of Tullia. Marcus was a disappointment to his father. An amiable spendthrift and souse, he proved to be a capable colonial administrator.

For reasons of health, in 79 Cicero went to Athens for study in the company of his brother, a cousin, and possibly another friend. Atticus was also in the Greek metropolis. After six months Cicero moved on briefly to Smyrna, where he met a friend of Scaevola Pontifex's, Publius Rutilius Rufus, also a Stoic—who, as we shall see, was later credited by Cicero with recalling at that time the discussions featured in the *Republic*. Then Cicero visited Rhodes to sit at the feet of his old professor of rhetoric, Molo. He also attended the lectures of Posidonius, the leading Stoic of the age and a pupil of the great Panaetius, and he returned to Rome in 77. The six-month sojourn in Athens, what little is known about it, is of interest for his intellectual biography. There he studied oratory and rhetoric with a friend of Atticus's, Demetrius of Magnesia, the author of a book on concord. He also heard the lectures of the Epicureans, Phaedrus and Zeno. To Cicero, however, the great intellectual attraction of Athens was the distinguished member of the Academy, Antiochus of Ascalon (ca. 130–120 B.C.–ca. 68 B.C.). Plato, the founder of the Academy, was Cicero's ideal of the philosophic mind, "our divine Plato" as he calls him, "my master Plato," "whose teaching I earnestly endeavour to follow," "that foremost of men in genius and learning."[16] Antiochus had been a pupil at Athens of Cicero's old admired teacher, Philo of Larissa, and was probably a companion in his flight to Rome. Rejecting, however, the skepticism of the New Academy, Antiochus returned to the orthodoxy of the Old Academy, attempting a synthesis of Academic, Perapatetic, and Stoic doctrines. Cicero, however, remained true to the moderate epistemological skepticism of Philo and always claimed to be a follower of the teachings of the New Academy. Apparently no basic contradiction existed for him between the skepticism of the New Academy and Plato's own position.[17]

Cicero had little interest in logic, and while he was willing to identify himself epistemologically with the New Academy and the dialectical approach of Plato, he turned primarily to Stoicism for ethical inspiration. Just as Philo had first given the youthful Cicero a taste for moderate skepticism, so his beloved house guest and tutor Diodotus seems to have inclined him to the morality of Stoicism. Much of Stoicism he rejected, in particular its epistemological and metaphysical dogma. Nevertheless, he was drawn to the austerity of its ethical outlook. The Stoic goal of the self-sufficient wise man striving for absolute virtue was always a cherished goal of Cicero's, although he was willing to tolerate moral compromise in the exigencies of everyday life. On Stoic ethics he turned for guidance to the writings of Panaetius (185–109 B.C.), the intimate of Scipio Aemilianus and his circle, the teacher of the conservative Roman notables, whom Cicero so revered. Panaetius tailored Stoic moral teachings to fit the practical needs of such accomplished warrior-statesmen as Scipio and Laelius. Consequently he gave priority in his theorizing to those virtues most becoming and helpful to the noble man of action in his quest for honor and glory. Emphasis is placed on such active virtues as greatness of soul or magnanimity, on generosity or liberality, on decorum or propriety, and on energy and industriousness, as against the traditional Stoic stress on fortitude and justice. Cicero, the consummate political animal, like his conservative heroes of the past, was to find in the ethics of Panaetius an ideology of the active and strenuous life and was to rely on him for his last philosophic work, *On Duties*.

Back in Rome, Cicero resumed his law practice and plunged into the politicking that in less than fourteen years would catapult him to the position of supreme power, consul of the Republic in 63. He followed the *cursus honorum* or path of honor expected of civic-minded gentlemen and held each public office (the election year preceded the year of incumbency) in turn at the minimum age: quaestor at 30 in 75, aedile at 36 in 69, praetor at 39 in 66, and consul at 42 in 63. It was an astounding feat, not only for one so young and without military skill or experience, but also for an equestrian, a gentleman certainly, but not one of senatorial family. Among the twenty quaestors, who were charged with financial duties and assisting provincial governors, Cicero was appointed to western Sicily, where he performed well in his single year of office and made many influential friends. Once quaestor, according to the procedure, he became a senator. Later, in 70, on behalf of the Sicilians he prosecuted C. Verres, governor of the province from 73 to 71, whose corrupt and extortionate administration had generated a scandal of considerable proportions. Cicero's oratorical skill brought down a judgment against Verres and did much to garnish an already promising legal career. In the year of his victory, Cicero decided to stand for plebeian aedileship, an urban magistracy charged with the supervision of the public games. His tenure was characterized by strict economy in the outlay of public funds for the games, and he carefully conducted himself so as to avoid any future accusations of having used the influential office to arouse the masses. Again he was successfully elected in 67 to a praetorship. Among the judicial functions assigned to Cicero was the presidency of the court of claims.

In his various electoral contests and in public office Cicero had skillfully forged links with the equestrian country gentry, with the *publicani,* and with the most important oligarchic families. He was always a painstaking organizer and canvasser and a most astute campaigner. No one could charge him with being a popular demagogue, and his scrupulous regard for finances, opposition to social reform, and belief in senatorial supremacy endeared him to the conservative aristocratic power-brokers, to country squires, and to businessmen, fearful of any major changes and desirous of uniting against popular leaders like Caesar and Catiline and the influential M. Crassus. So with an excellent record, having made few enemies and cultivating numerous friends in the right places by having carefully laid the political groundwork, Cicero was now in an advantageous position for seeking the consulship. Campaigning on a platform of unity and harmony between senators and equestrians throughout Italy as a whole,[18] with the slogan *concordia ordinum,* "concord of the orders," he was overwhelmingly elected in 64 along with a minor politician, C. Antonius.

Once in office, Cicero more than lived up to the expectations of the conservative oligarchy, successfully blocking any movement for reform, safeguarding landed and business interests, preventing the reduction and cancellation of debts, and raising penalties for bribery. One of his most noteworthy strokes in resisting social change was the defeat of the measure for land reform proposed by the tribune Publius Servilius Rullus. An unknown, Rullus was probably backed by the popular Caesar and M. Crassus. Cicero's *Three Orations Against Rullus* is the only extant source for the details of the bill. It was the culmination of the attempts at agrarian reform since Tiberius Gracchus. Public land now largely in the hands of great landlords was to be redistributed among landless peasants. Cicero, by what amounted to clever misrepresentation of the bill, seems to have duped the masses and won them over to his side in opposing it.[19]

Not unconnected with the defeat of the Rullan agrarian reforms was Cicero's most famous consular achievement, the suppression of the Catilinarian conspiracy. The minutiae of this exceedingly complex and still hotly debated episode need not detain us. After the failure of the Rullan measures and in the midst of a serious financial crisis involving the dangerous growth of indebtedness among all segments of the population,[20] L. Sergius Catilina, of impeccably noble lineage, who had previously been implicated in a number of dubious enterprises, unsuccessfully contested the consular election of 63 on a program of land distribution and debt cancellation. Affronted by his defeat and desirous of regaining his sullied honor, the fiercely ambitious Catiline plotted to seize power on October 28, with a small group of disgruntled and equally ambitious aristocrats, among whom were some bankrupts. They had the backing of the poorest urban plebeians and many of the dispossessed and debt-ridden peasantry who saw no alternative save armed insurrection. Getting wind of the conspiracy, Cicero decisively crushed the uprising before it could gain momentum, and under emergency powers obtained from the senate he summarily executed without trial five of the ringleaders. Catiline was hunted down and killed with his embattled forces in Etruria. Cicero clearly acted in the affair with the backing of the aristocracy united by the threat and of most of the urban masses who had supported him since his handling of the Rullan bill. For his key role in preventing the revolt, Cicero received the accolade of *pater patriae,* "father of his country." Although the exact nature of the conspiracy is still in doubt among scholars, it seems that Rome was not on the verge of social revolution, governmental overthrow, or civil war. Yet, in the words of Mitchell, it was not a "trifling episode," and Cicero must be praised for "skill-ful and effective leadership."[21] Cicero always considered it to be the high point of his political career, a fearless feat of statesmanship of which he was still unabashedly proud twenty years later: "For never was the republic in more serious peril, never was peace more profound. Thus, as the result of my counsels and my vigilance, their weapons slipped suddenly from the hands of the most des-perate traitors—dropped to the ground of their own accord! What achievement in war, then, was ever so great? What triumph can be compared with that?"[22] Unfortunately, the memoir he wrote of his consulship is not extant. Regardless of Cicero's rather smug self-acclaim, it should be remembered that Catiline was able to capitalize on the grievous conditions of the laboring poor, con-ditions whose alleviation Cicero had vigorously opposed and was to continue to oppose. Moreover, where a cooler head might have reacted more prudently and without sacrificing due process of law, Cicero, apparently misjudging the gravity of the situation and giv-ing way to panic, showed little respect for Roman liberties.

After his consulate and success in ending the career of Catiline, Cicero's political decline was far less spectacular than his rise. It was a story, not without pathos, of the steady and protracted erosion of power for two decades until his ultimate isolation and murder. Yet in the years immediately following office, he re-mained an important influence in the senate, having become first speaker in 62, and was a respected figure among the *publicani* and country gentry. His execution, however, of the five conspirators without according them the right of every Roman citizen to a fair trial, began to be increasingly questioned and condemned. The urban plebeians, previously his allies, deserted his cause and were gradually captivated by Publius Pulcher Clodius, a wealthy aris-tocrat who assumed their leadership and became their foremost spokesman for social reform. By slighting the honor of Clodius in 61, Cicero made a potent enemy for the future, who did not hesitate to capitalize on the increasing disaffection of the masses and their disillusion with Cicero. Moreover, the political initiative and the whole structure of power were shifting in the direction of his former foes, Caesar and M. Crassus. In 60, Pompey, who had been Cicero's conservative supporter, threw in his lot with them to form the First Triumvirate, with Caesar becoming consul in 59. Elected tribune in that same year and holding office in the next, Clodius, unrestrained even by the efforts of Pompey, vented his full wrath upon Cicero, managing to have him exiled in March for his alleged illegality in regard to the Catilinarian conspirators and razing both his Palatine palace and his Tusculan villa, ordering a temple dedicated to Libertas to be built on the former site. Instead of remaining in Rome and facing prosecution, Cicero fled to Thessalonica (Salonika) in Macedonia, where he may have suffered a suicidal breakdown. Following Clodius's tenure of office, and the easing of tensions, Cicero was restored, entering the capital on September 4, 57, and after a particularly eloquent plea was compensated for the destruction of his properties. Plunging once more into the legal fray, at the beginning of 56 he successfully defended his friend Publius Sestius who, with another associate, Milo, together with Pompey, had demanded his restoration. The Triumvirate was disintegrating by 54: Caesar had been in Gaul since 58, Pompey was in Spain, and in 53 Crassus was to lose his life in battle. In January of 52, shortly after Cicero, late in the preceding year, had been elected to the college of augurs which headed the state religious cult, Milo murdered Clodius and was unsuccessfully defended by his legal friend. To quell the rioting of a furious populace incited by Clodius' death, in an unprecedented move the senate brought Pompey and his troops into the city and appointed him sole consul.

It was customary for a consul after completing his term of office to serve for at least a year as proconsul in governing one of the provinces. This was supposedly so that the state could benefit from experienced officials in colonial administration, but in fact was largely the means of allowing former magistrates to recoup the enormous financial losses entailed in electoral politics. Although he had succeeded for years in delaying his expected term as proconsul, Cicero could no longer postpone it and was appointed governor of Cilicia. He left Rome in the spring of 51 to assume his new duties in Tarsus, the capital of the province that included the coast of southern Asia Minor, sections of the interior, what is now northwestern Syria, and the island of Cyprus. Cicero was in charge of the civil military administration and the nominal commander of two legions and the native auxiliary forces. His governorship was characterized by economic frugality, and he himself extracted much less profit from his subjects than was considered normal among more avaricious proconsuls. Although he had never before commanded troops in extended operations and did not personally do so now, he was credited with a Roman victory in a minor campaign against the Parthians, which garnered for him a *supplicatio* or thanksgiving from Rome, and the usual honor of the title of Imperator bestowed upon him by his soldiers.

Cicero came home in early January of 49, expecting the usual triumph for a victorious proconsul, only to find the Republic embroiled in civil war between the armies of Caesar and Pompey. In June, 49, some months after Caesar had crossed the Rubicon, Cicero decided to remain no longer a neutral spectator in the contest between the warlords; he joined Pompey in Macedonia. After the latter's defeat and assassination, Cicero returned to Italy in October, 48, where the following year he met Caesar in Brundisium, just back from his military successes. The victorious Caesar treated Cicero with the utmost courtesy and generosity, allowing him complete freedom of movement. Cicero saw Caesar's dictatorship as the end of his cherished Republic, indeed as the end of the state in any significant sense, and although he confessed that he had not personally suffered under the new regime,

still none the less, so crushing are my anxieties, that I do not think I am acting aright even in remaining alive at all. For I have lost not only numbers of my most intimate friends, either torn away from me by death, or dragged from my side by banishment, but also all those friends whose affection I had won by the part I once played, in conjunction with yourself, in the successful defence of the Republic; and all around me I see the shipwrecks of their fortunes and the pillaging of their possessions; and not only do I hear of it, which would in itself be a misery to me, but I actually see, and it is the most distressing sight in the world, the squandering of the property of those men with whose assistance we once extinguished that awful conflagration; and in the very city in which but lately I was richly blessed in popularity, influence, and fame, of all that there is nothing left me. I do continue to enjoy Caesar's extreme courtesy to me; but that cannot counterbalance violence and revolution in every relation of life and in the times themselves.[23]

Cicero retired completely from politics and turned to philosophy during the dictatorship that ended with Caesar's assassination by Brutus and his senatorial allies on the Ides of March in 44. A friend of Brutus's, but unaware of the plot, Cicero after the deed became closely associated with these liberators of the Republic, as they called themselves. Caesar's death gave Cicero one last political opportunity, and during the first half of 43, if anyone can claim the distinction, he was the virtual ruler of Rome in the name of liberation from tyranny. But his ferocious—and, as it proved, highly imprudent—onslaught against Marc Antony in the thirteen *Philippics,* named after Demosthenes' passionate attack against Philip of Macedonia three centuries before, sealed his fate. He was forced to give way to the superior power of the Second Triumvirate in their proclaimed goals of re-creating the Republic and destroying the liberators. Cicero and his allies were proscribed by the new junta, and after several vacillating and vain efforts to flee Italy he was murdered by their soldiers on December 7, 43. Twice before defeated by Caesar, Cicero was ultimately the victim of the process launched by his foe in 60.

Because of his voluminous surviving correspondence (over nine hundred letters from November, 68, to July, 43), more is probably known of Cicero's personal life than of that of any other major social and political thinker before Locke and Rousseau, and possibly of any prominent statesman before the nineteenth century. As a consequence of these revelations, Cicero tends to be more harshly judged—perceived as he is with all his warts and blemishes—than might otherwise be the case. About his patriotism and dedication to the common good as he perceived it, there can be no reservation. He was certainly an instinctive political creature who with Marius, Sulla, Pompey, Caesar, M. Crassus, and Octavian should certainly be called a leading statesman of the late Republic. Yet he lacked the ruthlessness, the single-minded determination, the supreme self-confidence, unrelenting courage, and spark of political genius to make him the equal in statecraft of Caesar or Octavian. His innate conservatism, extreme caution, and habitual temporizing were possible obstacles to the achievement of true political virtuosity, and in a state and age dedicated to war his failure to display military talent or to become a soldier of distinction may have been no less a hindrance. Of the seven premier statesmen of the century he was the only one without military expertise or experience. Despite his vacillation and procrastination on many occasions, and his lack of dependability, he could occasionally act decisively and not without courage. Essentially an exceedingly proud person, often self-satisfied and given to exaggerating his accomplishments, he could also be extraordinarily generous and loyal to others, displaying little or no envy at their successes, even turning his own polished wit against himself. Neither was he a particularly vindictive man toward his enemies, nor one who gloated over their failures. A certain detachment of manner, aloofness from the fray, and coldness in his personal relationships were perhaps political handicaps. The involuntary political retirement and transformation of his beloved Republic into a tyranny under Caesar did little to ease his last years. Moreover, his personal life in old age was one of deep disappointment: the divorce from Terentia, the unfortunate liaison with Pubilia, the tragic loss of Tullia, the profligacy of young Marcus, and the constant worry over money matters. At a time when toughness was a requisite for survival, he was remarkably deficient in that quality. By the standards of his age and class, he was an individual of honor and more humane than most, treating all his slaves well and freeing Tiro, his indispensable confidential secretary, librarian, and friend, to whom we are perpetually indebted for the publication of the voluminous literary remains of his former master and for writing his biography, which has not survived. Even though the personal imperfections may outweigh the strengths, Cicero will continue to be one of the most significant figures of European culture, a literary stylist without peer, an orator and advocate with few rivals, and an accomplished popularizer of complex abstract ideas. From our standpoint, he should be remembered and studied as the greatest interpreter of the political experience of the late Roman Republic, who possibly did more to influence early modern social and political thought than any other ancient.

2. *Philosophy as Solace and Guide*

The beginning of Caesar's ascent to power in 60, and correspondingly Cicero's descent, meant that with more leisure from politics, he increasingly turned to literary pursuits. Prior to his proconsulship in Cilicia in 51, he had completed and published the *Republic* and commenced work on the *Laws*. In the nearly two years of enforced political retirement under Caesar from late 46 or early

45 to the end of 44, he wrote his major philosophic works at a
furious pace, probably starting with the *Paradoxes of the Stoics.*
It was an erudite friend, Gaius Matius, ironically a loyal partisan
and admirer of Caesar, who, Cicero confessed, "urged me to write
these philosophical treatises."[24] In *On Divination,* published just
after the dictator's assassination, Cicero tells us that although now
politically inactive, he hopes to continue serving the state and con-
tributing to the public good by instructing his fellow citizens,
especially the youths, in the most noble learning.[25] We know that
for Cicero, the politician par excellence, philosophy was an important substitute, but only a substitute, for the life of action, a
means of solace in his isolation and exclusion from the public
forum. The works he lists in *On Divination* are *Hortensius, Academics, On Good and Evil Ends, Tusculan Disputations, On the
Nature of the Gods, On Fate, On Consolation, On Old Age,
Cato, On Oratory, Brutus,* and *Orator.* Of these, *Hortensius, On
Consolation,* and *Cato* have been lost. Another perished work,
On Glory, was written in the summer of 44, when he also began
his last philosophic tome, *On Duties,* completed in the autumn
and judged by many to be his masterpiece. His last writing, finished before the end of the year, *On Friendship,* was dedicated
to Atticus.

Cicero's disappointments in the political arena were aggravated
by the misfortunes of his personal life: his quarrel with Terentia
ending in divorce, the failure of his second marriage, and the death
of his treasured daughter, Tullia. Almost in presentiment of those
future years when he was to find comfort in his studies, in 62 in
defense of his old friend the minor Greek poet Archias, he explains
to the court the value of literature:

no mental employment is so broadening to the sympathies or so en-
lightening to the understanding. Other pursuits belong not to all times,
all ages, all conditions; but this gives stimulus to our youth and diversion
to our old age; this adds a charm to success, and offers a haven of consolation to failure. In the home it delights, in the world it hampers not.
Through the night-watches; on all our journeying, and in our hours of
country ease, it is our unfailing companion.[26]

Three years afterwards, he was forced to take seriously these sentiments in the conduct of his own life, writing to Atticus: "So,
Titus mine, let me throw myself into my studies, those wonderful

studies which I ought never to have left and to which I must now at last return."[27]

Cicero illuminates in a number of writings his reasons for taking up philosophy in retirement.[28] Now with ample leisure, free from the work and worry of public life, he believes that he has a duty to expound the principles of philosophy and to make his fellow countrymen less dependent on the Greeks in studying it. Latin is no less rich than the Greek language and more than adequate for conveying the ideas of Greek philosophy. His philosophic works are written especially for the moral instruction of the young, although men of advanced years may also find consolation in them. During a time of civic upheaval when the Roman state has degenerated into a tyranny, Cicero suggests that his thoughts, now that he is no longer at the helm of government, may provide direction and guidance for the personal lives of his contemporaries. However, he also considers that the study and writing of philosophy will resuscitate and elevate his own spirit, which has been crushed by his many tribulations. A dedication to philosophy, then, in such an annoying and debilitating time of trial may enable him to forget his sorrows and lift his flagging spirits:

O philosophy, thou guide of life, o thou explorer of virtue and expeller of vice! Without thee what could have become not only of me but of the life of man altogether? Thou has given birth to cities, thou hast called scattered human beings into the bond of social life, thou has united them first of all in joint habitations, next in wedlock, then in the ties of common literature and speech, thou hast discovered law, thou hast been the teacher of morality and order: to thee I fly for refuge, from thee I look for aid, to thee I entrust myself, as once in ample measure, so now wholly and entirely.[29]

Despite his eulogy to philosophy, Cicero confesses in a moment of candid despair that it is still second-best to an active life, and for one who scaled the pinnacle of politics his studies are of rather small comfort: "even with them, I hardly want to live; if I am robbed of them, then not even hardly."[30]

Cicero shares with most ancient thinkers the opinion that philosophy should always be of practical value, providing us with principles to be followed in our everyday lives.[31] As one might expect, he believes that politics should be guided by philosophy. Philosophy's role is to inform politics, to set the course, to provide orientation and order. Apart from its relationship to public life, philosophy has a crucial part to play as guide and mentor in our private affairs. Nothing contributes more to a good and happy life than philosophy. From its study we acquire strength of character and knowledge of virtue. Cicero conceives of philosophy as a mode of mental therapy. Philosophy purifies the soul, purging our tensions and anxieties, thereby supplying inner peace and harmony. Philosophy enhances self-sufficiency, increases independence from the outside world, offers refuge from our troubles, and allays and sublimates cares, fears, and passions. Philosophy is medicine for the disturbed psyche as well as requisite nourishment for the healthy soul.

Cicero fails to develop an original philosophic position. His philosophic outlook is derivative, characterized by eclecticism and moderate skepticism. Above all he is the commentator, interpreter, and popularizer for the Romans of the various important Greek schools of thought. While strongly attracted to much of Stoicism, as we have seen, to elements of its cosmology, ethics, and to its emphasis on an active public life, he rejects many of its more doctrinaire and esoteric views. He considers himself basically a follower of the New Academy, adhering to what are probably the teachings of Philo, the head of the school, under whom he briefly pursued his youthful studies in Rome. The skepticism of the New Academy must have been exceedingly congenial to a lawyer and politician of a pragmatic and empirically tentative temperament like Cicero. He no doubt found in Academic skepticism an attractive theory and method formalizing and justifying his approach to the conduct of public affairs: keeping an open mind and examining all sides of a question, weighing and comparing the evidence pro and con, calculating the advantages and disadvantages before deciding on a policy or course of action, and once reaching a decision, always ready to be flexible and seldom committing himself irrevocably to a fixed posture.

The New Academicians, by Cicero's account of their doctrines, hold that there can be no certain knowledge.[32] This does not mean the rejection of all reasons and principles and the advocacy of a life of indecision and vacillation. In place of certainty and uncertainty the Academicians substitute probability and improbability. Everything is suspect until a comparative estimate of the arguments and evidence of both sides is drawn up, and then a conclusion is reached as to what is "probable" and "improbable." By accepting the probable and rejecting the improbable the dogmatism of certainty and the "anything goes" attitude of uncertainty are equally avoided. Hence, Academic skepticism neither paralyzes human action nor sinks in a morass of relativism. The wise man simply follows probability rather than certainty, and dispenses with improbability. In fact, so it is argued, most of our lives are based on this principle. If we act only in terms of certainty, we can do very little. The wise man does not know with certainty that the ship will carry him to his destination. However, depending on what he can learn of its past voyages, its condition and the nature of the weather, the conduct of captain and crew, and the distance and route to be traveled, the wise man can judge the probability or improbability of its arrival. Utilizing a calculus of this kind, he then decides on action or inaction.

The testimony of our senses, according to the Academic skeptics, should be accepted until the contrary is demonstrated. The wise man withholds assent when either no evidence founded on sensory perception is offered or the evidence is inconclusive. In the latter case, he weighs the available sensory data in terms of probabilities and then acts or does not act, affirms or denies. Sensations possessing a particular "distinctness and clearness" (*insignem et inlustrem*) are probable and should serve to guide our activity, although we withhold our assent as to whether they are true and certain.[33] Cicero thinks the overall position of the New Academy stemming from the teachings of Arcesilaus is in harmony with the outlook of Plato, in whose works nothing is taken for granted, but instead everything is subject to minute analysis for and against, any conclusion of certainty being withheld.

Cicero is quite conscious that adherents of these tenets are less likely to be dogmatic, inflexible, and intolerant, more apt to display a humility about their own wisdom and opinions. In tackling any problem or in attempting to explain his attitude toward a specific matter the Academic skeptic does not act as if he "were the Pythian Apollo making statements to be regarded as certain and unalterable, but following out a train of probabilities as one poor mortal out of many."[34] Those who take the opposite course cling to some fixed position so tenaciously that for the sake of consistency they feel obliged to support normally unacceptable beliefs. In contrast, Academic skeptics, "whose guide is probability and who are unable to advance further than the point at which the likelihood of truth has presented itself, are prepared both to refute without obstinacy and be refuted without anger."[35] A wise man then is less a "manufacturer of words" than "a researcher into things."[36] Small wonder that John Locke, likewise skeptical about the certainty of knowledge, rejecting dogmatism and fanaticism of belief and contending that for most of the time our lives can only be based on probability, should have quoted on the title page of his masterpiece, *An Essay Concerning Human Understanding* (1690), a remark from *On the Nature of the Gods:* "How delightful it would be, Velleius, if when you did not know a thing you would admit your ignorance, instead of uttering this drivel, which must make even your own gorge rise with disgust."[37]

For Cicero philosophy possessed the power of consolation in distress and of relieving spiritual malaise and psychic tensions, functions we would normally associate with religious conversion and belief in God. Religion, he felt, was an absolute necessity, but less for spiritual than for social reasons.[38] He sincerely believed in God and in his rational presence in the universe but displayed little anxiety about life after death, rejecting the idea of punishment in the hereafter. The precise nature of his religious beliefs and their relationship to his philosophic perspective is an exceedingly complex one and remains a matter of continuing scholarly debate. Suffice it to say for our purposes that he apparently utilized his philosophic skepticism of the New Academy to combat two extremes: what might be called the religious nihilism of Epicureanism on the one hand, and the theistic absolutism of the Stoics on the other. His own position evidently attempted philosophically to steer a course between the two, between the untruth and truth of religion, in the form of a doctrine of the probable existence of the gods and their care of human beings. Ultimately he was led to fall back on authority instead of philosophy as the foundation of religious belief. Authority in this case, as one might expect, meant fundamentally the wisdom of the ancestors, the *mos maiorum,* in the form of the necessity of religious belief for the solidarity, loyalty, cooperation, and dynamism of the citizenry—

in a word, the civic virtue which had made the Roman state so great. Cicero was himself an augur who wrote a lost work on the subject, and explicitly upheld divination in both the *Republic* and the *Laws*.[39] In a philosophic context, however, from the outlook of Academic skepticism he severely criticizes divination as superstition, while at the same time acknowledging its invaluable social utility.[40] He seemingly is not making the sharp distinction between religion and superstition to which we have been accustomed in the Christian era. Instead of rejecting all divination out of hand as mere superstition, he again appears to have adopted a middle course to assure that religion will neither hamper political action nor obscure our perception of the rational order of nature. In sum, Cicero's religious views were entwined with his political ideas, finding both inspiration and intellectual legitimacy in the ancestral constitution.

3. *Principal Social and Political Writings*

Only the most casual treatment of Cicero's social and political thought can afford to neglect the ideas diffused throughout the full range of his many writings: the correspondence, forensic and political orations, the philosophical and rhetorical works. He never wrote a systematic treatise on society and politics, but four of his books are absolutely fundamental to any discussion of the subject. All were written after his fall from political power, in the leisure of the last decade or so of his life. In chronological order they are: *Defence of Sestius, Republic, Laws, On Duties*. Before proceeding, the reader must be warned of at least three problems in examining Cicero's writings, other than the fragmentary nature of some of them. The first concerns the fact that the philosophic works are in the main, together with the *Republic* and *Laws*, in dialogue form. Hence, care must be taken in differentiating Cicero's actual views from those voiced by others. This poses no special problem in the case of the *Laws* because Cicero is one of the participants; or for *On Duties*, an extended "letter" to his son. Among the numerous speakers of the *Republic*, Scipio Aemilianus, who is given the leading role, is usually thought to represent Cicero's own ideas, but even here caution should be exercised. For the other dialogues in which Cicero either does not appear or does not play much of a part, the reader must take care, "playing it by ear," as it were, keeping in mind the context of his other writings. A second problem pertains to the weight that should be given to the polemics of the orations vis-à-vis the more rational argumentation of the philosophic works. In case of a contradiction, the position of the latter should be given priority, with the proviso mentioned above. This is not to say, however, that the orations cannot be used to corroborate views in the philosophic works or to fill out and more fully develop opinions expressed in the latter. The third problem relates to Cicero's failure to write systematic political or philosophic treatises. As a consequence one should not give to his many ideas a greater logical consistency and coherence than they warrant. The temptation is to tie up loose ends into an architectonic whole, a danger that even the skillful interpreter cannot always avoid, and a defect to which this book, despite an acute awareness of the problem, may not be entirely immune.

The *Defence of Sestius* is a forensic speech delivered in court in early 56 B.C., just after Cicero's exile and restoration, and, as was his custom, revised for subsequent publication. The oration is a plea on behalf of Publius Sestius, whose trial began on February 10. Quaestor in 63, praetor in 54, and proconsul in Cilicia in 46, Sestius was closely associated with Caesar, although maintaining his relationship with Cicero. As a tribune in 57, he had collaborated with Milo against Clodius for the restoration of Cicero. Sestius faced two charges. The first, of which little is known, had to do with his candidacy for tribune. The second related to his use of an armed guard while serving in that office. The prosecution, while not in the name of Clodius, was due to his efforts, since he had been appointed aedile on January 20. M. Aemilius Scaurus, the son of Cicero's hero, served as presiding judge. Cicero headed a distinguished team of counsel for the defense, including Hortensius, M. Crassus, and the orator and poet C. Licinius Calvus Macer. Pompey was one of the character witnesses for the defense. Sestius was unanimously acquitted on March 11. The *Defence of Sestius* is primarily a manifesto, Cicero's first extant effort at outlining a political platform and presenting a justification of his past actions. He summarizes his view of the machinations of Clodius in regard to his own exile and restoration, and in so doing characterizes the *populares* and *optimates*—identifying

Clodius with the former, his own position with the latter—and traces the division in Roman society and politics back to the Gracchi. In this connection, the speech is an important example of Cicero's distinctive rhetorical formula directed against the *populares*—unique in late Roman republican political discourse—and employed in his numerous political and forensic orations in the twenty years between his consulate and his death.[41] His platform for the *optimates* is outlined in the speech, basic to which is the slogan *cum dignitate otium*. In sum, the oration is fundamental to an understanding of Cicero's political perspective as it pertained to Roman affairs.

Cicero's two dialogues, the *Republic* and the *Laws,* are together the *locus classicus* of his social and political ideas, and except for various lost pamphlets and essays they are the only works of their genre in the late Republic and, of course, the first in Roman history.[42] They are essential for his conceptions of man, law, and justice; his attitude to the state and politics; his typology of states; his notions of the mixed constitution, of tyranny, of the ideal statesman, and of the social utility of religion. Moreover, they are important for his anti-democratic bias and commitment to proportionate equality. Both works, in keeping with the sentiment expressed later in *On Divination,* were written primarily for the general reader, particularly a youthful audience, and not so much for the learned and wise.[43]

In addition to the actual disintegration of Roman civic life to which Cicero was responding, it has been persuasively argued that the "immediate intellectual cause" of both books and of the subsequent philosophic works was the publication of Lucretius's *On the Nature of Things.*[44] From Cicero's standpoint the brilliant poem of the Epicurean, which was being widely read by members of the Roman cultural establishment, threatened to subvert the Roman civic community and its foundation in the *mos maiorum.*[45] Cicero, then, turned to writing the *Republic* and *Laws* in an effort to enlighten his contemporaries by persuading them of the necessity of returning to the political and social values of their forebears and of recapturing something of the spirit of the ancestral constitution.

Probably less than half of the *Republic* has survived: what was discovered in the Vatican Library in 1820, after being lost for centuries with the exception of the concluding "Dream of Scipio," which was read throughout the Middle Ages. Nevertheless, portions of the work had long been known from the transcriptions and discussions of passages in the writings of Christians such as St. Augustine and Lactantius. Indeed, some of these quoted passages are necessary to fill in the fragmentary Vatican manuscript. Cicero probably began the tome, in the form of a dialogue, in May 54, when he wrote his brother Quintus that he found it "a very stiff and toilsome piece of work; but if it succeeds to my satisfaction, the labour will have been well laid out."[46] The dialogue was originally intended to take place during a holiday and to be divided into nine books, each representing a day's discussion. By the beginning of October of 54, two books had been completed on the "ideal constitution of the state and the ideal citizen,"[47] and Cicero was seriously considering assigning himself the role of leading participant in a current setting. He subsequently decided against the scheme and, in order to avoid offending his contemporaries, placed the dialogue in the previous century.[48] He also shortened the project to six books, two conversations per day for three days, with a preface to each day, one every two books. The work was apparently finished and published by the early summer of 51, before he went to Cilicia. In June of that year, a friend, M. Caelius Rufus, wrote of its popularity, and somewhat later we learn that Atticus was reading it.[49]

The *Republic* is dedicated to Quintus. Cicero maintains that when they were together in 79 on their grand tour of Athens and the eastern Mediterranean they were given a full account by Publius Rutilius Rufus, then living in exile in Smyrna, of the conversations presented in the book.[50] Rufus has a very minor part in the work. The scene of the dialogue is during the Latin holidays of 129 B.C. in the gardens of the villa of Publius Cornelius Scipio Aemilianus Africanus Minor, adopted grandson of the statesman and victor over Hannibal, Scipio Africanus Major.[51] Scipio Aemilianus, consul in 147, conservative opponent of the Gracchi, destroyed Carthage in 146. A friend and patron of Polybius and Panaetius, he is the principal speaker, voicing Cicero's own opinions. Although he was responding to the troubles afflicting Rome in his own age, Cicero substituted the period of the Gracchi for the disorders of his day as the reason for assessing the nature of the state. His choice of the historical setting for the dialogue was a stroke of genius, because he believed the conflict set in motion by the Gracchi was responsible for the deep fissures currently dividing the state.[52] Scipio Aemilianus, moreover, arch-foe of the Gracchi, was murdered in 129, the year in which Cicero had set the dialogue,[53] and it had long been rumored that their followers were responsible for the death. Another active participant is Scipio's close friend, Gaius Laelius, consul in 140, who shared Scipio's hostility to the Gracchi. Other speakers include Lucius Furius Philus, consul in 136; Marius Manilius, consul in 149, a distinguished jurist celebrated for being one of the three founders of Roman civil law; and Quintus Aelius Tubero, consul in 118, known for his legal erudition, nephew of Scipio and student of Panaetius. The group of friends, at least the older ones, belonged in actuality to the famed Scipionic circle, cultured pro-Hellenic gentlemen who gathered under the patronage of Scipio Aemilianus to exchange views on literary, philosophic, and political matters.[54] The brightest stars of the intellectual and literary firmament— Polybius, Terence, Panaetius, Lucilius—were attracted to the colloquia. Some scholars, however, now believe that the circle is simply a fiction of Cicero's.[55]

The dramatis personae of the *Republic,* consisting of nine distinguished historical figures including four with very small roles, are quite different from the political amateurs figuring in Plato's own *Republic.* Cicero's cast are all men of action, renowned warrior-statesmen, eight of the nine being of consular rank. They are also men of intellect. Six among them are serious Stoics; and three, legal experts. All had determinedly resisted the Gracchi, and one, Scaevola the Augur, the son-in-law of Laelius, with only a bit part in the dialogue, had been Cicero's teacher. It seems, therefore, that by the time and setting, the nature of the participants, the imminent death of the principal, Scipio, and the presence of a former teacher, Cicero wishes to establish himself as the legatee of the conservative anti-reformism of a venerable political tradition with roots in the pre-Gracchian golden age and to reveal to his struggling and anxiety-ridden contemporaries the *mos maiorum* as a preceptor of civic wisdom and virtue and a guide out of their present difficulties.

The *Republic* is a work on the state and its fundamental principles.[56] In Book I the state is defined and the three simple constitutions and their perversions are examined. Book II presents a "constitutional history" of the early Roman state and the development of the mixed constitution, and Book III offers a conception of natural law and justice. What little has survived of Book IV deals with the education and culture of citizens, and Books V and VI describe the ideal statesman, ending with the "Dream of Scipio." In conscious emulation of Plato, Cicero intends to offer a conception of the ideal state.[57] But from his standpoint, the Greek's portrayal of the ideally best state is unsatisfactory.[58] The problem with Plato, Cicero feels, is that he attempts to demonstrate the validity of his basic political axioms by creating a paper ideal, unfortunately a highly impractical one in terms of actual human conduct.[59] In other words, Plato's ideal is far too utopian to be of much service for guidance in the realities of politics. Plato's successors such as Aristotle and Theophrastus, Cicero maintains, analyze numerous existing states without coming to any definite conclusions about which might best serve as a model. Cicero hopes in a sense to combine the two approaches on the basis of experience and the generalizations derived from it. He proposes to use an actual state to demonstrate his political theorems, which he thinks are not essentially different from Plato's. Cicero also acknowledges his intellectual obligation to Panaetius and Polybius, "two Greeks who were perhaps the best versed of them all in politics." The model would be Rome itself, "the greatest State of all."[60] Rome is not only the best practicable state, but, with only slight modification, the ideally best state. Unlike Plato's Kallipolis of the *Republic,* therefore, Cicero's ideal was never to be only a mental construction, but an actual state, suited to men as they really are.[61] By emphasizing the ideal nature of the Roman state, Cicero is certainly not suggesting the Rome of his own era or that of the Gracchi. To the contrary, the ideal Roman state is a creation of countless men by trial and error over many years bequeathed to Cicero and his contemporaries, who have misused and defiled their priceless inheritance. So instead of devising an impractical utopia in the style of Plato, Cicero in his own *Republic* plans to discover in the historical experience of Rome, in the *mos maiorum,* the essence of the ideal state and its fundamental principles.

Although it was begun soon after, if not before, the completion of the *Republic,* perhaps in 52, the writing of the *Laws* was apparently delayed by Cicero's tenure in Cilicia and the Second Civil War. As late as 46 he was probably continuing to labor on the book,[62] which had still not been issued in 44 when he listed his works in *On Divination.* Whether he published it before his death or even finished it is unclear. Cicero is the chief speaker of the dialogue, his fellow participants being Atticus and Quintus. As in the case of the *Republic,* the work is probably dedicated to the latter. The scene is a long summer day at the family estate of Arpinum. Only the first three books of a possible projected six, like the *Republic,* are extant, and these contain gaps. Plato again is the model. Cicero designed the *Laws* to be a sequel to the *Republic,*[63] but this, of course, is not the precise relationship between the two works of the same name by Plato.

The purpose of the *Laws* is to set forth and explain the basic statutes of the ideal state of the *Republic,* the existing Roman Republic with some minor alterations. Cicero never intends to expound the laws in a narrow technical sense, for Roman civil law would be "confined to a small and narrow corner."[64] Instead his primary interest is in the broad question of the source and nature of law and justice. The first book, possibly derived from Panaetius or Antiochus of Ascalon, is devoted to this subject. Books II and III respectively contain the laws of the ideal state on religion and those concerned mainly but not entirely with the magistracy. The laws are presented in an intentionally abbreviated form, followed in each book by extensive comment and explanation.[65] Keyes's opinion that Cicero's enumeration of the laws amounts to the first historical instance of a written constitution in the modern sense seems somewhat exaggerated.[66] Cicero may have thought of the work in general and the detailed prescriptions of the laws in particular as constituting a set of legal norms that could serve, during Rome's disorders, to recapture something of the spirit of the ancestral constitution. Whatever his reasoning about the aim of the work, he admits to few differences between his model laws and those of the existing constitution.[67]

Popular commentators on Cicero's social and political thought often ignore *On Duties* and as a consequence fail to examine some of his most significant ideas. The neglect is symptomatic of the decline of Cicero's reputation as a philosophic thinker, but before the nineteenth century *On Duties* was usually thought to be his most important book. One classical scholar has written: "It is arguable that the *De Officiis* is the most influential secular prose work ever written,"[68] a verdict John Locke would probably not have disputed. A widely imitated work, it was read throughout the Middle Ages and was possibly the first book of classical antiquity to come from a printing press. From the sixteenth to the nineteenth century it was staple fare for young European pupils, a universally accepted manual for gentlemanly conduct. Apart from Cicero's position on moral obligation, the work is crucial because of its portrait of an ideal gentleman and the attitude expressed toward labor and various vocations. Nowhere are Cicero's positions on private property and its relationship to the state better or more fully explained. Furthermore, it is characterized by a pronounced individualism not only in economic but also in moral and political concerns. On strictly political matters, unless *On Duties* is scrutinized the student may miss Cicero's conceptual separation of state from government, his beginning distinction between state and society, and his notions of the trust of government, tyranny, and tyrannicide.

On Duties is Cicero's last philosophic work, probably started in the summer of 44 and finished in November. It is written in the form of a lengthy epistle for the moral edification of his twenty-one-year-old son Marcus, studying in Athens and indulging in the fleshpots of that ancient city. Cicero, in a letter of October 28 to Atticus, says: "Here I philosophize (what else?) and expound the subject of duty on a magnificent scale. I am addressing the book to Marcus. From father to son what better theme?"[69] Cicero admits that on the question of moral duty he will follow the Stoics not as a mere imitator, but with discretion as it suits his purpose.[70] His basic Stoic guide is Panaetius, who had written a no-longer-extant volume on duty. According to Cicero, Panaetius dealt in the two books of his work with the questions of determining whether an action is morally right or wrong, and whether it is expedient or inexpedient.[71] He never, however, fulfills his promise of dealing with a third problem, that of the possibility of a conflict between the morally right and the expedient. Cicero, then, prompted by Panaetius's failure, decides to devote

his third and final book of *On Duties* to this very problem. Although Panaetius's pupil Posidonius seems to have dealt with the
subject, Cicero evidently wrote his third book without seeing the
latter's treatment.[72] Cicero affirms that the question "which was
passed over by Panaetius, I will carry to completion without any
auxiliaries, but fighting my own battle, as the saying is," a fairly
clear indication that he did not rely on Posidonius.[73] Just as *On
Duties* is his last philosophical testament, his remarks to Atticus
about the book were to be his last known philosophical rumina-
tions to his friend, for Cicero had less than a year to live.[74]

CHAPTER FOUR

Law, Justice,
and Human Nature

1. *Natural Law and Natural Justice*

Because of its centrality to his thought as a whole, Cicero's natural-law conception of the universe and man is the most obvious
point of departure for any consideration of his social and political
ideas. His unshakable belief in the rational order of the universe
and man is perhaps his most basic value, the intellectual under-
pinning of his other fundamental norms. Far from being original,
however, Cicero's conception of natural law bears the unmistak-
able imprint of Stoicism. Yet he was the first major thinker in
whose extant works can be found something approaching a full
treatment of the subject, one which was to become the basis of
all future, more systematically developed natural-law theories
within the Christian tradition of discourse. In this chapter an effort
will be made to summarize his views—not, in the main, to comment critically on them—collected from a variety of his works,
a summary that should further our understanding of his social and
political ideas. It should always be remembered that the conceptions of *On Duties* were his last word on the subjects to which
this chapter is devoted, and that his previous efforts were by no
means conclusive, but were attempts to work out a position.
Hence, the following synthesis may appear to give to Cicero's
notions developed over time a greater logic and unity than they
in fact possess.

For Cicero, the mark of the divine intelligence on all things is
the law (*lex*). Law is the essence of nature. God rules the universe
by means of law, the law of nature. Law prescribes and prohibits

in regard to the functioning of all things. Law is the edict of nature and as such the highest expression of the supreme rationality and authority:

Law [*legem*] is not a product of human thought, nor is it any enactment of peoples, but something eternal which rules the whole universe by its wisdom in command and prohibition. Thus they have been accustomed to say that Law is the primal and ultimate mind of God, whose reason directs all things either by compulsion or restraint. Wherefore that Law which the gods have given to the human race has been justly praised; for it is the reason and mind of a wise lawgiver applied to command and prohibition.[1]

The law of nature is implanted in all things, giving to them their divinely ordained structure, purpose, and function. That portion of the law of nature applicable to humans consists of God's directives for the universal commonwealth or cosmopolis. In referring to this commonwealth of reason to which human beings belong, Cicero ascribes its governance to both God and the gods, often in the same passage. The reason for the apparent confusion is that he shared on this point the attitude of the Stoics, who allegorized the deities of the popular Greek and Roman religions. Their gods, for the Stoics, were different manifestations of the single God, the divine presence in nature.[2] The law of nature is inscribed on the souls of all human beings, directing them by a kind of innate apprehension, since they share in the universal rationality.[3] This law is absolute, eternal, immutable, and universal, knowing no limitations or modifications by people, place, or time. It is not only the embodiment of reason (*ratio*) but also, by definition, of right reason (*recta ratio*), of the ethical principles directing human action, because the source of law is God, the supreme all-wise moral good, the *summum bonum*. Cicero's classic definition of the law of nature is as follows:

True law is right reason in agreement with nature; it is of universal application, unchanging and everlasting; it summons to duty by its commands, and averts from wrongdoing by its prohibitions. And it does not lay its commands or prohibitions upon good men in vain, though neither have any effect on the wicked. It is a sin to try to alter this law, nor is it allowable to attempt to repeal any part of it, and it is impossible to abolish it entirely. We cannot be freed from its obligations by senate or people, and we need not look outside ourselves for an expounder or interpreter of it. And there will not be different laws at Rome and at

Athens, or different laws now and in the future, but one eternal and unchangeable law will be valid for all nations and all times, and there will be one master and ruler, that is, God, over us all, for he is the author of this law, its promulgator, and its enforcing judge. Whoever is disobedient is fleeing from himself and denying his human nature, and by reason of this very fact he will suffer the worst penalties, even if he escapes what is commonly considered punishment.[4]

The rule of nature applicable to humans is simply the divine reason ruling the soul of each of us, enabling us to distinguish between good and evil, the natural and the unnatural, and to direct our conduct accordingly. Cicero in his earliest work distinguishes the law of nature (*lex naturalis*) from both statutory law (*lex*) and customary law (*consuetudo*).[5] Statutory law is "that which in written form decrees whatever it wishes, either by command or prohibition,"[6] and is made available for the people to read.[7] It often confirms certain usages that have developed over time, proving to be advantageous to a people as registered by their consent. These usages constitute customary law: "either a principle that is derived only in a slight degree from nature and has been fed and strengthened by usage—religion, for example—or any of the laws . . . which we see proceed from nature but which have been strengthened by custom, or any principle which lapse of time and public approval have made the habit and usage of the community. Among these are covenants, equity and decisions."[8] All authentic law—natural, statutory, or customary—entails equity (*aequitas*) and choice or selection (*dilectus*) in the senses of granting to each his due and choosing what to prescribe and what to prohibit, what is just and what unjust.[9] Civil law (*lex civilis*), the statutory and customary law of a given state or people, should conform to the universal ethical principles of the law of nature. If civil law fails to do so, by definition it is not true law.[10] For Cicero law is basically a normative conception.

The reader is struck at first by Cicero's vagueness about the basic moral precepts of the law of nature. He fails to specify them in a single list, although he suggests what they are. In *Topics,* for instance, he stipulates that the law of nature has to do with the right of each to his own property and with revenge.[11] Earlier he wrote that the law of nature included religion, duty, gratitude, revenge, reverence, and truth.[12] But in his remarks on justice Cicero is more precise as to the moral commands of the law of nature. Reason, the omniscient intelligence of God as expressed through universal law, is the essence of nature, and the essence of that part of the law of nature applicable to human beings is justice. The moral commands and prohibitions entailed by natural justice are consequently those of the law of nature, which in turn reflect the universal divine reason.[13] Humans share in the universal reason whose source is God. Hence, they participate in the law of nature which is right reason, and accordingly they share in justice.

Like the law of nature to which it is essential, justice is absolute, universal, eternal, and immutable. In presenting his notion of natural justice in the *Republic* Cicero is contending with the opposing and exceedingly influential view of the Epicureans, among others, one that was most persuasively formulated by the Skeptic, Carneades, namely, that justice is not natural but conventional, originating in human weakness and self-interest.[14] From this perspective justice is an agreement or compact for mutual self-restraint between the masses and notables, each fearing the other. Since interest or utility changes with the context—from people to people, state to state, and time to time—justice is relative and conditional instead of being universal, eternal, and absolute. Law and customs differ, and hence justice varies according to time, place, and the inclinations of a people. Men obey the laws not from any instinct for justice but out of self-interest and the fear of punishment and of the consequences of any widespread breach of the law. In effect, a criminal is no more or less just than a legitimate ruler. Both are motivated by self-interest. Commenting on this view in a passage of which only a fragment survives, Cicero recounts a story of the meeting of Alexander the Great with a pirate, a tale used by St. Augustine in *The City of God*. When the pirate is asked by Alexander "what wickedness drove him to harass the sea with his one pirate galley, he replied: 'the same wickedness that drives you to harass the whole world.' "[15] The notion of justice so expressed, according to Cicero, is founded on self-interest and unprincipled self-aggrandizement. On the other hand, true justice prescribes that we "spare all men," consider the interests of mankind, give to each his due, and respect the property of others—private, public, and sacred.[16]

The basic precepts of the law of nature are for Cicero more

inclusive than those of natural justice because the former concern all living things, whereas the latter apply only to human beings. Every living creature, by virtue of the law of nature, possesses the instinct of self-preservation.[17] This is manifested in reproduction for the propagation of the species. Unlike plants, however, human and non-human animals strive to avoid injury to themselves, seek to acquire the necessities of life, and in varying ways care for their offspring. Humans differ from plants and non-human animals in that they possess reason and speech, *ratio et oratio,* as we shall see, and thus are moral creatures, subject to the moral prescriptions and prohibitions of the law of nature. Natural justice, therefore, which has to do with the moral principles that should guide the conduct of all rational beings, is the essence of that portion of the law of nature to which humans by virtue of their reason and speech are subject and that includes and transcends self-preservation, reproduction, and care of the young. Once Cicero's idea of natural justice is clarified, the moral tenets of the law of nature can perhaps be specified with greater certainty. On the whole, however, he fails to explain the ethical precepts of natural law as rigorously as St. Thomas does at a much later time.

Cicero began his literary career in *On Inventions* with a definition of justice and ended it in *On Duties* with a lengthy treatment of the subject. From the first work we learn that justice (*iustitia*)

is a mental disposition which gives every man his desert [*dignitatem*] while preserving the common interest [*communi utilitate conservata*]. Its first principles proceed from nature, then certain rules of conduct become customary by reason of their utility; later still both the principles that proceeded from nature and those that had been approved by custom received the support of religion and the fear of the law.[18]

The extensive discussion of justice in *On Duties* places great emphasis on its common utility.[19] Justice, Cicero argues, is absolutely necessary for the preservation of society. Justice is a natural inclination in humans, who because of their participation in the universal reason, which animates and gives form and purpose to the universe, are by nature gregarious or social creatures. No human society can exist without justice. Cicero's very definition of the state in the *Republic* as a partnership in right stresses the importance of justice as the foundation of society.[20] Justice is fundamental to all human relationships, in household as well as state, in respect to all commercial transactions, and between workers and employers. If they are to survive, even gangs of criminals must adhere to an elementary kind of justice:

> Its importance is so great, that not even those who live by wickedness and crime can get on without some small element of justice. For if a robber takes anything by force or by fraud from another member of the gang, he loses his standing even in a band of robbers; and if the one called the "Pirate Captain" should not divide the plunder impartially, he would be either deserted or murdered by his comrades. Why, they say that robbers even have a code of laws to observe and obey. . . .
> Since, therefore, the efficacy of justice is so great that it strengthens and augments the power even of robbers, how great do we think its power will be in a constitutional government [*constituta re publica*] with its laws and courts?[21]

In his insistence on the close connection between justice and the common interest Cicero notes in passing the statement attributed to Socrates by Cleanthes, the second head of the Stoic school, that the father of philosophy blamed all the mischief of the world on the first individual who divorced utility from justice.[22] Possibly Cicero is, among other considerations, trying to appeal to the obvious egoism of his contemporaries, by demonstrating that the way of morality is the pursuit of an enlightened self-interest.

Although Cicero believes that morality in the form of justice is advantageous and expedient, at the same time he maintains that it is always in our interest, no matter how unlikely it may seem, to act in a self-denying and altruistic fashion. We should constantly attempt "to make the interest of each individual and of the whole body politic identical. For, if the individual appropriates to selfish ends what should be devoted to the common good, all human fellowship will be destroyed."[23] In this almost Rousseauan formulation Cicero seems to mean that the individual will be truly acting for himself if he gives priority over his immediate interests to the preservation and well-being of society. When one acts only for oneself in the narrow sense, with no thought for the security and welfare of others, the society on which one's own life and happiness in the long term depend will be seriously weakened. Cicero never instructs us to abjure self-interest, but only to act as reasonable human beings, pursuing our own advantage in an enlightened and moderate manner, ever mindful of the possible consequences of our conduct.

What, then, are the essential principles of justice which should regulate our actions, thereby securing the common interest and as a result ensuring our own advantage? The moral obligation of natural justice, and hence of the law of nature as it pertains exclusively to humans, can apparently be reduced to four major duties: (1) not to injure others physically without cause; (2) to respect private and common property; (3) to fulfill obligations for which our word has been pledged; and (4) to be kind and generous to others, according to their worth and our means.[24] Each individual is duty-bound under the law of nature to render "to each his due" in reference to life, property, promises, and benevolence. But what is due to each depends on the worth of each. The human object of every moral duty prescribed by natural justice and the law of nature varies in value, some individuals being of greater worth than others. In practice, from Cicero's outlook, the differentials in the value or worth of humans correspond to their station in society. The life of the gentleman, his property, the promises given to him and made by him, and the generosity owed to and by him are of greater value than those of the humble laborer, and should appropriately receive higher priority. Should a conflict of duties arise, then, the gentleman has a greater claim than the laborer because of his superiority. Fundamental to Cicero's conception of natural justice and the moral dictates of the law of nature is his tacit aristocratic assumption of proportionate equality: more is owed to the superior, usually defined in terms of birth and wealth, and less to the inferior.[25] Natural justice in this sense favors the privileged few to the detriment of the underprivileged majority.

Aside from the question of Cicero's tacit assumption of proportionate equality, nothing about his four basic principles of natural justice per se poses a threat to his society of private property, enormous property differentials, and gross inequalities of privilege. Nor do these principles touch upon fundamental freedoms of speech, assembly, and thought. To the contrary, they seem to be what one might expect of a conservative who wishes to justify the maintenance of a hierarchical and authoritarian system of political and social inequality dominated by a wealthy landed class and to prevent any essential reforms from threatening the status quo. Morally good individuals, as perceived by Cicero, are obliged to resort to force, if no other means of redress are available, to defend their lives and possessions from all unprovoked attacks and violations. The converse is also expected: to refrain from threatening or harming the lives and properties of others under normal circumstances. All oaths, pledges, promises, agreements, contracts, compacts, and covenants should be meticulously honored, unless the situation has drastically altered from that under which they were made. Without common observance of these moral duties in regard to life, property, and promises, Cicero's whole world of landed property, wealth, commerce, and social inequality would collapse. Of course, any society is premised on the security of lives, possessions, and promises. But in Cicero's age what social group stood to gain most from the promise of such security? Was it those with little or nothing to lose, the overwhelming and virtually propertyless majority who labored under the most appalling conditions for the well-being of their superiors? Or was it those with everything to lose, the affluent and leisured minority whose domination might be undermined by protest from below, civil war, and policies of land redistribution and debt cancellation? Cicero's audience, of course, as was always true of that of his literary genre, was strictly limited, consisting of a select few of the upper classes and not of the masses. He wrote for a rapidly disintegrating ruling class, to raise their spirits and to provide them with moral encouragement; to revive, strengthen, and unify them; to offer them solace and justification during their tribulations; and to warn them of the perils of personal excess and self-aggrandizement and of the dire consequences of sweeping social reform. One comforting message suggested by Cicero to his peers was that Rome had in effect conquered the realm of nature as well as the world of man. In some ways he can be interpreted as having "Romanized" the cosmos by his identification of the essence of that law with the moral values of the Roman ruling class.

Finally, in regard to the last moral dictate of natural justice—generosity—mentioned by Cicero, our help and charitable attitude to others depend on the extent of our own property and the position of the others in society. We may be morally obligated to aid our fellows, but always within the limits of our own resources. To place our economic security in jeopardy for the sake of others would simply be reckless and intemperate. A healthy egoism is ever the condition of a wise and prudent altruism, or so Cicero seems to suggest. Nowhere is the assumption of proportionate equality clearer than in Cicero's recommendations on the subject of generosity. Help to others should be proportionate to their position in society, more to be reserved for those who by contemporary standards are the most deserving. A gentleman, therefore, if he must make a choice, would be better advised to succor another of the same status, particularly a family member, kinsman, close friend, or associate who has suffered misfortunes, than an indigent of the lower orders. Or, since Cicero believes that charity begins at home, our benevolence should be directed to our clients and *amicitiae* in gratitude for their support instead of to the poor in general.

Of the four cardinal virtues—wisdom (*prudentia*), justice (*iustitia*), courage (*fortitudo*), temperance (*temperantia*)—justice for Cicero is the highest. He believes that justice and its duties are in a way even more natural than wisdom and courage and their respective obligations, for their very existence and the possibility of their exercise depend on the maintenance of society and hence on the upholding of justice.[26] In justice is the "crowning glory of the virtues," he pronounces, later claiming that it is "the sovereign mistress and queen of all the virtues."[27] Nevertheless, in one passage Cicero rejects the idea that justice should take precedence over temperance.[28] There are, for example, evils so monstrous that a wise man could not commit them in order to save his country, that is, to uphold justice in the strict sense. Cicero, however, quickly dismisses the possibility of such a conflict between temperance and justice by saying that it can never be to the advantage of a country to make such a request of a wise man. He closes the discussion by stating that whenever a conflict among duties arises, "that class takes precedence which is demanded by the interests of human society."[29] In other words, authentic justice, by definition that which always promotes the interests of society, must be given priority over other virtues.

2. Conception of Man

We must now consider Cicero's conception of man or human nature (*natura humana*). Again, the reader should be warned that he offers no single systematic analysis of the subject. Man surpasses all living creatures. He is created by God; his soul is a gift from God. Unlike other animals, man shares in God's universal reason and possesses the divine faculty of speech (*ratio et oratio*). Virtue is also an attribute of man and God. For these reasons man bears a resemblance to God. Gods and men share reason and speech and live by law and justice. The universe forms a single commonwealth or state (*civitas*), of which gods and humans are citizens.[30]

Just because Cicero conceives of men as belonging, by virtue of their reason and speech, to a single world commonwealth does not mean that his view is similar to the later benevolent idea of a common humanity or the Christian spiritual belief in the brotherhood of man. In the past this kind of anachronistic approach to the attitude of Cicero and other Roman gentlemen on the matter has been popular. Cicero's conception of *humanitas,* it has been argued, "combines the humane with the humanistic," implying a notion of universal love or humanity.[31] Today, however, some scholars have concluded that Cicero's *humanitas* and *societas generis humani* (society of mankind)—both of Stoic derivation—have more to do with a common culture, a community of interests, or shared values originating in reason and speech than with an inner or emotional feeling of universal love or kindness.[32] Human solidarity, then, for Cicero, despite his sometimes misleading rhetoric of spiritual brotherhood and fraternal intimacy, implies not so much a loving sympathy or compassion for others as it does the kind of relations and shared interests existing in a community of citizens, with all the inequalities entailed by such a traditional social order.[33]

The universe, Cicero asserts, exists for the sake of rational beings, for gods and men. All things of the world that can be used by humans are divine creations for their convenience and enjoyment.[34] Because of their likeness to God, nature has been prodigal with its gifts to men. The heavens present a dazzling scene for them to observe and contemplate. By watching the movements of celestial bodies the individual learns to calculate the seasons, seasonal change, and irregularity. The earth lavishes men with an abundance of foodstuffs, with grain, vegetables, and fruit.

These are for humans and not for animals because the former have discovered and employed the art of agriculture. Nature has also provided humans with other bounties of the earth: the forests, mineral resources, and the seas. Moreover, the animals of the earth are fashioned by God to be the slaves of mankind. Some animals are used for food and others are trained by men to work for them by carrying burdens and pulling ploughs.

In addition to his emphasis on the earthly bounties created by God to serve and nourish human beings, Cicero dwells on the ingenious divine craftsmanship that allows them to make use of these gifts of nature.[35] God has skillfully designed man's bodily organs and their functioning to enable him efficiently to satisfy the biological needs of eating and drinking. The complex anatomy and physiology of the human body testify to divine inventiveness. To empower man to move and to maintain his stability, God has cleverly contrived his bones, cartilage, and sinews. Of all animals man alone is erect. God in effect has "challenged him to look up toward heaven," a gift allowing him to acquire knowledge of the gods, and men are endowed with senses, their "attendants and messengers," far superior to the comparable equipment of the animals.[36] The structure, location, and function of the sense organs render men more refined and discriminating than animals in regard to sight, taste, smell, sound, and touch. Man is the sole animal whose features are crafted by God to reveal his sentiments and emotions, and thereby his character. Only humans possess hands that manipulate with the greatest dexterity the objects provided by nature, thereby facilitating the development of the many arts and skills learned by imitating nature.[37] Men are indeed laboring animals, because of their agile hands set to purposeful activity directed by reason. By their manual skills and the cooperative employment of those skills, men have succeeded in constructing a civilized way of life with all its advantages and amenities. Through their labor and mutual helpfulness, men have raised themselves from a brute condition of isolated savagery to the material benefits and fraternity of the state.

The bounties of the earth, however, would be of no avail to man, and to his uniquely adapted physical constitution and laboring genius, without the guidance of reason, God's supreme and most glorious gift to humanity. Reason performs three primary and closely connected functions for man. It enables him to reason and acquire knowledge of different sorts, to live peacefully together in numerous and varied societies from the family to the state, and to be a creature of moral virtue. Human reason implies the power of speech. The two are intimately related and mutually dependent, as *ratio et oratio* denote. Language and its constituent elements are the raw materials of reason, the means by which reason is expressed and articulated, whether internally through thought and ratiocination or externally through the written and spoken word. The close kinship of reason and speech is apparent in Cicero's eulogy:

Then take the gift of speech, the queen of arts as you are fond of calling it—what a glorious, what a divine faculty it is! In the first place it enables us both to learn things we do not know and to teach things we do know to others; secondly it is our instrument for exhortation and persuasion, for consoling the afflicted and assuaging the fears of the terrified, for curbing passion and quenching appetite and anger; it is this that has united us in the bonds of justice, law and civil order, this that has separated us from savagery and barbarism.[38]

Whenever, therefore, reason and man as a rational animal are discussed by Cicero, he also has in mind, even when it is not mentioned, the divine faculty of speech.

Reasoning and the acquisition of knowledge comprise a basic function of human rationality.[39] By virtue of reason men draw inferences and understand a chain of consequences. Man because of reason is able to perceive causal relationships, to proceed by a series of steps from cause to effect and from effect to cause, to compare, collate, catalogue, and draw analogies. Reason enables each of us to comprehend and classify external objects and thus to perceive the order, harmony, and purposeful design of nature. Resulting from and facilitating these various processes of reasoning is the human ability to define terms concisely. Ratiocination in general means our power to solve problems, prove and disprove, come to conclusions, and eventually arrive at the truth. The result is the fabrication of a body of knowledge about various aspects of the world: religion, morality, politics, geography, astronomy, biology. Reason also governs the human hand responsible for the invention of the practical arts—agriculture, navigation, building, weaving, medicine—and those that contribute to our pleasure and amusement—music, painting, sculpture, dancing.

Men are also by nature gregarious and social creatures because of the divine gift of reason.[40] "We are born for justice," Cicero affirms.[41] Each of us shares with others in a sense of justice and transmits it to all. Man possesses an innate feeling of goodwill toward his fellow humans that apparently results from the ability to reason and the related self-consciousness and is advanced by the power of speech. Before they were united by the bond of speech, men lived solitary, subhuman lives. Cicero is at pains to point out, in opposition to Epicureans and Skeptics, that human society arose from man's natural reason and not simply out of human weakness and mutual advantage.[42] The natural friendship of man for man is the foundation of family and state and is responsible for their continuing existence. Writing to Atticus in 50 B.C., Cicero explains his outlook with an intimate example:

I am glad that your little daughter gives you pleasure and that you agree that affection for children is part of nature. Indeed if this is not the case there can be no natural tie between one human being and another, and once you abolish that, you abolish all society. "And good luck!" says Carneades—an abominable thing to say, but not so naïve as the position of our friend Lucius and Patro; when they make self-interest their only yardstick while refusing to believe in any altruistic act and maintain that we should be good only to avoid getting into trouble and not because goodness is naturally right, they fail to see that they are talking about an artful dodger, not a good man.[43]

Natural human kindness and gregariousness, stemming from reason and speech, lead men to exhibit a tender and loving care for their offspring, to provide for the future needs and comforts of their families, and to form many different societies and fraternities, not least of which is the state.[44] Human cooperation and social labor explain the growth and flourishing of civilized life and the arts.[45] The strength of the ties of friendship in binding man to man depends to a significant degree on proximity.[46] Fellow citizens have a greater attachment to each other than to aliens. The bond is closest among family members, kinsmen, and friends. Nevertheless, all men have fellow feeling because of their membership in the universal commonwealth of reason and speech. Although loyalties center on the circle of family and blood relationships and tend to weaken progressively in proportion to the distance from the nucleus, in specific circumstances allegiance to the greater communities of state and mankind take precedence over all other commitments.

Human participation in a universal brotherhood of goodwill and mutual aid and other fraternal endeavors would have been impossible without moral virtue, which, like knowledge and natural gregariousness, is the product of reason and speech. Virtue is natural to man, "nothing else than nature perfected and developed to its highest point."[47] The examination of Cicero's conception of virtue must begin with his notion of the human soul, which like so many of his other views is of Stoic inspiration. The soul consists of two parts: the rational, and the irrational or appetitive.[48] The rational portion of the soul participates in universal reason and is marked by peace and tranquillity. The irrational, with no share in reason and hostile to it, is the sector of the passions (*libidines*), of the strong emotions such as anger (*ira*), recklessness (*temeritas*), desire (*cupiditas*), delight (*laetitia*), fear (*metus*), and grief (*aegritudo*). Unlike the rational part, appetite is always turbulent and chaotic, in constant motion, forever pushing or pulling in one direction or another. Reason attempts to control the appetites, bringing them into conformity with the ethical standards inherent in nature itself. Cicero compares the virtuous or natural soul to a monarchy, in which kingly reason reigns supreme, imposing order on the unruly appetites.[49] Reason directs the desires in the healthy soul, and they in turn obey its edicts. The proper relationship between reason and desire is not only that of king over subjects but also comparable to the rule of a master over slaves, the general over an army, and a father over his sons. Self-mastery of the individual refers precisely to this domination of the rational over the irrational. The person with a soul ordered and managed by reason acts with temperance.

From Cicero's standpoint, how does reason enable us to be virtuous? Our rational faculty and our natural gregariousness account for the fact that humans can be virtuous whereas animals cannot be virtuous. To reason we owe a general sense of moral goodness (*honestas*) and greatness of soul or magnanimity (*magnanimitas*).[50] Furthermore, our rational perception of the external world—tracing causal connections, classifying, comparing, defin-

ing—reveals its order, harmony, and beauty. Out of recognition
of these elements emerges our *honestas,* which has to do with
orderly conduct, a sense of propriety, a balance and proportion—
neither too much nor too little—in all we do. In using our reasoning and explanatory skills in the constant pursuit of truth we
acquire an independence of mind, a feeling of superiority and pride
that prevents us from abjectly subjecting ourselves to others, allowing us to be disdainful of and aloof from worldly conditions.
In short, we acquire greatness of soul.

A further natural source of moral virtue is our inborn feeling
of friendship for our fellowmen. In fondly caring for his wife and
children, the husband and father overcomes obstacles in the quest
for things necessary to their comfort and needs. His efforts on
their behalf instill in him a sense of responsibility for them and
their welfare, in turn producing the virtue of courage.[51] Cicero
argues that virtue (*virtus*) is derived from the word for man, *vir,*
and hence the characteristic virtue of man as distinct from woman
is courage, a moral quality involving scorn of pain and death.[52]
From our natural gregariousness also arises those virtues that are
the foundation of justice, such as generosity, patriotism, loyalty,
an inclination to serve others, and gratitude.[53]

Once the individual, by nature rational and gregarious, acquires
an understanding of the general precepts of moral virtue, how
does he know where his moral duty lies in a specific situation? In
other words, how in practice does the individual apply the broad
theorems of the law of nature? To answer this question Cicero
affirms in *On Duties* that nature has endowed each human being
with two characters or *personae.*[54] One *persona* is universal, common to all because of their share in reason and superiority to the
beasts. "From this all morality and propriety are derived," Cicero
writes, "and upon it depends the rational method of ascertaining
our duty."[55] The other *persona* is individual, varying from human
to human, arising from the differences among men in physical
makeup and character. We should accept our own unique combination of strengths and weaknesses, make the best of them
within the limits of the moral law, choose a vocation suited to
our respective abilities, and strenuously pursue it. The differences
among human beings should be accepted by each of us; we should
respect those differences and treat each other with consideration.

Our moral duty, within the framework of the law of nature, depends on our individual *persona:* "For we must so act as not to oppose the universal laws of human nature, but, while safeguarding those, to follow the bent of our own particular nature."[56] Given this, a moral duty for one person may under the same circumstances be a moral transgression for another. In addition to the perception that a moral duty may vary from human to human because of differences in individual *personae,* differences in age, social standing, vocation, and circumstances are absolutely crucial. Since each of us shares in a universal *persona,* we can use our common reason to deliberate about how best we should act in terms of the law of nature, as unique individuals in the particular circumstances in which we find ourselves. Ethical conduct, consequently, depends on developing and applying a "moral calculus" enabling us to analyze a situation, taking into consideration the complicated mix of variables involved and ultimately choosing an appropriate course of action. "In every act of moral duty" we must "become good calculators of duty, able by adding and subtracting to strike a balance correctly and find out just how much is due to each individual."[57] A pronounced individualism is a feature of much of Cicero's thought, basic not only to his ethics, which relies heavily on Stoicism, but also to his economic and political outlook.[58]

It should be remembered that Cicero directs his efforts at moral instruction to showing how "everyday people" can be virtuous, how they can attain to "mean duties" (*officia media*) as against the humanly unattainable "perfect and absolute right" (*recta perfecta atque absoluta*) of the wise man, as is advocated by Stoics.[59] He seems to have in mind the practical and humanly possible standard of common usage applied to generally acknowledged "good men" like Cato and Scipio, not to "men as are nowhere to be found at all."[60]

The natural individual of rationality and virtue, even in the sense of "mean duties," however, is the rare exception. Most of us fail to realize our natural and rational potentials. Cicero is certainly under no illusions about the moral qualities of his fellow human beings. We are characterized by evil as well as good.[61] Every soul is tainted by a weakness and sensitivity which causes it to be readily disturbed and upset.[62] The fierce beast of our passions is tamed by reason only with the greatest difficulty.[63] Humans may be united by nature but because of their evil they are divided by constant conflict and war.[64] Man is man's worst enemy, for "there is no curse so terrible but it is brought down by man upon man."[65] All are subject to ambition, both a blessing and a potent cause of dissension and turmoil.[66] Few can resist the corruption of power and high office or the temptations of luxury and hedonism afforded by great wealth. Although we are the beneficiaries of divine reason, our rational faculties are often used for morally illicit purposes.[67]

What motive, according to Cicero, impels so many human beings, despite their rational and moral potential, to act irrationally and immorally? His answer is fundamentally that of the Stoics, beginning with the concept of pleasure (*voluptas*), which proves attractive to all and leads to vice (*pravitas*).[68] Pleasure is a good as well as an evil. The human proclivity for pleasure is the very foundation of life. Our fond attachment to pleasure forces us to avoid pain and death and to strive to preserve ourselves. The quest for honor and glory, feelings of kindness and gratitude, and hatred of the wicked and cruel—all essential to the shaping of civilized life—result from our overwhelming desire for pleasure. The unrestrained pursuit of pleasure, however, in the forms of sensual gratification, self-aggrandizement, avarice, and the lust for power, are mainly responsible for the evil of the world. Anyone succumbing to these pleasures suffers from a disordered or diseased psyche, an unnatural and intemperate soul.

Uninhibited endeavor for pleasure produces two major types of psychic disorder.[69] One originates in anticipating a good with lust (*libido*) and experiencing delight (*laetitia*), when the good has been attained; tranquil and healthy conditions of the soul in expecting and feeling a good are wish (*voluntas*) and joy (*gaudium*), in contrast to the lust and delight of the diseased soul. The other kind of psychic disorder appears in expectation of an evil, fear (*metus*), and ends in distress (*aegritudinas*) once the evil has been felt. An equable turning away from evil is caution, precaution, or foresight (*cautio*), but there is no equable state of distress. Both disorders occur because of an excessive desire to avoid pain and experience pleasure—in short, because of lack of temperance. Intemperance (*intemperantia*) thus is responsible for the unnatural or diseased soul, the failure of reason to control and guide the appetites: "just as temperance allays the cravings and causes them to obey right reason, and maintains the well-considered judgments of the mind, so intemperance its enemy kindles, confounds and agitates the whole condition of the soul, with the result that from it come distress and fear and all other disorders."[70]

Why, for Cicero, does intemperance, the abdication of reason from the government of the soul, occur in some humans and not in others? His answer is that those who fall victim to immoderation are corrupted by "bad habits" (*depravatio consuetudinum*) and "false beliefs" (*opinionum vanitas*). Cicero adds that "the sparks of fire, so to speak, which nature has kindled in us are extinguished by this corruption, and the vices which are their opposites spring up and are established."[71] Reason, our divinely ordained power of vision, if improperly cared for is blinded by error. It is within our capacity, nevertheless, to correct the ills of the soul caused by intemperance. They are matters of invalid belief and opinion and hence are owing to our misjudgment and misunderstanding of the morally right and appropriate.[72] He emphasizes that nature is not to be blamed for our psychic indispositions and the resultant evils. We alone are responsible. We suffer, as it were, from a "false consciousness" arising from improper training, education, and bad examples: "Do you not see, therefore, that evil comes from opinion and not from nature?" (*Videsne igitur opinionis esse, non naturae malum?*)[73] Cicero never explains what, if not nature, historically first caused the appearance of bad training and education which began the process of generating false opinions.

Nonetheless, Cicero suggests a cure for his own society of diseased souls. In fact his whole life can be said to have been dedicated to remedying what he takes to be the widespread malady afflicting his countrymen which he holds responsible for the serious troubles besetting the late Roman Republic. In a word, the potion he prescribes is "enlightenment," the eradication of false opinions by the education of the ruling classes and in turn their enlightened rule of the Roman people. Initially, the prevailing self-deception can be replaced by a return to nature and reason brought about by means of a therapy of increasing self-awareness and the purging of the psyche through philosophy:

But there is one method of healing both distress and all other diseases of the soul, namely to show that all are matters of belief and consent of the will and are submitted to simply because such submission is thought to be right. This deception, as being the root of all evil, philosophy promises to drag out utterly. Let us surrender ourselves therefore to its treatment and suffer ourselves to be cured; for when these evils settle upon us, not merely is it impossible to be happy but we cannot be in a sound state either. Let us then either deny that reason has its perfect work, although on the contrary the fact is that nothing can be done aright without reason, or inasmuch as philosophy consists in the collection of rational arguments, let us, if we wish to be both good and happy, seek to gain from it all aid and support for leading a good and happy life.[74]

This outline of Cicero's conception of man has not been offered simply out of deference to the conventional expectation that the treatment of any social and political theorist has to be so introduced. While Cicero's view of human nature is far from being systematically presented and suffers from a characteristic vagueness and lack of precision, it is crucial to an understanding of his social and political ideas. More significantly, the implications of some of the elements were to be more fully developed by later writers and were to inform their outlooks. At the core of the conception of man are the related notions of human rationality and human individuality, neither originating with Cicero. The first, typical of the teachings of Plato, Aristotle, and Stoicism, is expounded with variations by Cicero; the second, although basic to Stoic doctrine, is extended and refined. Humans possess at birth the potential for reason and speech, a capacity that if fulfilled will enable them to become moral creatures. Whether we are all equally endowed with this rational potential is not obvious from what Cicero says, but his belief in the moral (and hence rational) equality of all humans possibly implies it. He is clear, however, as to the vital roles of physiology and, especially, social environment in all efforts at self-realization. Each of us has a singular physical makeup, is born into unique circumstances, and experiences a different upbringing and education. Mankind, consequently, is comprised of unique individuals, each with a diverse character and dissimilar habits and beliefs. The moral principles guiding our lives remain unchanging and identical for all, but each must learn to apply these constant ethical precepts to every practical situation in the way most suited to his unique *persona*. Another result of different constitutions and environments is that some acquire bad habits and false beliefs and others do not, evidently a majority in the former case and a minority in the latter.[75] Those who do not acquire bad habits and false beliefs are naturally superior to those who do, who will in consequence be unable to realize their rational potential.

An individual's failure to fulfill his rational nature, according to Cicero, is largely the result of a defective social environment in the form of inadequate upbringing and education. Consequently, he offers a faint promise of enlightenment through education—at least to the upper classes—as the cure for social ills, a somewhat nebulous idea of mental hygiene as fundamental to any social therapy. While Cicero himself was to do little with this provocative suggestion, in centuries to come the idea was to captivate the European mind.

CHAPTER FIVE

Moral Equality and Social Inequality

1. *The Socially Superior and Inferior*

Cicero is often praised for being the first important social and political theorist to postulate the moral equality of humans, a notion basic to the theory of natural law and justice which he derived from Stoicism. A contradiction, however, exists between his basic ethical position and his acceptance in theory and practice of an inegalitarian society. He never appears to have been conscious of the discrepancy between the two stances, any more than did subsequent natural law theorists from St. Thomas to John Locke. They all take for granted that an inegalitarian society is the only feasible mode of ordering mankind, seemingly unaware that it is at odds with their fundamental moral egalitarianism. A demonstration of how Cicero is able theoretically to reconcile the two contrary views might be intellectually satisfying but could not be grounded on any substantial evidence from his works. The best perhaps that can be done is to delineate the two opposed conceptions as they appear in his writings, once more keeping in mind that he was not always a very neat and tidy thinker, and in the process a further confusion in his ideas related to the subject will become apparent.

Cicero's deep and lasting belief in the moral equality of human beings rests on his view that they are universally endowed with divine reason. The common participation of men and gods in divine reason renders them members of a single world commonwealth.[1] They are in effect blood relations. Humans who thus are godlike and joined together in a single fraternal order resemble each other. Each shares in a universal *persona* by virtue of his reason.[2] A single definition applies to all. Consequently each is a being of *dignitas*, of basic moral worth, and owes *reverentia* or respect to his fellow human beings. This and the fact that humans are superior to other animals and capable of living a civilized life together give them their characteristic *humanitas*. The reason common to all means that all share in right reason, thereby all are creatures of morality, justice, and law: "In fact, there is no human being of any race who, if he finds a guide, cannot attain to virtue."[3]

In addition to our common rationality and shared moral nature, Cicero stresses other egalitarian aspects of mankind. None of us can be sure of the validity of the knowledge informing our actions. Because all live equally in a world of epistemological uncertainty, no one should be overly dogmatic in his views or assertive in his conduct.[4] All individuals, no matter to what extent their *humanitas* is fulfilled, remain fundamentally flawed, albeit in different degrees.[5] Partiality to the self, the temptations of pleasure, and the corruption of power leave no one totally unscathed or completely innocent. Futhermore, all are destined by divine providence to take but a single path through life consisting of childhood, youth, middle life, and old age, with their respective qualities of weakness, impetuosity, seriousness, and maturity.[6] For all humans the cosmic path inevitably ends sooner or later in death, a divine finality to which the only wise response is resignation.[7]

Cicero's powerful and influential vision of the moral equality of all and their membership in a cosmic fraternity should not blind us to the fact that in actual life he condoned and justified the authoritarian rule of a leisured, wealthy oligarchy of landed gentlemen over a huge majority of laboring poor, with the vast differences in property, income, privilege, and mode of life that such rule entails. A sincere and dedicated egalitarian in moral principle, he is unquestionably an inegalitarian in social and political theory and practice, or, in Colish's recent judgment, "although he argues . . . that all men are equal by nature through their common possession of reason, he makes no attempt to apply this principle to politics. He defends an aristocratic polity laden with aristocratic privilege."[8]

In the first book of the *Republic* he states unequivocally that
the distinction between the highest or most distinguished individuals and the lowest or meanest ones is necessary in every people.[9]
This follows the affirmation that "nature has provided not only
that those men who are superior in virtue and in spirit [*animo*]
should rule the weaker [*imbecillioribus*], but also that the weaker
should be willing to obey the stronger."[10] A vital corollary of these
axioms is his doctrine of proportionate equality, for he opposes
the distribution of honors and offices in any state on the basis of
parity or numerical equality, a characteristic of democracy. Instead, the allotment, Cicero insists, should be premised on the
principle of proportionate equality, more to the superior and less
to the inferior.[11] Any commonwealth choosing to ignore this precept by choosing parity over proportionate distribution is in fact
violating true equality and is thus unjust, rendering more or less,
as the case may be, than is due to each. Proportionate equality
occurs in a state when citizens are divided by worth (*dignitas*)
from the lowest to the highest into a hierarchy of legal orders.[12]
Each citizen belongs to a distinct station or rank (*gradus*) in the
hierarchy. This arrangement is most effectively institutionalized,
Cicero thinks, in a mixed constitution like that of the Roman
Republic, with its system of differential rights, duties, and functions corresponding to rank.[13] Everyone, superior and inferior, has
some voice in government, but decisive power is in the hands of
the superior. Cicero's position, therefore, should be crystal-clear
and not subject to dispute. While believing strongly in the moral
equality of human beings, at the same time he argues that some
should be socially superior to others, that the superiors are entitled
to rule their social inferiors, that the latter are obliged to obey the
former, and that the division between superiors and inferiors is
essential to every state.

How then does Cicero, at least in theory, define or identify
those who are socially superior and are thus entitled to rule the
inferior? While he is never explicit on the subject, his Stoic conception of *persona* in *On Duties* may be a convenient point of
departure for ascertaining his meaning. In addition to the universal
persona shared by everyone, each possesses a unique, individual
persona.[14] By virtue of the former we are equally rational and
moral creatures; because of the latter each of us, due to our phys-

ical makeup, birth, and circumstances, differs from everyone else. To put it another way, we are born with equal rational potentials and thus are equally capable of being moral, but we do not equally realize our rational and moral natures. Some acquire bad habits and false beliefs preventing them from fully actualizing their rational and moral capabilities.[15] This indeed appears to be true of most of us in varying degrees, for only a few come close to complete rational self-fulfillment. We all would seem to possess roughly equal rational capacities at birth; nevertheless, we are all equally creatures of appetite. Because human beings are appetitive as well as rational, all are subject to desire, to the pleasure that accounts for our evil tendencies. Now this depravity (*pravitas*), as Cicero calls it in one passage,[16] is controlled in some men and not in others, owing to differences in circumstances. The result of this complex of causes is the development of the individual *persona* of each, as distinct from the universal *persona*. Some, but not all, with favorable circumstances and the proper upbringing and education subject their appetites to the rule of reason and by acquiring good habits and true beliefs realize their rational and moral natures. Therefore, in social reality, although all are of equal rational and moral potential, some manage to attain rational and moral superiority. Those who do are entitled to rule the inferior, whose rational and moral self-realization is stunted. Cicero is never clear as to whether the superior in virtue and wisdom are "naturally superior." One might surmise that they are, since they have more nearly realized their natural essence or being than the rest. At the same time, little said by Cicero—contrary to the positions of Plato and Aristotle—suggests that this superiority is in part innate or hereditary or is equated with good family and noble birth.

If, however, Cicero identifies the superior with individuals of wisdom and virtue, the truly best in the Greek sense of *aristoi,* how does he accommodate that conviction with his positive support of the oligarchical system of government dominating Roman society? Is this not a further contradiction in his social morality? Does not an obvious opposition exist between his belief in the rule of the wise and virtuous over the irrational puppets of lust, and his upholding the rule of the wealthy Roman aristocracy— many of whom by his own account were clearly not wise and virtuous—over a majority of impoverished and laboring citizens, many of whom were neither irrational nor morally evil?

Thus, we cannot fail to observe the further conflict in Cicero's social outlook, between his social ideal and his acceptance of the status quo. Ideally, Cicero seems to subscribe to the Socratic precept that social rank should be functional, corresponding to one's ability in performing the tasks necessary for life, tasks ordered in a hierarchy of the superior and inferior. Cicero's outlook on this point is to be expected, since as a *novus homo,* the son of a member of the country gentry, he rose to the senate by way of the magistracy and in the course of a remarkably rapid social elevation had often been exposed to the snobbery and envy of the entrenched Roman nobility. Cicero takes enormous pride in relating that he is the first *novus homo* for many years to be elected consul, preceded only by his fellow townsman Marius in 86, C. Caelius Caldus in 94, and Titus Didius in 98.[17] Of all the *novi homines* who attained the consulate, Cicero tells us, he was the first to be elected at the minimum age and to defeat by an overwhelming majority candidates of higher social rank. Consulate and senate in the past were open to all citizens regardless of birth and ancestry.[18] Why then, he asks, should *virtus, ingenium, humanitas* be penalized?[19] Why should citizens of lowly origin who have risen in society by their talent and industry be condemned and treated as enemies by the patriciate?[20] In 62, Cicero informs his listeners in court that "not all men are able to be patricians [*patricii*] and, to tell the truth, they do not even care about it; nor do men of your own age think they are your inferiors because they are not patricians."[21] Men from the country are no less able than the nobility. Witness the doughty Marcus Cato Major; Tiberius Coruncanius, consul in 280; the plebeian hero Manius Curius Dentatus in the first half of the third century—all from Tusculum. Cicero places in the same category Gaius Marius of Arpinum—Cicero's birthplace—the reorganizer of the Roman army and conqueror of Jugurtha; and Quintus Pompeius, consul in 141 and the first plebeian censor.[22] Marcus Cato, singled out as an heroic example, is eulogized at the beginning of the *Republic.*[23] *Virtus* or manliness, that vital energy becoming a man, is for Cicero the unique quality of the *novus homo,* just as *nobilitas* is the mark of the aristocrat. Not all *novi homines,* of course, display *virtus,* any more than all blue bloods exhibit *nobilitas*.[24] A noble like Catiline might be a complete scoundrel and inferior to the best *novi homines,* and no doubt Cicero would have said the same of Clodius and others. After all, birth is a matter of chance, but what we do with the circumstances into which we are born depends on our own choice.[25] A man of relatively low birth himself, Cicero claims that he could never have attained exalted office without preparing himself for it.[26] Men "very frequently achieve signal success who, though sprung from humble parentage, have set their aims high," he writes to his son in *On Duties,* no doubt thinking of his own career.[27]

Cicero may admire the self-made man of *virtus,* talent, and industry and believe ideally that the highest offices should be open to individuals of proven ability regardless of birth, but he shows in practice very little sympathy for those who have not ascended the ladder of worldly success. They are, in his mind, failures as humans, lacking the qualities of complete men, deformities who have not realized their full potential. He fails to perceive that there is little room at the top, that most men, through no fault of their own, cannot penetrate the order of the privileged few. If they were able to do so, the very kind of society that he cherishes, one of hierarchy, rank, and order dominated by a leisured propertied minority and served by a productive majority, would crumble. Most men are doomed to the humble position to which they are born, the human condition for which Cicero shows very little sensitivity or compassion. Quite the contrary, his social ideals and values and political outlook are derived from the very stratum that he managed to join—a characteristic of many self-made men throughout the ages. No matter how snubbed or slighted he may have been by the nobility, how much his career may have been hampered by their jealousy, his human ideal is theirs, that of the gentleman, *homo liberalis.* Among them the more enlightened might concede that one is a *homo liberalis* by disposition and conduct, not by birth. At the same time, however, they cling to the idea that like breeds like and that except for a rare few, gentlemen are of families of inherited wealth and property, and established lineage.

Like others for whom the notion of a natural aristocracy of virtue and ability is central, Edmund Burke among them, Cicero in practice compromised his ideal by accepting the status quo and the domination of the existing landed classes, recognizing, however, that they should reform their ways by acting in a more rational and less egotistical fashion. Despite rhetorical genuflexions to the *populus Romanus,* he shares with his peers a contempt for the lower orders, the *vulgus* or *multitudo.* If the supreme authority of the Roman state is vested in *senatus populusque Romanus,* the senatorial order, together with those of equestrian rank, is clearly the dominant partner that should be served by the laboring people, a situation almost comparable to the theoretical precepts of "parts" and "conditions" of Aristotle. In delineating his ideal *polis* in books VII–VIII of the *Politics,* he distinguishes between the "parts," a small elite of landed proprietors who fully participate in government, and the "conditions," the propertyless working majority without political rights whose labor, however, is necessary for the satisfaction of the needs of the parts.[28] "Conditions" are simply instruments for the well-being of the "parts."

While in principle Cicero does not necessarily identify social superiority with good birth, wealth, and property, he does so in practice. Worldly success in the form of riches and ancient family credentials is linked in his writing to honor and moral worth (*honestas*).[29] In keeping with the premium he places on the acquisition of private property, not only is poverty (*paupertas*) coupled with dishonor and disgrace (*ignominia, ignobilitas*), but also the impoverished (*egens*) are associated with the morally evil and profligate (*improbus, perditus, facinorosus*). Cicero is inclined to think of poverty as a crime and the propertyless poor as criminal.[30] He and his fellow notables maintain that the opposite of "gentlemanly" is *sordidus,* an adjective characterizing those of low station and meaning filthy, shabby, mean, base, vile. "Nothing," he insists, "is more fickle than the multitude," and he refers to the "dregs of the city populace" (*sordem urbis et faecem*) and "this wretched starveling rabble [*misera ac ieiuna plebecula*] that comes to meetings and sucks the treasury dry."[31] Another expression is "little better than laborers" (*paene operarios*).[32] Highly critical of Athenian democracy, he comments in the *Defence of Flaccus* on how easily the people are excited by unprincipled demagogues, who have no difficulty "in stirring up craftsmen, shopkeepers, and all the dregs [*faecem*] of a city."[33] These humble citizens clamor like ignoramuses. The word *faeces,* commonly used by Cicero and his contemporaries to label the lower classes, in addition to "dregs" means sewage, garbage, and quite literally "shit." In spite of the fact that Cicero praises many of the time-honored Roman worthies, recognizing that they are little more than peasants, and although peasants constitute the bulk of the population and are a source of Roman greatness, he shows typical urban disdain for humble rural dwellers. He uses the term *agrestis,* or countryman, in the pejorative sense—a convention among those of his class and values—implying "boorish" and "clownish"; and *rusticas* and *sub-rusticas* in the same way, as distinguished from *politus:* polished, refined, accomplished.[34]

2. *Vulgar and Gentlemanly Callings*

Occupations are classified by Cicero into the vulgar (*sordidi*) and those suitable for gentlemen (*liberales*).[35] Vocations such as commerce on a small scale—shopkeeping and retail trade—and those, such as tax-collecting and usury, that arouse hostility in others, do not befit gentlemen. Unlike these vulgar occupations, medicine, architecture, and teaching are respectable; however, they are for slaves and freedmen or those who must work for a living, not for true gentlemen.[36] The only callings for gentlemen are war, politics, law, philosophy, oratory, farming, and commerce on a large scale, particularly if the profits are invested in landed property.[37] Any occupation entailing labor for wages or the work of a craftsman is only for the vulgar. Wages, according to Cicero, are a mark of servitude, and a workshop by its very nature cannot be a gentlemanly atmosphere. The least respectable of all tradesmen are those ministering to our sensual pleasures, from the highest to the lowest in descending order: fishmongers, butchers, cooks, poulterers, fishermen, perfumers, dancers, and variety players. Hence, any labor that provides a livelihood and results in economic dependence is beneath a gentleman.

Cicero reflects the typical aristocratic contempt for banausic labor and predilection for self-sufficiency. But labor—the "execution of work or duty of more than usual severity"—can be mental as well as physical.[38] Of the two kinds, mental labour is thought by Cicero to be superior.[39] Objects striven for by the intellect win far greater appreciation than those realized by physical strength and skill. By mental labor, in effect, involving as it does reason and speech, one attempts to fulfill his natural essence or potential in a way not possible in physical labor, which is closer to the state of an animal than a human. Consequently, mental labor is characteristic of gentlemen; physical labor, of the vulgar.

Philosophy, the highest form of mental activity, is certainly appropriate for gentlemen. Cicero relates the famous Pythagorean story of the three types of men at a gathering such as the Olympic Games.[40] There are those who make money by selling various products—the avaricious. There are the contestants, who seek fame and glory for themselves—the ambitious. Finally, there are the spectators, who desire neither fortune nor fame—the contemplative:

a special few who, counting all else as nothing, closely scanned the nature of things; these men gave themselves the name of lovers of wisdom (for that is the meaning of the word philosopher); and just as at the games the men of truest breeding [*liberalissimum*] looked on without any self-seeking, so in life the contemplation and discovery of nature far surpassed all other pursuits.[41]

This link between authentic nobility and the self-sufficient, self-denying love of wisdom is an ancient one, predating Plato but attaining its fullest expression in the idea of the philosopher-king in the *Republic*. The Platonic Guardian is a soldier-philosopher of authentic gentlemanly conduct and outlook, who transcends the worldly self-interest of the multitude. Since the days of Plato, the genuine philosopher is ordinarily conceived of as being above ideology, one who pursues his calling in a dispassionate and disinterested fashion free from mundane motives, a notion so widely and unquestionably accepted and ingrained in our consciousness that it is seldom criticized and almost impossible to discredit. Yet we know that in actuality philosophers from the very beginning—Plato, Aristotle, and Cicero being cases in point—have been no more immune than ordinary mortals to worldly interests and prejudices, seeking to rationalize them as objective truths by clothing them in the fancy dress of abstract ideas, obscure terms, and erudite discourse.

Despite Cicero's aristocratic disparagement of physical labor and gentlemanly disdain for the manual trades, he expresses, as we have seen, a keen appreciation of the great debt of civilized life to manual work.[42] In *On the Nature of the Gods* he declares: "what clever servants for a great variety of arts are the hands which nature has bestowed on man! The flexibility of the joints enables the fingers to close and open with equal ease, and to perform every motion without difficulty."[43] Besides music and the fine arts, our hands make possible agriculture, building, the fashioning of clothes, and the working of metals. By applying our ideas and perceptions, the hand of the worker cultivates fields, sows, plants, fertilizes and irrigates, gathers foodstuffs, domesticates animals, mines the earth for metals, cuts trees for timber, and navigates the rivers and seas. Through the work of our hands we "create as it were a second world within the world of nature."[44] This paean of praise to manual labor and industry is repeated in *On Duties,* where we are informed that without the skill and physical work of man we would never enjoy all the benefits of our common life in society, concluding:

Think of the aqueducts, canals, irrigation works, breakwaters, artificial harbours; how should we have these without the work of man? From these and many other illustrations it is obvious that we could not in any way, without the work of man's hands, have received the profits and benefits [*fructus quaeque utilitatis*] accruing from inanimate things.[45]

Cicero is careful to point out that it is not the individual working in isolation, but mutual aid and cooperation that have rendered all this possible. A civilized life, as we know it, therefore, is the result of social labor, and men should be treated in such a way as to encourage them to work together for the supply of our natural wants.

From the laudatory passage, quoted above, on the human hand, it is not difficult to reconcile Cicero's admiration of manual labor and industry and our enormous obligation to them with his contempt for artisans and tradesmen and his haughty belief in the superiority of gentlemanly callings. For the hands are mere servants (*ministrae*) or instruments of the mind created to implement the ideas of reason, the characteristic faculty of human beings, just as the lower social orders exist to execute the commands of the rational and intelligent—the gentlemanly classes. Or, as Plato and Aristotle put it, the "instruments" and "conditions" of the naturally superior are manual laborers, naturally subordinate to those who live the life of the mind closest to nature. The natural master-servant relation existing in the soul of each human is duplicated in the best and most natural ordering of society, divided between the more rational, non-laboring masters and the less rational, laboring servants.

3. The Model Gentleman

But what of Cicero's conception of the gentleman, which is the key to his ideal of an inegalitarian society?[46] The true gentleman for Cicero is the person of *honestas*, which means both respectability and honor on the one hand, and moral virtue on the other. As such, the gentleman must possess the four cardinal virtues of wisdom, justice, courage, and temperance. For our purposes it will be sufficient in characterizing Cicero's ideal of a gentleman as distinct from the vulgar to concentrate on important elements of the last three of the cardinal virtues: *generosity,* a component of justice; *magnanimity,* part of courage; and especially *decorum,* an essential of temperance. Generosity, magnanimity, and decorum have long been considered the hallmarks of the gentleman.

The fact that Latin for generosity or liberality, *liberalitas,* is derived from *liberalis,* literally meaning free, and in a broader sense is the defining trait of the gentleman, *homo liberalis,* indicates something of its significance among the characteristics conventionally attributed to gentlemanly conduct. Since generosity has to do with what is given to others, if it is to be done properly, the principle of justice, "to each his due," must be the standard of action.[47] We should know how much, when, and to whom to give. True generosity is always just. It should serve to help our friends and should harm no one, including ourselves. Therefore, generosity must never outstrip our means. Family and kin should not be deprived or stinted because of gifts to strangers. If generosity exceeds the means, one may be tempted to act illicitly in order to acquire what is needed for a large gift. One should never be motivated to act generously simply for the sake of ostentatious display, for this is hypocritical. Most people tend to be generous if it is in their interest to be so. We naturally give help to those who are generous to us, to those who share our interests, or in exchange for service rendered; but these should not be our only considerations. A truly generous act is never solely a quid pro quo. When returning a kindness, however, care should be taken to give more than was received. In respect to the object of generosity, the gift should be in proportion to the need of the person and his proximity to us. It is proper to be more generous to those physically close to us than to those who are not. Family, kin, close friends—those who love us—should have a greater claim on our generosity than fellow citizens, and the latter should receive consideration over foreigners. Cicero and his peers rarely, if ever, feel any pressing moral duty or humanitarian impulse to be generous to the poor. If money is to be given to the destitute, they must be worthy. Generosity has little to do with pity.[48] In fact, the two are quite conveniently separated. Generosity is, rather, thought of as an investment in friendship or a method of winning friends for the future.[49]

The individual of magnanimity (*magnanimitas*), literally the great-souled person, is the opposite of what we call the pusillanimous, and for the Romans, of one who is marked by *animus timidus*.[50] The magnanimous individual is indifferent to external circumstances, performing important and useful deeds that are dangerous and arduous. To do so he must be free from passion and consider moral worth to be the only good. He is fearless, unmoved by desire for pleasure and riches, and displays both moral and physical courage. Public office is the highest duty and one that must not be shirked. Never vindictive toward enemies or rivals, the magnanimous person refuses to succumb to anger, always remaining calm and dispassionate. In times of prosperity and good fortune, he avoids arrogance, haughtiness, and pride. The higher he rises in society, the more humble he is. In retirement he manages his property honorably and honestly, increasing it by wisdom, industry, and thrift, and he employs his possessions generously and beneficently, eschewing all sensuality and excess. Thereby he is able to live a life of magnificence, dignity, and independence.

Decorum (*decorum*) or propriety, the third principal quality of the gentleman, emphasized by Cicero to a greater extent than either liberality or magnanimity, signifies in Latin "grace" and "comeliness" as well as the morally proper.[51] Cicero alleges that decorum characterizes true moral virtue as a whole and each of the specific virtues. In the first sense decorum is "that which har-

monizes with man's superiority in those respects in which his nature differs from that of the rest of animal creation"; and the second, discussed at greater length, is that "which harmonizes with
nature, in the sense that it manifestly embraces temperance and
self-control, together with a certain deportment such as becomes
a gentleman [*liberali*]."[52] Decorum, so fundamental to temperance
or moderation, denotes in the first place consideration toward all
men and reluctance to wound their feelings. Indeed, the essence
of decorum is reverence or respect (*reverentia*) toward others. To
act in accord with our worth as human beings, treating others
with respect, is to conduct ourselves with decorum. The person
of decorum conforms to his nature as a human—a rational creature superior to the brutes—and to his own individuality, which
differentiates him from the rest. Each individual is unique because
of his distinct physical endowment and character. We must follow
our individual nature, never fight against it, never wishing to be
other than we are and could be, choosing the part in life for which
we are best fitted, respecting the differences in others. Decorum,
then, is "nothing more than uniform consistency in the course of
our life as a whole and all its individual actions. And this uniform
consistency one could not maintain by copying the personal traits
of others and eliminating one's own."[53] One must decide the kind
of person one wishes to be, choosing a calling befitting one's natural and acquired talents and acting in accord with that role.

   To be decorous, all gentlemen as gentlemen are expected to
adhere to a specific pattern of conduct. Here the stress is on gravity, a sense of one's worth, a lack of affectation, and elegance,
polish, and refinement in all that we do. The young should respect
and show deference toward their elders, who in turn should counsel the young, acting as models for their emulation. Outward conduct should be characterized by beauty, taste, and tact, with the
avoidance of the coarse, boorish, and callous. All that is offensive
to eyes and ears should be shunned. Manners are to be simple and
unaffected. In conduct as in everything else a mean should be
struck. While not being coarse and callous, we should also abstain
from the other extreme, careful not to be effeminate or overly
nice or to exhibit a sensualism and fickleness that Cicero and his
contemporaries thought to be womanish traits.[54] Ever neat in appearance and dress, we should carry ourselves in a way becoming

to gentlemen, with dignity, refraining from hurrying or indulging in listless sauntering. Acting on impulse is unbecoming, as is every kind of immodesty. Our thoughts should be as elevated as possible; and our speech, clear and musical. Our manner must suit the subject of conversation, and should be easy, undogmatic, spiced with wit, courteous, and considerate of others. In joking we should cleave to the mean, be refined, polite, clever, witty, never rude, vicious, or obscene. Repressing passion and anger when provoked, we should act instead with firmness and sternness. While the young are expected to sow their wild oats, on maturing they should put away childish ways and be serious about life.[55] The gentlemanly quality of decorum perhaps represents nothing so much as an aesthetic approach to human relations, one in which consistency, harmony, and symmetry are uppermost. Decorous action is graceful, tasteful, elegant, discriminating, in contrast to the typically awkward, uncouth, crass, and loutish conduct of the vulgar.[56]

The decorous individual should also set his sights as high as possible, endeavoring to win the esteem of others by performing acts of true glory through manly, spirited, and energetic conduct in war and politics.[57] Cicero and his fellow Roman gentlemen cherish the life devoted to the pursuit of true glory as one of the highest human ideals. But in devoting ourselves to glory, we should keep in mind that it is only won through just actions and is not to be confused with a mere reputation that can be gained without virtue. Cicero warns his readers not to be mistaken in this regard:

For true glory is a thing of real substance and clearly wrought, no shadowy phantom: it is the agreed approval of good men, the unbiased verdict of judges deciding honestly the question of pre-eminent merit; it gives back to virtue the echo of her voice; and as it generally attends upon duties rightly performed it is not to be disdained by good men. The other kind of glory, however, which claims to be a copy of the true, is headstrong and thoughtless, and generally lends its support to faults and errors; it is public reputation, and by a counterfeit mars the fair beauty of true honour. By this illusion human beings, in spite of some noble ambitions, are blinded and, as they do not know where to look or what to find, some of them bring about the utter ruin of their country and others their own downfall.[58]

In aspiring to achieve true glory, as well as in our day-to-day actions, we should always be generous and liberal and treat others humanely, giving to each, even the humble and unfortunate, his due.

The disparity between Cicero's conception of the gentleman and the actual conduct of Roman aristocrats is probably no greater than the gap between most social ideals and reality. Nevertheless, we must ask how Cicero in terms of his high ideal could possibly justify his own attitude and behavior and those of his peers toward the lower social orders? He evidently sees no serious conflict between the two. If asked to explain what we take to be the broad discrepancy, he might have replied that gentlemen should give to each his due, meaning equal treatment to equals and unequal treatment to unequals. Since Cicero and his kind think that the populace are inferior, little more than irrational instruments, in effect, subhuman, to serve the rational, they are not to be dealt with on a par with their natural superiors, the fully human gentlemen. As far removed as Cicero's gentlemanly code is from our own standards, it is somewhat less austere and forbidding and in principle somewhat more benevolent than Aristotle's aristocratic prescriptions in the *Nicomachean Ethics*. Both gentlemanly ideals are basically ethics for noble landed proprietors in essentially peasant societies, and as such reflect little feeling or compassion for the wide circle of ordinary people beyond the privileged few. It is understandable how attractive Cicero's ideal was to future gentlemanly classes wishing to maintain their dominant positions in slightly more humane environments.

CHAPTER SIX

Private Property
and Its Accumulation

1. *The Finances and Properties of Cicero*

If for Cicero the quintessential consequence of man's rational nature is his potential for moral virtue, another significant result is the human propensity to acquire and accumulate private property. Our natural instinct for self-preservation forces us to acquire possessions for the survival and well-being of ourselves and our families. Human reason not only guides man in his pursuit of possessions by enabling him to determine what is necessary and how it can most satisfactorily be gained, but also serves as a moral regulator, prohibiting the individual in his drive for accumulation from making it the *summum bonum* and from injuring his fellows in the process and violating their properties or interfering with their own acquisitive activities. Moreover, Cicero believes, as we shall see, that reason enables humans to create the state for the chief purpose of securing private property. Because he is the first major thinker to give such emphasis to the notion of private property and to make it a central component of his structure of social and political ideas, the neglect of the subject by most commentators is strange. Plato, Aristotle, and Polybius do, of course, recognize the significance of private property. Nevertheless, they do not give it Cicero's close attention, neither defining it so clearly nor assigning it such a crucial role in their thought.

Cicero's concern with private property is by no means confined to the realm of theory. A child of his time, he displays a pronounced desire for the acquisition of possessions and his own economic advancement. His preoccupation with property in public and private life and in his writings places him squarely in the social context of the late Roman Republic. The ruling classes of the day were no less devoted than he was to amassing real and movable property: buying and selling country estates, city mansions, and blocks of flats and shops at a frenzied rate, hiring architects to refurbish the new acquisitions to their taste, and obtaining objets d'art for their decoration.[1] Real property was the major form of capital investment for the gentlemanly classes as well as a mark of prestige and social status. In the absence of proper banks and an institutionalized system of credit, real estate was one of the few safe financial resources. Notables like Cicero, who lacked the security of a salary or fixed income (taken so much for granted by us) and had to live off their capital, were perpetually short of cash not only because of their extravagant life-styles and huge property investments, but also because of the immense outlays on public entertainments and the enormous political expenses required of their station. Consequently, they were compelled to borrow large sums, often from each other. Such debts could be repaid by enrichment from a variety of sources, not least of which was plunder from successful warfare and loot from colonial office. A booming property market with a rapid turnover resulted from frequent proscriptions and persecutions, leading to the rise and fall of prominent families. Other factors contributed to the constant quest for property, among the most important being the absence of any uniform regular procedure of primogeniture and entail, and the fashionable desire for holdings convenient to the capital. Moreover, since the slave revolts, Roman gentlemen preferred a number of relatively small holdings to a single vast one. Nor should it be forgotten that Roman law, unlike the legal norms of ancient Athens, provided dignitaries with a precise and rigorous definition of private property and an undisputed right of private ownership, in addition to strict guarantees of contract and exchange.

In public affairs and in the domestic sphere, Cicero's abiding interest in the accumulation of private property should be obvious to anyone familiar with his correspondence. Finley's judgment that Cicero was "a consistent protector of the rights of creditors" is borne out by his comment in 60 to Atticus that his "army" consists of "the well-to-do."[2] As barrister and magistrate, senator, consul, and governor of Cilicia he champions the cause of tax-farmers and *publicani* of the order of equestrians, and in turn receives their favors and firm backing. In Cilicia he calls himself a "prime favourite with the tax-farmers." "In a word," he writes to Atticus, "they are all my friends and each man thinks himself preeminently so."[3] He frequently recommends prominent bankers and businessmen to influential public officials of the highest rank.[4] He diligently defends well-known *publicani* in court and forges important links with leading country gentry throughout the Italian municipalities.[5] Ever the shrewd politician, he makes a point of championing the property interests of fellow-townsmen of his birthplace, Arpinum. For instance, he requests M. Brutus, governor of Cisalpine Gaul, to ensure the collection of rents of Arpinum property-holders in the province, remarking: "how conscientiously it is my habit to support my fellow-citizens, the inhabitants of Arpinum."[6]

In regard to his own circumstances, his letters to friends, particularly to Atticus, abound in detail about personal finances: the purchase and sale of houses, estates, and tenements; surveys of prospective properties; improvements to properties and their decoration and furnishings; income from property, dowries, inheritances; debts and loans, interest rates, investments, and profits. Often heavily indebted, Cicero plunged from one financial plight into another, occasionally on the verge of bankruptcy. Indeed, his last surviving letter to Atticus, written in 44 from Arpinum the year before his assassination, ends on a characteristic note of optimism, despite his toubles: "So come I must, even if it means moving straight into the furnace. Private bankruptcy is more dishonorable than public. I am too much worried on this account to reply in my usual fashion to the other matters of which you write so agreeably. Join me in this anxiety I am in to get clear of debt— as to how, I have ideas, but can decide nothing definitely till I see you."[7]

Cicero collected properties just as our own wealthy amass paintings. In addition to the ancestral holdings in Arpinum, he acquired, with the blossoming of his political fortunes, a magnificent palace on the Palatine Hill that once belonged to Livius Drusus, tribune in 91. Cicero paid 3,500,000 H.S. for it to the current owner, the wealthy Marcus Licinius Crassus. He also obtained a villa—previously owned in turn by Sulla, Quintus Lutatius Ca-

tulus, and the rich freedman Vettius—at Tusculum, the birthplace
and home of Marcus Cato Major. He purchased residential properties at Antium, Cumae, Formiae, Astura, Puteoli, Pompeii;
lodges at Anagnia and Sinnessa; and a farm at Frusino. He once
described his rural retreats as "those pearls of Italy, my little
houses in the country."[8] At least some of them seem to have been
bought with an eye to their political usefulness, since they provided opportunities to establish closer connections with the local
gentry. Although never exceptionally knowledgeable about farming, as a youth he translated into Latin Xenophon's classic treatise
on estate management, the *Oeconomicus,*[9] and he always displayed
a keen interest in the architecture and rebuilding of his villas. For
example, he wrote to Atticus:

About the property, I have received your letter and Chrysippus' report.
In the house, which I well knew to be unattractive, it seems that little
or nothing has been changed. He does however speak well of the larger
baths; the smaller ones he says could be made into winter apartments.
So a covered path needs to be added. Even if I make it the size of the
one I made at Tusculum, it will cost hardly more than half as much in
that locality. For the model temple that I want the grove, which I remember, seems ideal.[10]

A great deal of thought, energy, and money was devoted to furnishing his mansions with art treasures from abroad:

out of all your purchases there is absolutely not one that I should really
prize. You, however, in ignorance of my regular practice, took over your
four or five statues at a price beyond what I set on the whole collection
of statues in the world. You compare your Bacchantes with Metellus's
Muses. Where is the analogy? In the first place, I should never have
thought those Muses themselves worth all that money, and all the Muses
would have agreed. Still it would have been suitable for a library, and
would harmonize with my literary pursuits. But as for Bacchantes, where
is there room for them at my house? Ah but, you will say, they are
beautiful little figures. I know them perfectly well, and have often seen
them. Had I fancied them, I should have specifically commissioned you
to buy statues that were known to me. For I often buy the sort of figures
that would adorn a place in my palaestra, and make it look like the gym-
nasia. But a statue of Mars! What do I, the advocate of peace, want with
that? I am glad there was not one of Saturn, for I should suspect these
two statues of having brought debt upon me. I should rather there had
been some sort of a statue of Mercury. I might have had better luck
perhaps in my transaction with Avianius.[11]

His deep attachment to his properties is evident from the pain he felt when during his exile in 58 the Palatine residence was confiscated by his arch-foe, the tribune Clodius, who intended the site to be used for a sacred monument to Libertas. Cicero laments to Atticus that "my property has been crippled and dissipated and pillaged,"[12] and in a heartfelt plea to the College of Pontiffs asks for the restoration of the palace:

the house which has been wrested from me by crime, seized by brigandage, and built over by lawlessness masquerading as religion, even more wickedly than it was overthrown, cannot be lost to me without the infliction of the direst disgrace upon the state, and the deepest grief and ignominy upon myself. If, therefore, you conceive that my restoration is a source of pleasure and gratification to the immortal gods, to the senate, to the Roman people, to all Italy, to the provinces, to foreign nations, and to your own selves, who have always been first and most influential in working for my welfare, I beg and conjure you, gentlemen, as I have been restored by your influence, enthusiasm, and suffrages, so now also, since it is the will of the senate, let it be your hands that install me in my own home.[13]

Despite frequent financial troubles, Cicero was a man of means, but not wealthy by Roman standards. Although advocates were prohibited by law from accepting fees, they customarily received substantial inheritances from those who had benefitted from legal services. In his last year Cicero estimates that he had thus gained more than twenty million H.S. throughout his legal career,[14] by no means a paltry sum, when it is remembered that the minimum annual wage for an unskilled laborer was about five hundred sesterces. Apart from this source of riches, Cicero, like so many of his peers, was able from time to time to loan money at interest, and made a profit of over two million sesterces during his one year as governor of Cilicia.[15] His wife, the well-born and wealthy Terentia, brought a large dowry to their marriage. She owned woodlands when timber was at a premium, rented *ager publicus* for pasturage, and possessed other properties, including income flats.

Cicero's own landed holdings should not be discounted as sources of income. If nothing more, they rendered him and his various households self-sufficient. The tenant farmers on the estate of Arpinum paid rents, as did the market gardeners who cultivated the land at Tusculum, where tiles were manufactured, although whether for Cicero's own use or for the market is not clear. An effort was made to improve and increase the value of at least some of this land, as a letter to his secretary, Tiro, at Tusculum indicates:

Wake up Paredrus to hire the garden for himself. Your doing so will give the present gardener a shaking-up. Why, that hopeless rascal Helico used to pay me 1,000 sesterces, when there was no sunny-corner, no water-drain, no wall, no garden-shed. Is he to have the laugh of us, when we have gone to all that expense? Warm the fellow up, as I do Motho here, with the result that I get a glut of cut flowers.[16]

Cicero also derived appreciable income from urban rental properties. He was, in fact, a slum landlord owning *insulae* or blocks of flats in the Argiletum and on the Aventine, lower-class districts of Rome, and one-eighth of an *insula* near the temple of Strenia. Besides the villa at Puteoli, he possessed tenements, gardens, and other properties there. As was customary, leasing the tenements was supervised by middlemen, dealt with directly by Cicero in Puteoli and in Rome through Atticus. What little is known about Cicero the landlord suggests that he was an exacting one, constantly anxious about rents and always expecting punctual payment.[17] The Puteoli tenements, inherited from a client, the wealthy banker Cluvius, were apparently profitable, yielding 80,000 H.S. in 44, with the prospect of even more in the future, despite their decaying condition.[18] This large sum was sufficient for the annual allowance for his son, Marcus, who was sojourning in Athens and succumbing to its many expensive enticements.[19] Cicero's attitude toward income property in general is nicely illustrated by his comment to Atticus about these Puteoli tenements:

I am quite delighted with the Cluvius property. But you ask me why I have sent for Chrysippus: two of my shops have collapsed and the others are showing cracks, so that even the mice have moved elsewhere, to say nothing of the tenants. Other people call this a disaster, I don't call it even a nuisance. Ah Socrates, Socratics, I can never repay you! Heavens above, how utterly trivial such things appear to me! However, there is a building scheme under way, Vestorius advising and instigating, which will turn this loss into a source of profit.[20]

Four days later, he writes: "The collapse of the building has not lowered the returns, indeed I rather think it may actually have increased them."[21]

2. *An Enlightened Economic Individualism*

Against this background the emphasis given to private property and its accumulation in Cicero's writings, especially in *On Duties,* is understandable. Every living creature, he affirms, is endowed by nature with the instincts of self-preservation and of obtaining those things, such as food and shelter, necessary for the wants and comfort of himself and his dependents. So, in fact, the accumulation of possessions is rooted in man's nature. Cicero agrees with the Stoics that the fruits of the earth exist for the use of man. Nature has given to men the common right to all things created for common use. But each person is expected to appropriate from the commonness of nature the things needed by himself and his family. At the very beginning of time and before the institution of the state, therefore, a distinction was made by men between common property and private property.[22]

Although Cicero suggests that men have some kind of natural entitlement to property which takes precedence over the claims of the state, he stops short of postulating a natural right to property. Private property, he explains, exists by agreement or convention rather than by nature, but—and the qualification is significant—the law of nature as well as civil law protects and secures private property. Long occupancy, conquest, due process of law, bargain, purchase, and allotment are the various means, upheld by civil law, by which private property is legitimately acquired. Nevertheless, above and beyond civil law, the law of nature safeguards one's claim to one's own, as distinct from what is common. Any infringement upon the possessions of one's neighbor or any effort to acquire property through force and fraud is a transgression of the law of nature, of reason, and of civil law, providing it is truly law, that is to say, in keeping with the dictates of nature.[23] Sharp practices in buying and selling real property are immoral—violations of natural justice—and misrepresentation should be prohibited in commercial intercourse.[24] Cicero maintains in *Topics* that of the two parts of natural law, the first is the right of each to his own property, the second being concerned with revenge.[25] Justice itself means "to each his due," and due to each are his rightful possessions.[26] While Cicero never contends that men have a natural right to property, one's entitlement to one's own possessions appears to be more than a civil right. The state, if it is an authentic state, conforming to the precepts of natural justice, legally formalizes and protects, so it seems, what we legitimately acquire for our own use from the common bounty of nature. The primacy of private property is underwritten by the law of nature and institutionalized by civil law.

Cicero obviously has no desire to equalize property. He constantly and vigorously attacks agrarian laws that would redistribute property, most of which he believes are designed by demagogues to plunder the rich for the sake of the poor. Property differentials are as natural as equalization is unnatural.[27] He evidently thinks that the individual with large possessions, by the very fact of the size and value of his holdings, demonstrates industry, skill, and even rationality superior to the smallholder and the impoverished, and, hence, has a natural claim to a greater share.[28] Certainly he insists that a decisive role in government is the prerogative of the former. The Stoics' condemnation of economic collectivism and their doctrine of the naturalness of private property and property differentials must have been congenial to Cicero.[29] Although he holds that property is a convention, he does not dispute the Stoic notion of the naturalness of property. But, as we have seen, Cicero's view of the convention of property is scarcely in opposition to a "naturalist" position.

In all fairness to Cicero, nevertheless, it should be stressed that he is highly critical of avarice; and in practice, despite his financial difficulties, he was probably among the least avaricious, venal, and corrupt of his peers. He opposes acquisition and accumulation for their own sake, and he calls for moderation in all things.[30] He feels that the moral decline of his own times can be explained by the unbridled pursuit of riches, that public office should be held out of a sense of duty instead of profit, power, and glory, and that wisdom is superior to wealth. This last point, made in the *Republic,* becomes the theme of the sixth paradox, "That the wise man alone is rich," of the *Paradoxes of the Stoics.* The paradox is commonly thought to be an attack on Marcus Licinius Crassus, a close colleague of Julius Caesar's and reputedly the wealthiest person of the age, from whom Cicero had bought his Palatine mansion. Condemning in the sixth paradox the unscrupulous use of riches for venal purposes in courts and elections, the unprincipled passion for unrestrained acquisition, and extravagant expenditure on art, furniture, and clothes, Cicero concludes:

> but it is one's mode of life and one's culture, not one's valuation for rating, that really fixes the amount of one's money. Not to be covetous is money, not to love buying things is an income; in fact contentment with one's own possessions is a very large and perfectly secure fortune! . . . Those endowed with virtue alone are rich, for they alone possess property that both produces profit and lasts for ever, and they alone have the special characteristic of wealth—contentment with what is theirs.[31]

Perhaps, however, these words should not be taken too seriously, since so much of their author's life tends to belie such criticism of wealth and luxury. Crassus, political foe and ally of Caesar, was from Cicero's standpoint using his fortune to foment social unrest and to upset the social and constitutional balance of the Republic for which good men had so diligently labored.

Cicero does not oppose the accumulation of riches as long as it is within the moral limits prescribed by the law of nature and used for morally good ends, as he defines them. He clearly accepts the extremes of wealth and poverty existing in the Republic and endorses the rationalization of property differentials offered by the Stoic Chrysippus, whom he paraphrases:

> And the nature of man, he said, is such that as it were a code of law subsists between the individual and the human race, so that he who upholds this code will be just and he who departs from it, unjust. But just as, though the theatre is a public place, yet it is correct to say that the particular seat a man has taken belongs to him, so in the state or in the universe, though these are common to all, no principle of justice militates against the possession of private property.[32]

The implication of the passage is clear. Although all men possess their own private realm within the public sphere, some individual holdings are superior to others. We should be content with our lot and not envy the better fortune of our neighbors. Hence, property differentials are to be accepted without complaint, for they are ordained by nature.

Cicero may castigate the immoderate accumulation of possessions, but at the same time he insists that men are morally obliged

by nature to employ their resources and forward their own
interests. No fault should be found with acquisition as long as it
is done with moderation, fairness, and honesty. We must safeguard and enlarge our own property and take every precaution
not to lose it. However, we must avoid meanness and avarice,
striving to be liberal and generous in all that we do. We should
try to enlarge our property, but ever in a reasonable, industrious,
and thrifty manner. Our duty is to make and increase our wealth,
but always in an honorable way.[33] So Cicero urges men, within
the bounds of natural justice, to look to their own advantage and
pursue their own interests. Life is, indeed, a strenuous contest
among self-interested individuals, each of whom should energet-
ically and conscientiously seek victory. In making his point, in a
passage that may have inspired Hobbes's use of a similar analogy
in *The Elements of Law,* Cicero again approvingly quotes the Stoic
Chrysippus, who compares life to the rigors of a highly competitive race:

"When a man enters the foot-race," says Chrysippus with his usual apt-
ness, "it is his duty to put forth all his strength and strive with all his
might to win; but he ought never with his foot to trip, or with his hand
to foul a competitor. Thus in the stadium of life, it is not unfair for
anyone to seek to obtain what is needful for his own advantage, but he
has no right to wrest it from his neighbour."[34]

Cicero, like John Locke much later, sees no contradiction between
the imperative of morality and the demand of self-advancement
as long as the latter is accomplished in a reasonable fashion and
not at the expense of others, although both have a rather broad
interpretation of what this means.[35] Man is morally obliged to
preserve and forward with industry and perseverance his worldly
station.

Cicero's economic individualism, especially noticeable in *On
Duties,* is a new element in the social and political thought of the
major figures, clearly alien to the speculations of Plato and Aristotle.[36] Two fundamental sources—one intellectual, the other
practical—of Cicero's individualism seem to be elements of Stoicism and what was actually happening in the Roman social world.
Suggestive is the Stoic stress on the physical and circumstantial
differences among humans and respect for these differences, on
the ideas of reconciliation with one's own lot whatever it may be
and the diligent pursuit of one's own calling, and on the impor-

tance of duty and fortitude. Acquisition of wealth and material possessions are to Stoics natural activities, although neither moral goods nor positive evils. Certainly, such "indifferent things" are not necessary conditions of true virtue, yet possibly they enable a person to attain a more complete virtue than would otherwise be the case. Such a perspective may have contributed to or at least reinforced—and perhaps was even used, by some, to rationalize— the mounting acquisitive individualism in Roman society.[37] The acute competition and struggle of members of the ruling class for power and riches, the unbridled exploitation of the provinces, the resort to violence and the proscription of great families, and the rapid rise and fall of family fortunes are all manifestations of an increasing social atomism that brings to mind a Hobbesian state of nature.[38] What may surprise some about such a prevailing "possessive individualism," to use C. B. Macpherson's felicitous expression, is that it occurs in a precapitalist social formation characterized neither by a capitalist nor a quasi-capitalist economic structure, nor by a capitalist mentality.[39] Cicero, just as Hobbes possibly does, owes much of his theoretical perception of the human condition not to an incipient capitalism or budding capitalist spirit, but to a crisis of the landed aristocracy.[40] Amid the political, social, and economic anarchy in which he participates Cicero raises his voice in a plea for reason. His message to his contemporaries is to seek their own economic advantage, but always in a rational and enlightened way.

3. *Town versus Country*

Since landed property and wealth, ownership of a country mansion, and leisure for the pursuit of rural pleasures were fundamental to gentlemanly rank and an aristocratic way of life, it is not inappropriate to conclude this discussion of Cicero's views on property by briefly examining his attitude toward town and country and their respective merits, a subject on which he tends to be somewhat ambivalent. The son of a country gentleman, he spent his early youth on the ancestral estate of Arpinum, lovingly recalled in the *Laws*:

Yonder you see our homestead as it is now—rebuilt and extended by my father's care; for, as he was an invalid, he spent most of his life in study here. Nay, it was on this very spot, I would have you know, that I was born, while my grandfather was alive and when the homestead, according to the old custom, was small, like that of Curius in the Sabine country. For this reason a lingering attachment for the place abides in my mind and heart, and causes me perhaps to feel a greater pleasure in it. . . .

But here we are on the island; surely nothing could be more lovely. It cuts the Fibrenus like the beak of a ship, and the stream, divided into equal parts, bathes these banks, flows swiftly past, and then comes quickly together again, leaving only enough space for a wrestling ground of moderate size. Then after accomplishing this, as if its only duty and function were to provide us with a seat for our discussion, it immediately plunges into the Liris, and, as if it had entered a patrician family, loses its less famous name, and makes the water of the Liris much colder. For, though I have visited many, I have never come upon a river which was colder than this one.[41]

His treasured country properties were visited whenever he could free himself from the duties and demands of Rome. The writings contain numerous references to agriculture and farmers as the backbone of the fatherland's strength and greatness. On the other hand, much of Cicero's time seems to have been spent in or near the capital, engaged in his cherished urban activities of law, government, and politics. The busy metropolis on the Tiber was the hub of the universe, for which he pined when in Greece and Asia.[42] Like a true townsman, he occasionally lost patience with countrymen and disparaged them for being crude, unrefined, and boorish.[43] Unlike English gentry of the seventeenth and eighteenth centuries, who were constantly planting, grafting, and gardening, Cicero seldom displays any special attachment to the family estate, thinking of his country holdings primarily as investments. Other than this, the major concern is over their rebuilding, decoration, and furnishing. He knew little of husbandry and its practical technicalities. Typical pursuits of the country gentlemen such as hunting and riding hold little fascination for him.[44] Nor do his writings and correspondence generally display unusual sensitivity to the beauties of the countryside and the glories of nature. Perhaps his is the rural nostalgia of the dedicated townsman with roots in the country but with no very profound devotion to it. Cicero affords an obvious contrast to another ancient country gentleman, Xenophon, a lover of rural pastimes and a writer on rural subjects, who is keenly interested in estate management and farming.

Cicero, however, acknowledges with considerable eloquence and passion that agriculture is the foundation of civilization.[45] The results of man's clever and skillful use of his hands have been the arts of recreation and utility. Chief among the latter is agriculture, providing us with an abundance of food and the variety of our diet. In addition to the mining of metals, the cutting of timber, the building of dwellings and ships, and the navigation and fishing of the seas, the work of our hands means that "the entire command of the commodities produced on land is vested in mankind. We enjoy the fruits of the plains and of the mountains, the rivers and the lakes are ours, we sow corn, we plant trees, we fertilize the soil by irrigation."[46]

If agriculture is so fundamental to our way of life, of all occupations none surpasses farming: "none more profitable, none more delightful, none more becoming to a freeman."[47] Cicero generally suspects commerce and the commercial way of life. Commerce has a corrupting influence on morals, leading to the degeneration of society by the widespread pursuit of pleasure and luxury.[48] The decline of Greece and Carthage, Cicero maintains, is basically the result of their neglect of agriculture for commerce. Moreover, farming is the nursery of good arms, as commerce can never be, of the soldiers necessary for the security and power of the state. Commerce on a small scale is suitable only for the vulgar.[49] On a large scale involving international trade and wholesaling, commerce is not unbecoming a gentleman, particularly if he invests his profits in a landed estate.

Praise of farmers is scattered through Cicero's works. They are "one of the most worthy, honest and respectable sections of society,"[50] "the best and most respectable division of the human race."[51] The farmers of Sicily exhibit the "stern old Roman manners."[52] In contrast to the Greeks, such husbandmen are patient, virtuous, frugal, and conscientious. The people of Apollonis "are the most thrifty and honest men in the whole of Asia, completely untouched by the extravagance and unreliability of the Greeks, heads of households content with their lot, farmers and countrymen. Their land is naturally fertile and made more so by their careful toil and cultivation."[53] Even the practical wisdom of peasants receives a good word.[54]

Cicero, in these remarks, does not reserve his praise for gentlemen farmers, but is thinking of humble peasants who toil with their hands. He delights in referring to the great heroes of the Roman past who, according to tradition, were little more than peasants themselves, working and living on their small farmsteads.[55] Among them are C. Atilius Serranus, consul in 257 B.C., "the great Serranus of the plough,"[56] found, by the deputation sent to offer him the consulship, sowing with his own hand; Manius Curius, consul in 290, 275, 274, and censor in 272, who was called from his farmhouse to the senate; Cincinnatus, who left his plough for the dictatorship in 458 to save the Roman army from the Aequians; and Valerius Corvinus, consul six times between 348 and 299, who reputedly cultivated his fields until his hundredth year. These men, according to Cicero, acted "on such principles that, in place of a very small and poor state, they have left us one that is very great and prosperous. For they cultivated their own lands diligently, they did not covetously desire those of others; and by such conduct they added lands and cities, and nations to the republic, and made this dominion and the name of the Roman people greater."[57] To show that no stigma attaches to gentlemen engaging in manual labor, he repeats the story (to be so often repeated after Cicero) told by Xenophon in the *Oeconomicus* of Cyrus the Great of Persia, who planned the layout of his palace gardens and planted many of the trees with his own hands.[58] How seriously does Cicero take these examples? Although he emphasizes the vital contribution of the manual arts to civilization, he also displays the typical gentlemanly contempt for manual labor. Far from believing that his kind should emulate the humble, frugal lives of these "peasant heroes," he is perhaps doing little more than providing a nostalgic reminder that past rustic virtue was the foundation of present glory and grandeur.

In *On Old Age* Cicero stresses the merits of agricultural life.[59] His idealized picture is presented in the dialogue through the person of Marcus Cato Major, who rose from being a small farmer to a person of wealth, and who wrote a classic treatise on agriculture. Country life is full of pleasure and satisfaction, suitable to old men and wise men. Because of its undeniable benefit to mankind and great charm, no life can be happier than the farmer's. Nor is there a more attractive sight than a well-kept farm. Elsewhere Cicero describes country life as the fount of virtue in comparison to urban iniquities: "The city creates luxury, from which avarice inevitably springs, while from avarice audacity [*audacia*] breaks forth, the source of all crimes and misdeeds. On the other hand, this country life, which you call boorish, teaches thrift, carefulness, and justice."[60]

The reader of these sentiments can only conclude that Cicero laments the passing of an era to which no return is possible. At a time when the fields of the smallholder are being expropriated by the wealthy to be amalgamated into *latifundia* manned by slave gangs, when peasants are increasingly forced into the town in search of a livelihood, when the *ager publicus* is being enclosed by greedy landlords, when the urban masses are beginning to fill the ranks of the former peasant legions, and when Roman Italy is no longer agriculturally self-sufficient, Cicero looks back wistfully to an idealized past. He recognizes the importance of agricultural life for fashioning men of civic virtue and martial qualities. But, powerless to turn back the clock, Cicero seems guilty of wishful thinking. For him a farm is basically a capital investment to help maintain the standard of life to which he is accustomed. He himself is too much in love with the excitement and variety of the town ever to forsake it for the country, despite his penchant for romanticizing the latter. Despite his rural roots and possibly because of them, Cicero, the *novus homo* who had become a cultured urbanite and renowned statesman, could never accept the provincial gentleman's ideal that Augustus did so much to realize and secure and that was so basic to his power. Cicero was always an active *Roman* gentleman, never a dormant country squire. Not for him were the sentiments of Augustus's poet laureate: "O happy husbandmen! too happy, should they come to know their blessings! for whom, far from the clash of arms, most righteous Earth, unbidden, pours forth from her soil an easy sustenance. . . . Theirs is repose without care, and a life that knows no fraud, but is rich in treasures manifold."[61]

CHAPTER SEVEN

The Idea of the State

1. *Dedication to the State and Politics*

In view of the revival of interest in the state among social scientists, and rehabilitation of the notion by many students of politics, Cicero's thought on the subject is of fundamental significance. He is the first important social and political thinker to give a succinct formal definition of the state,[1] and to conceive of its major purpose largely in non-ethical terms, as the protection and security of private property. He is, furthermore, the first to distinguish state from government conceptually, and possibly to take the initial step in differentiating state from society. Thus his contribution to the early modern idea of the state worked out by such figures as Machiavelli, Bodin, Grotius, Hobbes, and Locke should not be underestimated and warrants serious study. Cicero's conception of the state can be most appropriately introduced by reference to his impressive commitment to the state in principle and his fervent dedication to the Roman state in particular, and to his passionate belief in the superiority of the active political life.

All that is distinctively human, according to Cicero, depends on the existence and well-being of the state. Within the security instituted and maintained by the state, civilization was born, grew, and flourished. Through the state men are able to fulfill their rational and moral being, rising above their original animal condition. The state also assists nature by enabling men to acquire possessions, to enlarge them, and to protect them. The state provides an environment conducive to the flourishing of culture and its highest manifestation, philosophy. Without the state, philosophy would not have been born, and without philosophy's guidance the state is like a rudderless ship.

Cicero's deeply patriotic devotion to the Roman state cannot be fully explained by any utilitarian purpose he attributes to it. He writes that "nothing in the world is more precious to me than the Republic herself."[2] Later, on two separate occasions, he exclaims that he cherishes the state more than life itself,[3] and further contends that "so great is love of country [*patriae*] that we measure it not by what we feel but by the salvation of our country itself."[4] True honor (*verum decus*), he asserts, rests on virtue (*virtus*) and the highest virtue, and hence the greatest honor, is won "in serving the state with distinction."[5] Service to the state brings out supreme *virtus* in men of ability, who in governing wisely and prudently are far superior to those who do not participate in politics. Indeed, the noblest use to which *virtus* can be put is the governing of the state. Founding new states, and their preservation, of all human activities most closely resembles the activity of the gods. A special place in heaven and a life of eternal happiness is awarded by them to men who have preserved, maintained, or enlarged their fatherland. In a manner somewhat reminiscent of the argument employed by Socrates in the *Crito,* Cicero declares that we owe service to our fatherland in exchange for all the advantages it bestows on us: birth, education, and security.[6] Hence, our country is quite justified in taking from us the greater part of our courage, wisdom, and talent for the satisfaction of its own needs.

In the introduction to the *Republic,* Cicero meets point by point current arguments—most probably those of Epicureans—opposing political activism and service to the state.[7] To the objection that the labor entailed by politics is taxing, Cicero replies that in comparison to such lesser matters as studies and business, the effort and energy expended for the sake of the fatherland would not be so for the industrious and vigilant, especially in concerns of the greatest importance. In respect to the dangers necessitated by an active political life, most men, Cicero reasons, seem more fearful of dying through the natural process of old age. Those, of course, who act heroically for their country often suffer at the hands of thankless citizens, for instance, Miltiades and Themistocles of Athens, and Camillus, Gaius Marius, and other Roman notables. Cicero cites his own public career as an example of the ingratitude of the people but insists that the honor and glory he reaped are far greater than the troubles and vexations incurred by the fickleness of the populace. Politics, some might say, is degrading and dangerous because of the participation of so many worthless individuals who incite the mob, exposing the good and well-meaning to its abuse, vituperation, and fury. But can there be a better case for an active political life? Why should we sit idly by, allowing the state to become the prize of evil men? And to the one exception made by quietists for political intervention—a situation of emergency—Cicero counters by asking how good men can possibly manage successfully in such circumstances, since without previous political experience they would lack the requisite degree of skill.

No one, therefore, should doubt that Cicero prefers the active political life to that of study, philosophy, and contemplation,[8] although occasionally during his last, inactive years he suggests the superiority of the latter. Men who pursue either the *vita quieta* or the *vita activa* are wise: "one nourished nature's first gifts to man by admonition and instruction, while the other did so by institutions and laws."[9] Nevertheless, the active life of the statesman is more praiseworthy and yields far greater fame and glory than the contemplative life: "And if we consider how many praiseworthy commonwealths exist now and have existed in the past, and remember that the establishment of a state which is stable enough to endure for ages requires by far the highest intellectual powers that nature can produce, what a multitude of great geniuses there must have been, even if we suppose that every state possessed only one!"[10] The wisdom of the great statesman clearly surpasses the genius of the philosopher. There is no just and honorable principle of philosophy that was not discovered and instituted by notable lawmakers.[11] Statecraft contributes more to the good of mankind than does philosophy.[12] Through politics, it seems, man is able to realize more fully his characteristically human essence. Philosophy is less burdensome than politics, safer, easier, more tranquil, and less subject to the whims of fortune. In politics no room exists for the faint of heart, the overconfident, and the easily discouraged. *Virtus* or manliness is subjected in politics to the paramount test, and greatness of soul is most decidedly required if one is to pass the test.

Ideally, a life combining statecraft with philosophy is the best, Cicero suggests, a life like his own.[13] He illustrates his precept by reference to Demetrius of Phalerum, who

> had remarkable success in bringing learning out of its shady bowers and scholarly seclusion, not merely into the sunlight and the dust, but even into the very battle-line and the centre of conflict. For we can mention the names of many great practical statesmen who have been moderately learned, and also of many very learned men who have had some little experience in practical politics; but who can readily be found, except this man, that excelled in both careers so as to be foremost both in the pursuit of learning and in the actual government of a state?[14]

Demetrius, a student of Theophrastus and possibly of Aristotle, was an enlightened despot who ruled Athens with the backing of Macedonian might from 317 to 307, and introduced anti-democratic reforms favoring oligarchy.[15] He was the first Socratic philosopher-king to achieve power, the most able philosopher in the ancient world to govern a state. Cicero thinks very highly of Demetrius, comparing him to famous ancient founders and lawgivers such as Romulus, Theseus, Lycurgus, Solon, and Kleisthenes, and perhaps seeing in Demetrius's life a parallel to his own: both were philosophers who ruled, who were deprived of their power, and who returned to philosophy in their retirement.

2. Definition of the State

Following the Second World War and until the last decade, a prevailing intellectual fashion has been to discredit the conception of *state* and to label anachronistic its service as a descriptive term for political entities prior to the emergence of the modern nation-state.[16] Accordingly, *state* is considered an inappropriate designation for such diverse political phenomena as Oriental despotisms, *poleis,* tribal kingdoms, and feudal monarchies. Although the pros and cons cannot be examined here, despite the criticisms leveled at its use, *state* remains a meaningful conception in ordinary discourse, and in scholarly analysis it appears that state can be employed legitimately in both generic and specific senses.

Generically, *state* usefully denotes a variety of institutional

forms from Oriental despotism to nation-state. Utilized in this
manner, *state,* as Morton Fried suggests, represents "the complex
of institutions by means of which the power of the society is organized on a basis superior to kinship," characterized by its claim
"to paramountcy in the application of naked force to social problems" through "formal, specialized instruments of coercion."[17]
From this standpoint every type of historical state, notwithstanding the many differences, displays certain similar features. Each is
a hierarchical structure of power over a defined membership and
usually a specified territory, consisting of a network of recognized
rules, some kind of centralized administrative apparatus, an armed
force for the maintenance of internal and external security, a
means for appropriating and redistributing surplus labor, and a
mechanism for the resolution of disputes. So conceived, any state,
whether *polis* or Renaissance city-state, can be analyzed in a number of related ways—for example, legally and institutionally, politically, sociologically, and economically.

On the other hand, *state* in a specific sense can refer to the
object of the early modern conception that appears between 1200
and 1600 (or to the twentieth-century industrial capitalist state)
and begins to be expressed in the latter part of the period in Italy,
France, Germany, and England by such words as *stato, état,
république, Staat, state, commonwealth,* or *political society.* The
early modern theory of the state created by the efforts of such
thinkers as Machiavelli, Bodin, Grotius, Hobbes, and Locke—to
list only the most prominent contributors—stresses legal and institutional characteristics.[18] The state is identified as possessing an
abstract existence separate from the people it comprises. It begins
to be thought of as a distinct legal and constitutional order characterized by the principle of sovereignty, a locus of perpetual,
supreme, and absolute lawmaking power resting on the exclusive
exercise of coercive sanctions. The state is endowed with a cor-
porative being or personality that acts like an individual in buying,
selling, loaning, borrowing, and contracting. A fundamental aim
of the state is not the ethical or religious shaping of human souls
to conform to some pattern of moral virtue, but the purely secular
and amoral guardianship of the lives and possessions of its citizens.
The state exists apart from the government, the officials acting in
its name and with its authority. Governments come and go; states,

as it were, remain forever. The state is also differentiated from the people or citizens under its law, that is, from society; and in constitutionalist versions of the conception, the state is ultimately the creature of and responsible to the full members of society—however they are defined. Important components of the early modern conception, then, are its non-ethical and secular nature and the separation of the state from both government and society, all of which have a beginning in the thought of Cicero.

How, then, does Cicero conceive of the state? He wrote a single work, *De Re Publica*, commonly translated as the *Republic*, on the nature of the state and its best form; and a second book, *De Legibus*, the *Laws*, in which he sets forth his view of the ideal state. The most appropriate title in English of *De Re Publica* might be simply the *State* instead of the *Republic*, since *republic* in our vocabulary denotes a non-monarchical state, usually with a popular or representative assembly. For *state* Cicero employs *res publica* and *civitas*, terms rendered by English translators often interchangeably as *republic, state, commonwealth, civil order, government*. In using *res publica* (or *respublica*), literally "public thing" (property or affair), or *res populi*, "property (or affair) of the people," to designate what we call *state*, Cicero is adhering to the common usage of his day.[19] The Romans gave to the state their own name, *populus Romanus*, "Roman people," or *res populi Romani*, "property of the Roman people," because they had no abstract notion of the state, thinking of it as the collectivity of citizens in much the same way as the ancient Greeks did with their *polis*.[20] As we shall see, however, Cicero, at least, tended to conceive of the state in somewhat more abstract terms. To be official, Roman state documents must bear the initials *S.P.Q.R.* (*Senatus populusque Romanus*), "the senate and the Roman people," indicating not only the importance of the people but also the preeminence of the senate in the Roman state. In Roman private law of Cicero's time, *res publicae* are contrasted to *res privatae*, public things or property in comparison to private things or property.[21] Public property is state property such as the *ager publicus* or common land, or such property as the seashore and banks of navigable rivers, which no individual can rightfully claim. *Res* in *res publica* or *res populi* is possibly best translated "property," because this suggests something of the importance of property ownership in the Roman mentality and of the idea that the state is the possession of the citizens. In general, it is worth remembering that in Rome the state was considered to be a "thing" (another meaning of *res*), a property to be owned. Under Roman law, of course, an owner is not merely a possessor of property but has an absolute right of property, a claim of ownership under civil law against all others. The owner can do with his property as he sees fit, within the limits of the civil law. Roman notables sometimes even think of *res publica* as their possession, to be used as they would their own property.[22]

Cicero seems most typically to employ *res publica* when he wishes to emphasize the idea of the common interest and the responsibility of the state to the people. *Civitas,* on the other hand, only rarely during the period denotes "city" (*urbs*). It has to do with citizenship, the state as a union of citizens, in much the same way as the Greeks employ *politeia,* and hence stands for the state viewed institutionally and constitutionally; and so it is often used by Cicero in preference to *res publica*. In thinking of the state not so much in terms of the common interest and right, as in consisting of a complex of laws, courts, and magistrates, he chooses *civitas*.[23] *Civitas* tends to be a somewhat less normative and emotive term than *res publica*.

Cicero repeats several times in the opening pages of the *Republic* that since his primary subject of inquiry is the state, it will be necessary to define it precisely and to arrive at some agreement as to its meaning.[24] Then follows his classic definition of the state, the first of its kind in the history of political thought. Plato, Aristotle, and Polybius, of course, write at great length on the state or *polis;* nowhere, however, do they clearly or precisely identify it in a formal definition. Cicero begins his definition by identifying state or *res publica* with *res populi,* an equation he subsequently emphasizes.[25] He then asserts that a people (*populus*) are not any random collection of human beings, but "a union of a large number of men in agreement in respect to what is right and just and associated in the common interest."[26] By defining *populus* in this way, he also in effect defines the state or *res publica*, since he identifies *res publica* with *res populi*. The state, then, is the property of a people joined together by justice or right (*ius*) and common interest (*utilitas*). Justice and common interest are the two crucial characteristics of Cicero's definition of the state that must be examined in due course. The *populus,* for Cicero, consists of citizen heads of households. Citizen women and children are not, strictly speaking, part of the *populus;* and aliens and slaves do not belong to it. Nor, at least in his definition of the state, does Cicero evidently intend to exclude the lower classes from the *populus.* The "people" consist of all male adult citizens, regardless of property, rank, class, or status.

Cicero's definition of the state in terms of right or justice (*ius*) is clearly normative, as is his view of civil law. Law (*lex*), he writes, is the bond uniting the state, the "mind and soul" (*mens et animus*) of the state.[27] In other words, where natural right or justice is absent, neither genuine state nor law exists.[28] Any state consistently violating the principles of natural justice ceases to be a state by definition, and the same is true of civil law failing to conform to the ethical precepts of nature. An unjust state is a tyranny, not a state but a pseudo-state. Rome under Julius Caesar, according to Cicero, was a state in form, not substance.[29]

Because a state to be a state must embody the principles of the law of nature, a state cannot be just any collection of people. As he maintains in the *Paradoxes of the Stoics:*

> For what is a state? every collection even of uncivilized savages? every multitude even of runaways and robbers gathered into one place? Not so, you will certainly say. Therefore our community was not a state at a time when laws had no force in it, when the courts of justice were abased, when ancestral custom had been overthrown, when the officers of government had been exiled and the name of the senate was unknown in the state; that horde of bandits and the brigandage that under your leadership was a public institution, and the remnants of conspiracy that had turned from the frenzies of Catiline to your criminal insanity, was not a state.[30]

Prior to the historical state, men live by brute force instead of reason.[31] They lead a scattered, nomadic, animal existence without religion, morality, or law. Men first come together in locations naturally suited for defense and seek shelter by building dwellings, calling each group of them a town or city (*oppidum vel urbem*) with its common property in the form of shrines and meeting places.[32]

Cicero disputes the Epicurean view, however, that the state is a convention arising from the weakness of men who institute it by mutual agreement in order to ensure their protection and safety. Although accepting the notion that the state is founded on consensus, he believes that it originates in nature, not convention.[33] The fundamental reason or *prima causa* of the state, of the grouping together of people in such an institution, is the natural gregariousness or sociality of man, stemming from the common human bond of reason and speech, *ratio et oratio*. This link among men is the initial impetus for all associations, families as well as states. The state is also natural because it satisfies certain human needs such as virtue and the desire for preservation and security.[34] The family, itself the basic natural human association in which all things are held in common, is the foundation of the city (*principium urbis*) and the nursery of the state (*seminarium rei publicae*).[35]

Every state possesses a government (*gubernatio*) to conduct its day-to-day affairs.[36] The state is governed (*regenda est*) by some deliberative body (*consilium*) arising from the same causes that produce the state. The ruling functions of the *consilium* are performed by one, the few, or the many. Hence states are commonly classified by the nature of their governments as either kingdoms, aristocracies, or democracies, or to use the Latin terms of Cicero, *regni, optimatii, civitates populares*.

3. Purpose of the State

The objective of the state given in Cicero's formal definition is the common interest, utility, or advantage (*utilitas communis*). In a first immature and derivative work, written about 91, he defines *utilitas* in reference to the state:

Advantage [*utilitas*] lies either in the body or in things outside the body. By far the largest part of external advantages, however, results in advantage of the body. For example, in the state there are some things that, so to speak, pertain to the body politic [*ad corpus pertinent civitatis*], such as fields, harbours, money, a fleet, sailors, soldiers and allies—the means by which states preserve their safety and liberty—and other things contribute something grander and less necessary, such as the great size and surpassing beauty of a city, an extraordinary amount of money and a multitude of friendships and alliances. These things not only make states safe and secure, but also important and powerful. Therefore, there seem to be two parts of advantage—security and power [*incolumitas et potentia*]. Security is a reasoned and unbroken maintenance of safety [*salutis*].

Power is the possession of resources sufficient for preserving one's self and weakening another.[37]

The theme of security or safety, so basic to the common interest served by the state, is found in the *Laws,* in which Cicero maintains that laws "were invented for the safety of citizens, the preservation of states, and the tranquillity and happiness of human life."[38] He later affirms that "the safety of the people shall be the supreme law" (*salus populi suprema lex esto*).[39] A similar view appears in *On Duties,* where we learn that the first kings (Cicero is following Herodotus) are established to protect the weaker classes from the strong and that cities (*urbes*) arise to satisfy human wants.[40] From Cicero's standpoint, therefore, the reason for the existence of the state is the common interest of those concerned, interest defined in terms of security, protection, and well-being, fundamental to which, as we shall see, is the preservation of private property.

Finally, it should be remembered that for Cicero no contradiction exists between the two key elements of his definition of the state: *ius,* right or justice, and *utilitas,* interest. The state is an association in justice for the common interest. Without justice there could be no true state, and the common interest cannot exist without justice. The man (or state) who acts rightly, in conformity with the principles of natural justice or the law of nature, would always be acting in his (or its) true interests, and the converse is also the case.[41] The foundation of the common interest, and hence of the state, is always justice. Unless the duties required by the law of nature—respecting lives and possessions, keeping promises, and being kind and generous—are generally observed, the state as a framework of security and order for the common interest will disintegrate.[42]

Cicero's idea that the basic function of the state is the protection of private property and the security of the dominant propertied classes requires several prior theoretical presuppositions that by his day were accepted as part of the conventional wisdom. First, the distinction between rulers and ruled is natural to mankind, a division that always existed and would continue to exist, beginning in the family and continuing in any organized human grouping. Second, just as natural and perpetual as this distinction is the one between the non-laboring propertied and the laboring propertyless. These propositions need only depend on a belief that a social division of labor is necessary, and not on any idea of the natural inequality of man. The two precepts—that the divisions, on the one hand, between rulers and ruled, and on the other hand, between the non-laboring propertied and the laboring property-less, are inevitable to the human condition—are united in the conception of the rule of the non-laboring propertied over the laboring propertyless. From this axiom is derived the inference that the natural end of the state is to safeguard the property of its citizens, in practice the property of a minority, since the majority are often without property.

While Plato and Aristotle maintain quite explicitly that direct economic producers should not rule,[43] they are by no means equally explicit that the primary purpose of the state is the protection of private property. They think that the chief goal of the well-ordered *polis* is to encourage human beings to fulfill their rational nature by the achievement of true moral virtue. Whatever its other ends, the *polis,* from their standpoint, is primarily a school in ethics. However, so their reasoning goes, true moral virtue can in practice only be attained by a promising few among the non-laboring propertied. In turn, if this is to occur—or such seems to be the inference—the *polis* must protect the property of the ruling classes and maintain property differentials.[44] But nowhere do Plato and Aristotle—or Polybius—clearly spell out this conclusion.

Considering that the Romans, unlike the Greeks, had a view of private property as a distinct and absolute claim against all others—a central feature of Roman law—it is not surprising that Cicero, a lawyer and magistrate who rose to the oligarchic senatorial order dominating the Republic and shared in his peers' passion for the acquisition and accumulation of landed property, is the first to be exact about the relationship of property and state, indeed making it the linchpin of his conception of the state. For this basic reason, Cicero, instead of Plato or Aristotle, is the significant ancient influence on early modern political thinkers and their idea of the state.

As early as 69, Cicero maintains that law defines and safeguards property rights, enabling us to distinguish between *meum* and *tuum,* what is mine and what is thine:

no institution in our state deserves to be so carefully preserved as the law. Abolish law and there can be no means whereby the individual can ascertain what belongs to him and what to other people. . . . If law be overthrown, nay, if it be neglected or insufficiently guarded, there will be nothing which anyone can be sure either of possessing himself or of inheriting from his father or of leaving to his children. What does it profit you to possess a house or an estate left to you by your father or legitimately acquired in some other way, if you are not certain of being able to keep that which the law of ownership now makes yours, if the law be inadequately safeguarded and if our public code be unable to maintain our rights in the face of some private interest? . . . Believe me, the property which any one of us enjoys is to a greater degree the legacy of our law and constitution than of those who actually bequeathed it to him. . . . A man can inherit an estate from his father, but a good title to the estate, that is, freedom from anxiety and litigation, he inherits not from his father but from the law. . . . Wherefore you ought to hold fast what you have received from your forefathers—the public heritage of law—with no less care than the heritage of your private property; and that, not only because it is the law by which private property is hedged about, but because the individual only is affected if he abandons his inheritance, while the law cannot be abandoned without seriously affecting the community.[45]

A quarter of a century later, after the many vicissitudes of public life, he reaffirms these sentiments in *Topics:* "The civil law [*ius civile*] is a system of equity [*aequitas*] established between members of the same state [*civitatis*] for the purpose of securing to each his property rights [*res suas*]."[46]

If law is the cohesive force of the state, the bond joining together its members, and the chief function of law is to secure private property, then the inference is that the state's fundamental function is the same, with one addition. Not only is the major aim of the state, like that of law, to protect property from all internal transgressions, but also to protect it from all external threats. The validity of the inference is confirmed by *On Duties,* written about the same time as *Topics.* In *On Duties* Cicero says that "although it was by nature's guidance that men were drawn together into communities [*congrebantur homines*], it was in the hope of safeguarding their possessions [*rerum suarum*] that they sought the protection of cities [*urbium*]."[47] Consequently, "the chief purpose in the establishment of states and constitutional orders [*res publicae civitatesque constitutae*] was that individual property rights might be secured [*sua tenerentur*]." A few pages later he repeats this sentiment: "it is the peculiar function of state and city [*civitatis atque urbis*] to guarantee to every man the free and undisturbed control of his own particular property [*suae rei*]."[48]

There can be no doubt that Cicero means precisely what he says in these unambiguous formulations. Moreover, there appears to be no basic contradiction between his insistence on the naturalness of the state and its cardinal end of preserving private property. States are natural in that they arise out of human sociality. States are also natural insofar as they satisfy natural human wants and, as we have seen, the desire for possessions seems to Cicero basic to human nature. Nor is Cicero's conception of the authentic state as the embodiment of justice at odds with the purpose of securing property. Any violation of private property is unjust. Hence, in order to be just the state to be a true state must guarantee the security of each citizen in his possessions. This means, of course, that property differentials, which are characteristic of human society, must likewise be maintained and protected if the principles of natural justice are not to be violated.

Cicero, consequently, is the first important social and political thinker to affirm unequivocally that the basic purpose of the state is the protection of private property.[49] Thereby he is the first, with some qualification, to offer a non-ethical conception of the chief end of the state. Unlike Plato and Aristotle, he does not conceive of the state fundamentally in moral terms, that is, as a means of shaping human souls, of creating men of virtue.

4. *State, Government, and Society*

The ancient Greeks or, more exactly, the Athenians never very precisely distinguished the state as a collection of citizens from those individual citizens chosen to fill public offices and to perform public functions, that is, the government. Cicero and the Romans, in contrast, begin to separate government from state conceptually, endowing both with a more "collective" and abstract character than did the Athenians. Of importance in this regard, a matter to be discussed shortly, is that Cicero seems to differentiate between the person and office of magistrate. Once offices of state are thought to be independent of the individuals holding office, a notion of government as the totality of offices arises. Such an abstract idea of government, in itself, implies a more abstract conception of the state. Government as the totality of offices is conceived of as serving the ensemble of citizens, a distinct entity, perhaps approaching something more than the sum of its parts.

Government, for Cicero, generally comprises those officials and administrators who are agents of the *civitas,* acting in its name, as distinct from the *civitas* itself.[50] The state does not govern, but those responsible for its management and policy do. Magistrates and their authority are absolutely essential to the state, to an important extent determining its character.[51] The Romans use *gubernaculum* to denote the totality of public officials, or government as a whole, distinct from *civitas* or *res publica.* The original meaning of *gubernaculum* is "rudder" or "helm"; just as the helm cannot be identified with the ship, so *gubernaculum* differs from *civitas. Gubernaculum,* helm or government, and a related word, *gubernatio,* steering or government, are differentiated from *gubernator,* the helmsman or individual official who administers and governs. Officials such as helmsmen can be changed without altering either helm or ship of state. Cicero employs expressions like *civitatis gubernatio* and *procuratio rei publicae* for management or administration of the state.[52] More frequently than using one of the abstract terms for government, however, he refers to the individual official, *magistratus* (or *procurator*).[53] Magistrates acting in the name of the state exist by stipulation of the civil law and are themselves subject to the law, just like any ordinary citizen.[54] Magistrates should be the living embodiment and expression of the law: "For as the laws govern the magistrate, so the magistrate governs the people, and it can truly be said that the magistrate is a speaking law, and the law a silent magistrate [*magistratum legem esse loquentum, legem autem mutum magistratum*]."[55] Individual magistrates, then, are joined together into a whole— *gubernaculum* or government—through their common application of a single body of law.

State officials perform public functions not for their own advantage, but for the benefit of all under their jurisdiction. No one should be deprived of his civic privileges and property without due process of law.[56] Government, therefore, in *On Duties* is likened to a guardianship or tutelage committed to the welfare of those for whom the "trust" is created:

For the administration of the government [*procuratio rei publicae*], like the office of a trustee [*tutela*], must be conducted for the benefit [*utilitatem*] of those entrusted [*qui commissi sunt*] to one's care, not of those to whom it is entrusted [*quibus commissa est*]. Now, those who care for the interests of a part of the citizens and neglect another part, introduce into the civil service a dangerous element—dissension and party strife.[57]

In the course of his prosecution in 70 of Verres—an ancient prototype of Warren Hastings—who was charged with the corrupt administration of Sicily, Cicero illustrates the "trust" of the magistrate by recalling his own tenure as quaestor in the province:

My election as quaestor meant for me that the office was not only conferred upon me but committed and entrusted [*creditum et commissum*] to me. While I carried out my duties of quaestor in the province of Sicily, I felt all men's eyes directed upon me and me only. I fancied myself and my office staged in a theatre where all the world was audience; I refused all the accepted methods of gratifying not only the abnormal passions but even the most natural and inevitable desires.[58]

It is significant that Cicero uses the abstract legal conception, *tutela,* guardianship or trust, to describe the proper relationship of government to citizens under its jurisdiction.[59] By Roman law a guardian was required for children under puberty (twelve years of age for girls and fourteen for boys) and independent (*sui iuris*) women of any age. So in respect to the former, the father of the family (*paterfamilias*), in case of premature death, would specify in his will the name of a guardian (*tutor*), not necessarily a kinsman. Originally *tutela* functioned to maintain the family property intact and secure, but later entailed the public obligation for the well-being of the children. In applying the notion of *tutela* to the role of government, Cicero apparently has in mind a number of things. The creators of the *tutela* of government—those who elect public officials—are also its wards. Government is duty-bound to serve them and is accountable to them—as is also true of the *tutela*—for their welfare. Chief among the responsibilities of government, just as of those of the *tutela,* is the security and preservation of the possessions of its wards. Like the tutor who has been entrusted with his function by the *paterfamilias,* government has been given the confidence of the state, *res publica* or *res po-puli*. The abstract conception of government as *tutela,* hence, seems to imply an abstract idea of state, above and beyond a mere sum or collection of individuals.

In a further passage in *On Duties* Cicero returns to the important idea of the trusteeship of government: "It is, then, peculiarly the place of a magistrate [*magistratus*] to bear in mind that he represents the state [*se gerere personam civitatis*] and that it is his duty to uphold its honour and its dignity, to enforce the law, to dispense to all their constitutional rights, and to remember that all this has been committed to him as a sacred trust [*ea fidei suae commissa meminisse*]."[60] The sentence is very important. First, Cicero affirms as clearly as possible that public officials are not identical with the state. Instead, they bear in themselves the character or *persona* of the state, implying that as soon as they give up their official function or position, they cease to represent the state. A public office, then, carries with it the *persona* or mask of state authority. This is also testified to by the preceding quotation, in which Cicero compares his office as quaestor in Sicily to being on stage before an audience, for the *persona* was the mask worn by actors. The implication, of course, is that the public official plays a role, and offstage he is like anyone else; that is, he has a public and a private role. Second, to return to the quotation from *On Duties,* government as the ensemble of such public offices or *personae* has the duty of upholding state authority. Third, officials hold their posts in trust to those under their care and are obliged to serve them by protecting their interests, the security of private property being the most vital. To continue the theatrical analogy, the role or *persona* of the magistrate is like that of the actor. It is for the benefit and edification of the audience. By accepting his role of public office, the magistrate in effect promises in the name of the state to protect the lives and possessions of citizens under his authority. Again, we find a connection between Cicero's basic commitment to private property and his conception of government as distinct from state. Since the primary goal of the state is the security of private property, magistrates acting in the name of the state are obliged to safeguard private property. If they do not do so, their actions constitute a breach of trust, a violation of their role, and they forfeit their office. The state provides procedures for their removal and continues as before, but with new magistrates. In these remarks, Cicero not only differentiates government from state but also endows both with an abstract character. Each of the officials composing government, by wearing the same masks, in effect loses his different individual identity in a single common role or function. By his reference to each official bearing the same *persona civitatis,* Cicero is basically treating the *civitas* itself as one person whose likeness can be simulated by a single mask.

The use of *fides,* "trust" or "faith," stressed by Cicero to describe the relationship between magistrate and citizens, is also salient. Trust, as he and the Romans see it, is central to all the business of society: buying, selling, hiring, letting; in trusteeships, partnerships, and commissions. Trust is also the foundation of *amicitia,* that special brand of friendship and loyalty linking together groups of members of the senatorial and equestrian orders; and of the patron-client relationship between these notables and those of lower station. Any violation of a trust threatens to undermine the whole of social life. Trust is at the very heart of justice itself.[61] Justice, the basis of human society, absolutely necessary for its existence and preservation, is concerned with allotting to each his due and with seeing that each individual meets his obligations *(rerum contractorum fide).* Where immense power reposes in a single individual such as a king, there can be no trust in or responsibility of government, and the social bonds joining men are placed in jeopardy.[62]

The use of *fides* in regard to government recalls in particular the common Roman fiduciary nexus between patron and client. In a way, Cicero's idea of the relationship between magistrate and citizens parallels that between patron—a notable of social standing and means—and his clients, persons of the lower orders. The patron holds a trust for his clients just as the magistrate does for citizens under his jurisdiction. In exchange for the protection and benefits offered by patron or magistrate, clients or citizens are expected to support and serve him.

From what has just been said there can be no doubt about Cicero's conceptual differentiation of state and government, but his separation of state from society is another matter. His distinction between the two is far from being clear and precise. Little more than the germ of the idea is present in his thought, but the seed he sows is of the utmost significance in contrast to previous theorizing and because of its tremendous import for future social and political speculation. In Greek thought, at least in the cases of Plato, Aristotle, and Polybius, state and society are fused in the single conception of the *polis,* considered to be the supreme human grouping, subject to no other association or sphere of value. Cicero, influenced by the common Roman view of their own polity and by Stoicism, takes a first step toward dissolving the unity of state and society that typifies Greek political thought and practice, a direction continued by the architects of the early modern conception of the state.

An essential part of Cicero's notion of the state seems to be little more than the articulation of Roman conventional wisdom on the subject. The state, as we have explained, is the public thing or property, *res publica,* in turn identified by Cicero with *res populi,* property or thing of the people. He thus closely associates state and *populus* in order to emphasize that a state as state in the true sense must always be aimed toward the common interest, one of two basic components of his classic definition. Now if the state is viewed as an object or thing belonging to the *populus,* then the *populus* represents a greater whole, in a manner of speaking, to which the state as a complex of laws and institutions (*civitas*) is subordinate and from which it derives authority. Moreover, the common interest, a defining characteristic of the genuine state and interpreted in terms of protection, security, and well-being, originates in the members of the *populus,* as their natural desire to preserve themselves and their possessions. The common interest and hence its source, the *populus,* are superior to the state. The state is in a fashion a function of the "society," constituted by the *populus,* that exists historically and logically prior to the state and concurrently with the state as a monitor of its activities.

Cicero, of course, never maintains that the individual interests composing the common interest are of equal worth, for he cherishes the principle of proportionate instead of numerical equality. The common interest for Cicero is not simply the sum of the desires of the people regardless of rank and status, the desires of each individual on a par with those of every other member of the *populus.* The common interest in his view, however, differs conceptually from the Platonic *summum bonum,* whose perception and practical application are completely beyond the ken of most citizens, except for a select handful of rarefied intellects. All things considered, in Cicero's nebulous idea of the *populus* and the common interest is the implication, however faint, of a larger entity than the state, comprising individuals joined together by vital personal interests and values; in short, a "society" to which the state is subject.

According to Cicero's definition, however, the state is not only subordinate to the greater whole of the *populus* and the common interest, but also to the superior orb of the right and just. Each individual by virtue of his natural essence, his *ratio et oratio,* or at least his rational potential, can claim membership in a moral community, a universal society taking precedence in its directives over those of the state. Our word *society* is derived, of course, from the Latin, *societas* meaning partnership, companionship, fellowship, fraternity, association. Cicero contends that because of a natural gregariousness arising from their endowment of reason and speech, men associate, forming various types of societies for common purposes. The most comprehensive society is humanity (*societas hominum*) itself, the Stoic commonwealth of reason to which all men belong, united in a partnership of natural justice and right.[63] Regardless of race, tribe, language, or citizenship, men as rational beings are subject to the natural principles of equity and right, which take precedence over civil law and custom and to which they must conform.

Cicero's universal commonwealth of reason should not be confused with our own notion of society or, for that matter, with the different forms of human association that he places under the rubric of *societas.* During the early modern period, society began to be thought of as a sphere of human activity and intercourse distinct from the state, neither public nor private, one of economic production, distribution, and exchange; of cultural relations; and of the competition, conflict, and cooperation of individuals and groupings. The *societas hominum* is certainly not society in this sense; yet there are several resemblances. Cicero viewed it not so much as a rarefied and transcendent realm of moral values, as a common culture of citizens bound together by mutual interest instead of brotherly love or fraternal devotion.[64] *Societas homi-*

num was conceived of as an idealized version of Roman society itself. And because Cicero in this way suggests that the universal society is not simply an abstract world of ethical norms, he can refer to all things being held in common except that which is needed for one's own use, a distinction, he claims, existing by nature and institutionalized by civil law.[65] Property and an individual natural "claim" to property, then, are central to universal human society, just as private property is fundamental to Roman society. While Cicero's *societas hominum* is not identical with the modern idea of society, it does in these ways convey a faint intimation of the later conception.

Cicero describes other kinds of societies from the standpoint of the quality of their associational ties. Those of our common humanity are the loosest, and then in ascending order to the ones with the closest bonds: people, tribe, tongue, state, friends, kin, and family. This specific hierarchy listed in *On Duties* omits *patria*, "fatherland" or "homeland," but Cicero often uses it interchangeably with *res publica*. Occasionally, however, *patria* seems to be a more inclusive term than *res publica*, almost in the sense that we might use *society*, for example:

And what of our country [*patria*] herself? Heaven knows that words can scarce express the love and joy which she inspires! How beauteous is Italy, how renowned are her cities [*oppidorum*], how fair her landscapes, her fields, and her crops! How splendid is her metropolis [*urbis*], how enlightened her citizens [*civium*], how majestic her commonwealth [*rei publicae*], and how great the dignity of you her children![66]

But normally *patria* and *res publica* seem to be two aspects of the same whole. *Patria* tends to be more emotive, *res publica* more practical in meaning, designating actual political institutions and arrangements aimed at justice and the common interest. In the *Laws* Cicero asserts that all natives of Italian towns possess two fatherlands (*patriae*), their birthplace—a *patria* of nature—and the state—a *patria* of right and citizenship.[67] Commitment to the *patria* of law takes precedence over the *patria* of birth:

But that fatherland must stand first in our affection in which the name of state [*rei publicae*] signifies the common citizenship of all of us. For her it is our duty to die, to her to give ourselves entirely, to place on her altar, and, as it were, to dedicate to her service, all we possess. But the fatherland which was our parent is not much less dear to us than the one which adopted us. Thus I shall never deny that my fatherland is here, though my other fatherland is greater and includes this one within it.[68]

After loyalty to state and fatherland comes our moral duty to parents, and then to family, kinsmen, and friends. But duty to state and fatherland must always give way to our loyalty to the universal human community. When duties conflict, "that class takes precedence which is demanded by the interests of human society."[69] For Cicero "there are some acts either so repulsive or so wicked, that a wise man would not commit them, even to save his country. . . . The wise man, therefore, will not think of doing any such thing for the sake of his country; no more will his country consent to have it done for her."[70] Cicero, therefore, differentiates *res publica* and *patria* from the universal commonwealth of reason of which they are a part and to which they are morally subordinate, particularly in respect to the immunity of private property. The state exists to forward and safeguard the distinctly human values of the members of the universal society. If the *societas hominum* is in some sense, as has been suggested, Roman society and culture idealized and "writ large," then the Roman state is its instrument.[71]

The two major elements of Cicero's definition of the state—common interest and justice—have but a single subject—the human being—who is a member both of the *populus* and of the *societas hominum*. By acting genuinely in one capacity, he fulfills his other role. If a citizen adheres to the law of nature, he promotes the common interest. Natural justice implies the common interest, and in turn the common interest presumes natural justice. From Cicero's perspective, no fundamental contradiction exists between the two. In an important sense the good citizen of the state, by advancing the common interest, conforms to the law of nature, thereby being a good member of the universal moral community. Such is Cicero's rather tentative suggestion of a single society—one with two mutually related aspects—that is superior to the state and has a prior claim on the loyalty of the individual.

A crucial factor in all this from the standpoint of the link between Cicero's embryonic conception of society and that of the early modern era is the primacy he assigns to property and the claim to property. Membership in Cicero's universal society means that each of us is entitled to his own property and can expect the state to formalize and secure the claim. The state in effect legitimizes and preserves what is already ours as part of the universal society. The state is meant to implement the principle of natural justice, "to each his due." Perhaps the somewhat clearer practical distinction in Roman than in Greek law between public law and private law is relevant.[72] Public law is concerned with the relationship of citizen to the state, with the common interest, our civic duties, and public offices and officials, and it includes the criminal law. Private law has to do with ordering intercourse between individuals and the securing of individual interests, and it regulates matters pertaining to the family, property, and property relations. In a sense, then, the distinction is to a limited degree an institutionalized recognition of the rudimentary differentiation between state and society that Cicero seems to be implying, and at the foundation of the differentiation is the question of individual property and property interests. At any rate, he thinks of the state as being accountable to us as members of the universal society. Any violation of property by the state without due cause, any rule without right that threatens our lives and possessions is tyrannical and can be legitimately opposed by force.[73]

Before the early modern idea of the state is possible, state has to be further separated in conception (and practice) from society, and the latter has to be more clearly and precisely demarcated. Thus Bodin conceives of family and property as constituting a distinct sphere—incipient society in the modern sense—safeguarded by natural law, and for whose security and well-being sovereign power exists. Hobbes's state of nature, a condition without government and law, is a society characterized by households and family possessions, despite the *bellum omnium contra omnes*. The head of the household is a little sovereign. Locke's "society" is the state of nature, one meaning of which is the secular condition of man without the civil order imposed by the state, an historical situation marked by a natural right of property, by family and family life, monetary exchange, wage labor, and commercial intercourse. Thus he brings Cicero's universal moral society down to earth, so to speak, and assigns to law and government the major task of ensuring the right of property. The next stage in the transformation of Cicero's moral commonwealth and *populus* with a common interest into a non-ethical conception of society is the idea of civil society in the writings of eighteenth-century Scottish philosophers and of Hegel: a realm of free economic exchange activated by the pursuit of self-interest, in which private property is supreme, the whole governed by the natural law of the market.

CHAPTER EIGHT

Types of State

1. The Three Simple Constitutions

In the *Republic,* before Cicero shows that Rome is the ideal polity he surveys other forms of state, catalogues their strengths and weaknesses, and indicates why they do not measure up to his standard of the best. This project in political science entails some sort of typology of historical states. Cicero classifies them in two broad ways: according to the origin of the constitution, and by the nature of the government. From the standpoint of the origin of the constitution, a state is either founded by one man who gives it a system of laws and government, or is developed by many men over a lengthy period of time.[1] Examples of the first given by Cicero are such ancient lawgivers and hero-founders as Minos of Crete, Lycurgus of Sparta, and Theseus of Athens, to be followed in that *polis* by Draco, Solon, Kleisthenes, and Demetrius of Phalerum. Cicero's only illustration of the second mode of creating a constitution is Rome itself. Because of the fallibility of men, even of geniuses like the famous founders and codifiers, Cicero believes the second way to be superior. A constitution drafted at one time cannot provide for all future contingencies, whereas one like the Roman embodies the collective genius of many men and is worked out by experience to meet the test of time. Such a constitution is comparable to a living organism, flexible enough to adapt to changing conditions and circumstances, learning from others but utilizing their experience in a creative and experimental fashion. The Roman constitution, therefore, advancing "by a route which we may call nature's road, finally reaches the ideal condition."[2] As Cicero visualizes the Roman constitution, it is the living embodiment of the *mos maiorum,* the fount of wisdom, the criterion of truth, and the measure of morality—indeed, the supreme authority over civil life.

A second method of categorizing states, one emphasized by Cicero far more than the first, is by the nature of government. Every state possesses some kind of government, in the form of a deliberative body or *consilium* that arises from the same causes that account for the origin of the state itself.[3] It is the type of government that determines the nature of the state, its constitution: "For you must understand that a government consists of its magistrates and those who direct its affairs, and that different types of states are recognized by their constitution of these magistracies."[4] The function of the *consilium* or deliberative body forming the essence of government and differentiating one state from another can be assigned to one man, a *regnum* or kingship; to a select few, an *optimatium* or aristocracy; or to the whole body of citizens, a *civitas popularis* or democracy. These, then, are the three simple types of states.

Since the simple types are subject to decay and corruption, described in each case by Cicero, one would expect that in addition to the three types he would name their three corresponding corrupt forms, as do the Greeks: tyranny, oligarchy, and ochlocracy, or "mob rule." Cicero usually calls a king (*rex*) who rules unjustly a *tyrannus* or tyrant.[5] Occasionally he refers to a tyrant as *dominus* (master, despot) and to his rule as *dominatus* (despotism), explaining in one passage that *dominus* in this context means "master of the people" (*dominus populi*), or what the Greeks call a tyrant (*tyrannus*).[6] Once he employs "power of a faction" (*potestas factionis*) to describe corrupt types of aristocracies or oligarchies like the rule of the Thirty Tyrants in Athens and the third year of the rule of the decemvirs in ancient Rome.[7] The unjust government of the people, the corruption of democracy, when it "inflicts punishment on whomsoever it will, when it seizes, plunders, retains, and wastes whatever it will" is labeled in one passage *dominatus multitudinis,* "despotism of the multitude."[8] So Cicero's three simple constitutions and their degenerate forms, if systematically classified (which he himself never bothers to do), are something like the following:

	Just States	Unjust States
Rule of One	*regnum* (kingship)	*dominatus* (tyranny)
Rule of the Few	*optimatium* (aristocracy)	*potestas factionis* (oligarchy)
Rule of the Many	*civitas popularis* (democracy)	*dominatus multitudinis* (mob rule)

Cicero is never concerned about an exact nomenclature for the unjust or corrupt forms of the simple constitutions, probably because they are not genuine states at all according to his definition. All unjust states, whether they possess governments of one, the few, or the many, are simply tyrannies or pseudo-states.[9] Wherever unjust rule exists, either of one, or the few, or the many, there can be no *res populi,* which is essential to his notion of *res publica.* Even the unjust rule of the people, *dominatus multitudinis,* "is just as surely a tyrant as if it were a single person, an even more cruel tyrant because there can be nothing more horrible than that monster which falsely assumes the name and appearance of a people."[10]

Consequently, two broad categories of state are offered by Cicero. The first is that of the three simple constitutions that are just. The second, to be discussed in the next chapter, is that of the mixed constitution, in which elements of the three simple types are mixed (*mixta*) or combined in a "moderate and balanced" (*aequatum et temperatum*) way, represented by Sparta, Carthage, and Rome.[11] By default, there is a third form, the pseudo-states, tyrannies of one, the few, and the many that comprise the unjust versions or corruptions of the simple constitutions. The mixed constitution, at least the one of Rome, is the best state; tyrannies as pseudo-states are the worst; and the simple constitutions fall somewhere in between. This chapter will begin with the simple constitutions and end with a consideration of tyranny and Cicero's attitude toward it.

Of the three types of simple constitution, none, Cicero thinks, is perfect or the best of states, but all are tolerable provided they endure. Cicero is clearly lukewarm about all of them, preferring a mixture. He gives a few examples of historical states that have such simple constitutions, just and uncorrupted. Kingships are limited to Cyrus of Persia and three ancient Roman monarchs: Romulus, Numa Pompilius, and Servius Tullius. The only aristocracy mentioned is that of the Massalians; and Athens and Rhodes are the sole democracies.[12] Democracy is in Cicero's view "the least commendable type," a judgment he repeats by saying that it "deserves less approbation" than the others.[13] But in respect to the other two, he appears hard-pressed to make a choice, although he asserts that kingship is by far the best and that aristocracy is not superior to it. Elsewhere, he admits that if forced to indicate a preference, he would choose kingship as the best of the simple forms. When absolute power is given to one man, however, even to a good and just monarch like Cyrus, one can hardly speak in terms of *res populi*. Moreover, such absolute rule easily degenerates into a tyranny of one—for instance, that of the cruel and infamous Phalaris of Agrigentum. Like all dedicated Roman Republicans, Cicero, despite his qualified praise, distrusts monarchical government. If wisdom in government is sought, then aristocracy proves wiser than a monarchy, but if one and the few are equally wise, it really makes little difference who rules.[14] So, while Cicero thinks least of democracy and explicitly affirms that kingship is the best, he sees little basis for choice between kingship and aristocracy.

Through the words of Scipio, Cicero presents at some length the case for each of the three simple forms.[15] Of the three simple constitutions, democracy, from the standpoint of its partisans, is the only true *res populi*, because all citizens may participate in decision-making and hold public office. On the other hand, aristocracy is the rule of the best men, those of wisdom and virtue. In principle, Cicero emphasizes that rule of the best does not mean government by the wealthy, for there exists no "more depraved type of state than that in which the richest are accounted the best."[16] Along with other adherents to the ideal of a natural aristocracy, Cicero steers a difficult course between accepting and rejecting the rule of the wealthy. In principle, as we have seen, he believes in the political supremacy of the best; in practice, he accepts the traditional domination of the Roman oligarchy, although he must have realized that many of the oligarchs, even the vast majority, did not meet his requirements for the best.[17] A regime of moderation, aristocracy is a mean between the weakness of kingship and the recklessness of democracy. In addition, aristocracy corrects the unfairness of the democratic egalitarianism of leveling through a system of differential rights, assigning more rights to the worthy and fewer to the less worthy, what Aristotle terms proportionate or geometrical equality. Spokesmen for kingship, according to Cicero, defend it as being a more natural kind of rule than the other two. For just as a single divine mind works in the universe, just as reason rules the passions and the master presides over the household, so monarchical government is best. When ill we rely on one physician; when boarding a ship we place our safety in the hands of the pilot; and in time of war and civil emergency we appoint a dictator. Hence, the rule of a king is preferable to any of the others, or so its supporters believe.

Each simple type, however, Cicero stresses, suffers from the serious defect of instability arising from an inherent tendency to become corrupt. In a kingdom, because of the concentration of power in the hands of a single ruler, he may be tempted to govern in a capricious, arbitrary, and unjust fashion, thus becoming a tyrant in the mold of Dionysius of Syracuse or Phalaris of Agrigentum. When this occurs, a group of the best men overthrow the tyrant and establish an aristocracy, the most usual change from such a tyranny. (Cicero seems to have in mind the rising of Roman notables under Junius Brutus against Tarquin the Proud.) Or, as sometimes happens, the people depose a tyrant and create a just regime. Artistocracies tend to degenerate into oligarchies, like the Thirty Tyrants of Athens or the decemvirs of Rome; democracies, into anarchy and mob rule, ultimately giving birth to the tyranny of a single ruler.[18] If just kingships or aristocracies are overthrown by the people, the inevitable consequence is the breakdown of law and order, the disintegration of all authority, eventuating in a war of all against all. Out of this chaos a tyrant such as Pisistratus of Athens emerges, who in turn is replaced by an aristocracy or an oligarchy. And so the oscillations and changes of government to which the simple constitutions are prone continue unabated.

The crux of the problem of instability of the simple types is the question of liberty (*libertas*).[19] In a nutshell, kingships and aristocracies offer too little liberty to their subjects, and democracies, too much: a deficiency on the one hand and an excess on the other. In kingship and aristocracy, a monopoly of power by one or a few and a lack of liberty for the citizens as a whole inevitably spell change and degeneration. In democracy, the excess of liberty involves a diffusion of power, since all citizens share in the political process and the holding of public office. The result, from Cicero's perspective, is bound to be disastrous. For democratic *libertas* entails democratic equality or *aequabilitas* that ceases to be just and is little more than leveling or parity, what the ancient Greeks call *isonomia*.[20] Each man is considered to be as good as any other, with social distinctions among individuals obliterated in a system of identical rights and duties for all.

Cicero believes this to be the principal and most dangerous characteristic of democracy. Even, for instance, where the people wield power justly and moderately, "the resulting equality itself is inequitable, since it allows no distinction in rank" (*tamen ipsa aequabilitas est iniqua, cum habet nullos gradus dignitatis*). The verdict is repeated at the end of the same section: "and even though the Athenians at certain periods, after they had deprived the Areopagus of its power, succeeded in carrying on all their public business by the resolutions and decrees of the people, their state, because it had no definite distinctions in rank [*quoniam distinctos dignitatis gradus non habebant*], could not maintain its fair renown."[21] Presenting the case for aristocracy, Cicero returns to the injustice of numerical equality:

For that equality of legal rights [*nam aequabilitas quidem iuris*] of which free peoples are so fond cannot be maintained (for the people themselves, though free and unrestrained, give very many special powers to many individuals, and create great distinctions among men and honours granted to them), and what is called equality is really most inequitable [*quae appellatur aequabilitas, iniquissima est*]. For when equal honour [*cum enim par habetur honos*] is given to the highest and the lowest—for men of both types must exist in every nation—then this very "fairness" is most unfair [*ipsa aequitas iniquissima est*]; but this cannot happen in states ruled by their best citizens [*ab optimis reguntur*].[22]

Later, in discussing the virtues of a mixed constitution, one based on some liberty for all citizens and a true and just proportionate equality instead of parity, Cicero insists that under such a system "there is no reason for a change when every citizen is firmly established in his own station [*ubi in suo quisque est gradu firmiter collacatus*]."[23]

The key term for understanding the significance of these passages is *dignitas:* worth, merit, or reputation.[24] *Dignitas,* in Cicero's scheme of things, is clearly at odds with the excessive *libertas* in a democracy. As early as 91, he writes: "Justice [*iustitia*] is a disposition of mind which accords to each his worth [*dignitatem*] while preserving the common interest [*communi utilitate*]."[25] In the same work he defines *dignitas* as "some honour, reverence, respect, and modesty deserving authority [*digna auctoritas*]."[26] A gentleman and *novus homo* like Cicero, as we have seen, is exceedingly sensitive to the differences, both acquired and inherited, among human beings, to the uniqueness of each, and consequently to the question of station, rank, and privilege.[27] Justice in his view rests essentially upon the principle of proportionate equality, more to the meritorious minority and less to the unworthy majority. On his return from a year's exile in 57 he reveals in his speech to the people how much he cherishes and welcomes the restoration of the *dignitas* given to him by the state.[28] The premium he places on *dignitas* is aptly summarized in his last great political oration by his characterization of M. Antonius, the renowned grandfather of Marc Antony: "To him life, to him prosperous fortune, was equality in liberty with the rest, the first place in honour" (*Illa erat vita, illa secunda fortuna, libertate esse parem ceteris, principem dignitate*).[29]

Any government, therefore, according to Cicero, seeking to blur or eradicate social distinctions among men, to reduce all to a common denominator, is to be condemned for violating the principles of natural justice and true equality. Those who merit more, by Cicero's own gentlemanly standards, should have more political power and privilege than the minimal rights granted to all. He firmly believes in a constitution in which some liberties are given to all; more to some—those of superior *dignitas*—than to most—those of inferior *dignitas*. The only political arrangement for accomplishing this is one instituting and maintaining a hierarchy of social orders with a corresponding differential scale of political rights such as exists under the mixed constitution in general and in the Roman Republic in particular.[30]

Cicero, however, not only links *dignitas* to *libertas* in this special way, but also to *auctoritas* or authority.[31] *Dignitas,* for Cicero and the Romans, endows a person with *auctoritas.* Hence, a state failing to acknowledge differences in *dignitas* and to build its political structure on those differences undermines the vitality and cohesion of the civic order, whose very foundation is recognition of and deference to authority. Democracy, precisely because it confers too much liberty on citizens, a liberty productive of a spurious and unjust equality, is as susceptible to tyranny—if not more so—as are states with too little liberty. Once democratic *libertas*—in reality, little more than *licentia* or license—sweeps away all rank and privilege resting on *dignitas, auctoritas* disappears. Law and order are destroyed by mob rule, anarchy, and terror, and all sense of justice and moderation is lost. Indeed, democracy is doubly dangerous because a democratic people, obsessed by their power, confusing *libertas* with *licentia* and *aequabilitas* with leveling, become a collective tyrant, the renowned "many-headed beast" of Plato, and eventually, out of desperation and the need for some return to peace and stability, they subject themselves to the rule of an unprincipled and despotic leader.[32]

There are even more complexities to *libertas*—a multifaceted conception in the Roman mentality—and its relationship to *dignitas* and *auctoritas.*[33] In the broadest formal sense *libertas* denotes the freedom of all citizens, regardless of status, to minimal participation in government, basic to which is the right to vote. To the elite, however, *libertas* means essentially their own freedom to rule the masses without impediment and to accumulate riches without hindrance. No one has bettered Syme in describing the outlook: "*Libertas* was most commonly invoked in defence of the existing order by individuals or classes in enjoyment of power and wealth. The *libertas* of the Roman aristocrat meant the rule of a class and the perpetuation of privilege."[34] For the downtrodden and exploited multitude, however, this *libertas* spells their own servitude (*servitus*), and they eagerly support *populares* like Clodius and Julius Caesar who give them some hope of redressing the balance by acting in the name of *libertas,* one for all instead of a select few. But to those in the saddle, like Cicero, the clamor of the people for *libertas* and their action under a popular leader in the service of that ideal is *licentia* rather than *libertas,* in reality political subjection. Cicero, indeed, condemns Clodius, who as tribune had confiscated his Palatine mansion and built a shrine to Libertas on the property, for erecting "a temple to Licence" (*templum Licentia*), and accuses him of instituting servitude.[35] Once a popular leader attains power, he invariably uses the slogan of *libertas* in the manner of his former opponents to authorize his rule just as they had done, and he brands all resistance as *licentia*. The displaced notables feel that the restrictions placed by the new regime on their *libertas*—the former freedom to voice publicly and to implement practically their social and political opinions— is a direct assault on their *dignitas* and hence a blow to their authority. Cicero bitterly complains about his loss of *dignitas* in such a way under Caesar, but if we can believe his friend Marcus Brutus, he would have willingly endured this kind of enforced subjection to Octavian and the Second Triumvirate without open protest or opposition, provided he could have maintained his honor, a view evidently shared by many of his peers in a comparable position.[36]

Clearly, then, for Cicero, democracy and full popular participation constitute the prime political danger. He makes the classic conservative argument against democracy, one that has scarcely been improved. Even though his *Republic* was lost until the nineteenth century, the kernel of his anti-democratic case could readily be culled from the *Laws, On Duties,* and the orations and letters. Indeed, his attack on democracy has probably been more influential than Plato's, perhaps because Cicero was a dedicated republican and an active statesman whose political writings tended to be more succinct and less encumbered with philosophical analysis. Moreover, they appear to have been more widely read than Plato's works by members of the upper classes in the modern era when democracy was proving to be a distinct threat to the established social order.

As one might expect, Cicero, so disdainful of popular rule as to show no hesitation in terming it the worst of the simple constitutions, severely criticizes the democratic institutions of Athens. That ancient city is a warning, cited by Cicero and anti-democrats in subsequent ages, of the dire consequences of power in the hands of the people, a specter to haunt all gentlemen. Cicero's criticism of Athens is directed against the Athenians as well. They are fickle, quick-tempered and mercurial, unstable, untrustworthy, extravagant, and generally deficient in character. In comparison to the slothfulness and self-indulgence of the Athenians, the Sicilians of his own day, like the Romans of yore, are paragons of virtue: hardy, industrious, upright, and honest. Athenians may recognize the meaning of civility but they do not practice it and are less respectful than the Spartans toward the aged. Outstanding citizens of Athens who serve the state with distinction, like Themistocles, Aristides, and Miltiades, are often treated shabbily and even exiled. In this regard Cicero refers in the *Defence of Sestius* to the "so many instances of hasty temper and fickleness shown by the people," a view repeated at the opening of the *Republic*.[37]

In Athens all differences in social rank were abolished and every citizen was eligible to hold public office. The result was government by the vulgar and uneducated, and a disastrous public policy: "When untried men, totally inexperienced and ignorant, had taken their seats in the theatre, then they would decide on harmful wars, put trouble-makers in charge of public affairs and expel from the city the citizens who had served it best."[38] He castigates "those cobblers and belt-makers" of the assembly and mentions the ease with which "craftsmen, shopkeepers, and all the dregs" of the *polis* were excited by some facile and unscrupulous demagogue.[39] "Remember, then," he cautions, "that when you hear Greek resolutions, you are not hearing evidence; you are hearing the wild decisions of a mob, the voice of every nonentity, the din of ignoramuses, an inflamed meeting of the most unstable of nations."[40] Cicero hopes his bitter attack on Greek democracy will serve as a lesson in his own day for those dependent on the support of the Roman masses and wishing to base their power on public meetings.[41] He, of course, expresses the highest admiration for Greek culture, so at least some of his criticism reflects an obeisance to Roman political chauvinism.[42] Although much of the evidence rests on a forensic speech of 59, the *Defence of Flaccus,* in which Cicero is attempting to discredit Greek witnesses, it seems to reflect his genuine antipathy to Greek democracy and gentlemanly dread of the specter of rule by the vulgar that might result from current efforts at social and political reform in Rome.[43]

In his belief that the major deficiency of the three simple constitutions is the inevitability of their corruption, Cicero seems to

be following the theory of *anacyclosis* of Polybius: he and Panaetius were called in the *Republic* the "two Greeks who were
perhaps the best versed of them all in politics."[44] Because of his
lack of systematic formulation, complicated by the fragmentary
condition of the relevant text of Book VI of *The Histories,* Polybius's conception of *anacyclosis* is difficult to unravel, exercising
the attention of a number of scholars.[45] Only the briefest and most
simplified account of his treatment is necessary for the purpose of
determining the extent to which Cicero was indebted to it. Advancing the conception in order to render constitutional change
intelligible and that of the future predictable, Polybius fuses several
Greek theoretical components: a probable Sophistic notion of the
emergence of culture, a conventional doctrine of the corruption
of the simple constitutions found in Plato and Aristotle, and the
idea of a biological cycle as old as Anaximander. Every state, for
Polybius, is subject to the inexorable life cycle or natural history
of constitutional change, passing through successive stages from
birth through youth, maturity, and senility to death. State formation began in what amounted to an historical "state of nature"
where humans, living like animals in herds, from weakness submitted to the strongest of their number. These first primitive
"monarchs" who dominated the others through fear, as collective
life and morality developed, were forced to give way to "kingship" and the rule of law. Over the course of time, kingship degenerated into tyranny, to be replaced by aristocracy, which deteriorated into oligarchy, followed in the inevitable sequence by
democracy, ochlocracy or mob rule, the eventual disintegration
and death of the state, a return to a stateless society, and then
possibly a repetition of the total process. The empirical models
used by Polybius were evidently Greek history from the mythical
hero-founders to the age of democracy, and the legendary record
of Rome's past commencing with the monarchical chieftain, Romulus, succeeded by Numa Pompilius and subsequent kings, to the
institution of the tribunate and the Twelve Tables of the Law of
451 B.C. Polybius seems to attribute the cause of constitutional
degeneration in each of the three cases to man's basically defective
nature: the corrupting influence of power on the rulers leading to
their injustice, insolence, lawlessness, and greed.

A number of questions are never dealt with very clearly by

Polybius. Does the return and repetition of the cycle occur for all former constitutional orders or just for some? In what ways is the primitive period prior to the original foundation similar or dissimilar to that between the death and the rebirth of a state? Which of the uncorrupt constitutions represents the acme or prime—the high point of growth—of the cycle as a whole? If each of the uncorrupt constitutions attains an acme, is it legitimate to apply the notion to the corrupt forms, to speak of the stage of perfection of tyrannies, oligarchies, and ochlocracies? The crucial problem, however, arises from Polybius's effort to weld the theory of *anacyclosis* to his doctrine of the mixed constitution of Rome. How precisely does he integrate the two? Trompf interprets Polybius as holding that the Roman mixed constitution—breaking out of the regular cycle, as it were—arose in the early fifth century sometime after the banishment of the tyrant Tarquin the Proud. The mixture is first dominated by the consulate, then reaches its acme under the senatorial aristocracy during the Second Punic War, and finally in the second century moves in the direction of popular hegemony. Polybius possibly concluded that the Roman mixture was in the process of shifting back to the normal constitutional cycle, beginning with oligarchy and then adhering to the predetermined course until the death of the state.[46] Whatever Polybius had in mind, it seems fairly clear that in his view the mixed constitution itself was not immune to cyclical change and decay, but served to slow down the natural process.

Cicero, therefore, appears to conform to Polybius's theory in maintaining the corruptibility of the simple constitutions: "before every one of them lies a slippery and precipitous path leading to a certain depraved form that is a close neighbour to it."[47] Likewise he is generally following the Greek historian in a comment on the termination of the reign of Tarquin the Proud and the various constitutional changes in the next century:

At this point begins that orbit of development with whose natural motion and circular course you must become acquainted from its beginning. For the foundation of that political wisdom which is the aim of our whole discourse is an understanding of the regular curving path through which states travel, in order that, when you know what direction any state tends to take, you may be able to hold it back or take measures to meet the change.[48]

Cicero, however, only rather loosely applies the Polybian *ana-cyclosis* and its combination with the doctrine of the mixed con-stitution to his constitutional history of Rome. He agrees with Polybius that the principal cause of the degeneration of each of the simple types is the frailty of man's nature, the human lust for power and the corrupting effect of too much power. In addition he argues that too much liberty is a basic factor in the decay of states.[49] The result of both factors, at least as Cicero reasons in Book I of the *Republic,* is an even greater instability of simple constitutions than that accorded to them by Polybius, and a far less regular course of rise and decline than he plotted: "Thus the ruling power of the state, like a ball, is snatched from kings by tyrants, from tyrants by aristocrats or the people, and from them again by an oligarchical faction or a tyrant, so that no single form of state ever maintains itself very long."[50] Yet generally in Book II Cicero seems less reluctant to be guided by Polybius, if hardly precisely and explicitly, in tracing the "history" of Rome from the rule of kings and the tyranny of Tarquin the Proud to the institution of the mixed constitution.[51] Cicero's closer adherence to the Polybian pattern is scarcely surprising, since the Greek thinker in devising his cyclical theory was probably inspired by the same traditional "historical" sources employed by Cicero. One can only conclude, however, that Cicero is indebted to Polybius on the question of constitutional change only in a vague and un-systematic way, deferring to him or not as occasion demands. This verdict is confirmed by Trompf: "Tullius Cicero certainly used cyclical language very loosely. . . . Polybian frames of reference had only a slight impact on Cicero."[52]

2. *Forms of Tyranny*

Cicero's third type of state (in addition to the simple and mixed constitutions) in terms of the nature of government—tyranny—is in fact not a genuine state at all, according to his definition, but a pseudo-state. Any state whose government is unjust, ruling for its own rather than for the common interest, is a tyranny. The unjust sovereignty of one, the few, and the many are all tyrannical. Cicero illustrates the tyranny of one by the examples of Tarquin the Proud, Pisistratus of Athens, Dionysius of Syracuse, Deme-trius Poliorcetes, Phalaris of Agrigentum, Alexander of Pherae, and Julius Caesar; and the tyranny of a few, by the Thirty Tyrants of Athens and the short-lived faction of the decemvirs in ancient Rome. He is less specific about instances of tyranny of the many. Most probably he is thinking of Athens at various periods under such popular leaders as Kleon.[53] Cicero's description of mob rule relies more on the famous passage from the eighth book of Plato's *Republic* than on historical reality, although he may have contemporary Rome in mind. One possible reason for the lack of concrete examples is that Cicero apparently considers tyranny of the many to be a highly unstable situation of short duration. It tends to be a brief and anarchic transitional phase from one of the simple just constitutions to either the tyranny of one or the tyranny of a few. So, in fact, for Cicero, these two are the basic types of tyranny.

Of the two, the capricious, arbitrary, and unjust government of one is the most characteristic and the worst sort of rule.[54] With Tarquin the Proud in mind he writes that

no creature more vile or horrible than a tyrant, or more hateful to gods and men, can be imagined; for though he bears a human form, yet he surpasses the most monstrous of the wild beasts in the cruelty of his nature. For how could the name of human being rightly be given to a creature who desires no community of justice, no partnership in human life with his fellow-citizens—aye, even with any part of the human race?[55]

Although monarchies in their pure and uncorrupted form are the best of the simple constitutions, they are potentially dangerous because of the great power of the single ruler and the ever-present temptation to wield that power illegitimately. A king becomes tyrannical, not by seizing new power, but by abusing the power he already holds.[56] Furthermore, the power of a monarch is so great and so attractive to ambitious men of high rank that notables of the kingdom ruthlessly compete with each other for it, thereby rending the state asunder with their struggles and dissension.[57] Like all good Roman republicans, Cicero is highly suspicious of kingship, despite his praise of it in a pure and just form.

Tyrants hold power by instilling fear in their subjects with the use of force.[58] This proves to be the tyrant's undoing, because his rule of fear generates in his subjects a deep and fierce hatred inevitably leading to their resistance and his overthrow:

The death of this tyrant [Julius Caesar], whose yoke the state endured under the constraint of armed force and whom it still obeys more humbly than ever, though he is dead, illustrates the deadly effects of popular hatred; and the same lesson is taught by the similar fate of all other despots, of whom practically no one has ever escaped such a death. For fear is but a poor safeguard of lasting power; while affection, on the other hand, may be trusted to keep it safe for ever.[59]

The tyrant, then, who thus governs must in turn live in constant dread of the governed, ever fearful of assassination, conspiracy, and revolt instigated even by members of his family, friends, close associates, and servants. The force employed by a tyrant does not necessarily entail actual physical harm to his subjects. Force is far more effective if it is covert and psychological, striking terror into the hearts and souls of those whose behavior is to be controlled.[60]

Julius Caesar exercised tyrannical power after Cicero wrote the *Republic.* Had the dictator appeared before, Cicero might have been less sanguine about the merits of the mixed constitution. But even at the time of writing the work, he expresses doubts about the strength and substance of the Roman state, which seems to have been transformed into a mere shadow of its former strength and stability.[61] In private he has no hesitation in expressing his concern over the rot that had already set in, at the signs of degeneration and disintegration everywhere before his eyes. He writes to Atticus: "Hurry back to Rome, come and look at the empty husks of the real old Roman Republic we used to know. For example, come and see money distributed before the elections tribe by tribe, all in one place openly, see Gabinius acquitted, get the smell of a dictatorship in your nostrils, enjoy the public holiday and the universal free-for-all."[62]

Although dissociated from Caesar's autocracy, Cicero was allowed by the regime to live in peace, and remained in Rome or in one of his country houses nearby, just as he says Socrates had stayed in Athens under the Thirty Tyrants.[63] The leisure afforded by his exclusion from public affairs gave him the opportunity to return to his studies as a means of escaping his worries and of serving his fellow countrymen.[64] Living in Rome at the time also afforded an unprecedented opportunity to observe a tyranny at first hand and to ask some vital questions about it, just as relevant today as they were then:

Ought a man to remain in his country under a tyranny? Ought he to strive for the overthrow of a tyranny by every means, even if the existence of the state is going to be endangered thereby? Ought he to beware of the overthrower lest *he* be set up as a tyrant? Ought he to try to help his country under a tyranny by taking opportunity as it comes along and by words rather than by war? Ought a statesman to live quietly in retirement while his country is under a tyranny or ought he to take every risk for freedom's sake? Is it right to make war against one's country and blockade it when it is under tyrannical rule? Ought a man to enrol himself on the side of the best citizens even if he does not approve of overthrowing the tyranny by war? Ought he in politics to join in the dangers of his friends and benefactors even though he does not approve of their actions in capital matters? Ought a man who has rendered his country great service and has on that account brought himself irreparable suffering and hostility voluntarily to incur danger on his country's behalf, or may he be allowed to begin to think of himself and his family, giving up political opposition to those in power?[65]

While remaining aloof from politics and taking no active part against Caesar, he loudly hails the assassination of the tyrant by their mutual friend Brutus. Cicero is acclaimed throughout history not only as a foe of tyranny but also as an ardent spokesman for tyrannicide. His position on tyrannicide, however, must be considered later, within the broader context of his views on the art of politics.[66]

CHAPTER NINE

Essentials of
the Mixed Constitution

1. *The Doctrine prior to Cicero*

The doctrine of the mixed constitution is one of the most important legacies of ancient political theory to modern times. Not only did it have a decisive impact on the general development of the idea of constitutionalism since the Middle Ages, but also, in the early modern period, especially on the theory of mixed monarchy, the English Classical Republicans, and on Montesquieu and the American founding fathers, who devised and instituted the notion of the separation of powers. Basic to that notion is the historical interpretation of the Roman constitution as a mixture, expounded by Polybius, Cicero, and other writers both ancient and modern. The mixed constitution was thought to combine the merits of the three simple forms of monarchy, aristocracy, and democracy without their defects into a balanced whole that would be resistant, if not entirely immune, to corruption and would impede tyrannical rule.[1] Of the various ancient treatments of the mixed constitution, Cicero's in the *Republic* and *Laws* is perhaps the definitive and clearest one in respect to intention and constitutional operation. Before considering his view of the mixed constitution, however, it may be helpful to summarize briefly some aspects of the "doctrine" as it evolved before Cicero.

The most obvious and fundamental assumption of the doctrine of the mixed constitution is the typology of the three simple constitutions and their degenerate forms. Herodotus provides the first recorded instance of the typology, which probably had become

159

conventional and was later systematically presented by Plato and Aristotle.[2] Once the classificatory scheme was generally accepted, it was not long before the idea of a mixture of elements of two or all three of the good forms appeared. Thucydides is usually acknowledged to be the first to describe an actual governmental arrangement as a mixture, and both Plato in the *Laws* and Aristotle in the *Politics* briefly discuss various existing constitutions as a combination of three simple forms. Each of the two latter thinkers in their respective works also recommends a mixture for their best practicable or second-best constitutions: Plato's constitution for Magnesia mixes monarchy and democracy; Aristotle's "polity" fuses oligarchy and democracy.[3] The early Stoics prescribed for the best state a blending of the three simple constitutions, or so Diogenes Laertius informs us.[4] Polybius is commonly thought of as the classic theorist of the mixed constitution, because of his detailed analysis of the Roman state as a synthesis of monarchical, aristocratic, and democratic components.[5]

The doctrine is socially and politically conservative, fashioned by and appealing to those of aristocratic values and interests and aimed at securing their own privilege and domination by averting tyranny and paying lip service to democracy. As it developed, the notion of the mixed constitution came to be informed by a number of basic and closely connected principles. The first, the precept of the mean or "middle way" which shuns excess, can be traced as far back as Solon's poetic utterance that he "stood with a strong shield thrown before the both sorts," the rich and the poor.[6] Theognis's "midst is best in everything" is reflected in such diverse phenomena as the Athenian social ideal of the self-sufficient farmer, neither rich nor poor, and as the philosophic themes of the Delphic *sophrosyne* and the "golden mean."[7] When applied to politics, the idea of the mean and the avoidance of excess gives rise to a psychological assumption that too much power corrupts, or, to paraphrase Acton, all power corrupts and absolute power corrupts absolutely.[8] Hence the power of state officials must be balanced and checked institutionally by an appropriate mixture to prevent them from acting capriciously and irresponsibly. Another fundamental principle is the preference for proportionate over numerical equality.[9] In regard to the distribution of offices, honors, and awards in the state, this signified in practice some combination of the two conceptions of equality or a "mean" between the two. All citizens would be granted a minimal function in government, such as membership in a popular assembly or suffrage, but decisive political power would be a monopoly of the well-born and wealthy. A related principle is the idea that the social unity of the state depends on governmental arrangements that would create a balance or harmony of social classes—rich and poor, landlords and peasants. "Balance," of course, in this context, as in the case of the "equality" of the principle of proportionate equality, favors the rich over the poor. Since ancient societies were peasant societies, in the main governed by gentlemanly landed proprietors, a central theme of ancient political thinkers is the problem of constructing a durable modus vivendi between the two classes. This concern with class harmony is associated with a further principle. Untainted by modern notions of the benefits of human progress, the advantages of social change, and the positive value of social and political conflict, the ancients sought an immortal form of constitution, one that would be relatively impervious to the passage of time and generate conditions of lasting unity, order, and stability. In the opinion of ancient theorists, the properly mixed constitution was an ingenious contrivance for the practical implementation of these principles.

The doctrine of the mixed constitution, as it was fashioned in varying ways by the major thinkers before Cicero, was designed for the protection of the propertied status quo and the maintenance of property differentials, and for securing the political domination of the wealthy, while at the same time giving the vast majority of direct economic producers a nominal voice and stake in government. As a kind of middle ground between the extremes of tyranny and democracy, the purpose of the mixed constitution was the obstruction, by complex institutional and legal arrangements, of tyranny from above and tyranny from below. Preservation of the propertied status quo and their continuing political domination could be assured, according to the ancient theorists, by an intricate governmental mechanism that would inhibit, on the one hand, any faction or individual of the landed class from seizing power and ruling despotically; and, on the other hand, any drift of the multitude toward democracy—in their view, synonymous with mob rule—and the eventual emergence of a popular tyrant. This could be accomplished through a hierarchical system of rights and duties allocated differentially to landlords and peasants. The supreme governing function would be reserved for the gentlemanly landed minority, and the majority of peasant producers would be allotted a minimal supportive role. After a development of four centuries, the doctrine of the mixed constitution, in effect, amounted to a conception of autocratic government resorting on occasion to popular approval. Cicero, then, had a rich legacy of ideas, as well as Roman experience, to draw upon for his own notion of the mixed constitution.

2. *The Roman Mixture*

The second major type of state described and analyzed by Cicero is the mixed constitution that, in the form of the Roman Republic, he judges to be by far the best kind.[10] Cicero rejects the simple constitutions, as we have noted, because of their tendency to degenerate into tyranny, preferring a mixed constitution like the Roman that combines the three simple types into a "moderate and balanced form of government."[11] In such a state there is a supreme or royal element, with power (*potestas*) for the magistrates, authority (*auctoritas*) for the notables, and liberty (*libertas*) for the people.[12] Rights, duties, and functions are balanced in an equitable fashion, with each citizen in his own rank and station. In addition to a true and just equality, a mixed constitution produces great stability, since the causes of its degeneration are held in check by structural constraints. The net result is a harmonious state and a peaceful social order:

> For just as in the music of harps and flutes or in the voices of singers a certain harmony of the different tones must be preserved, the interruption or violation of which is intolerable to trained ears, and as this perfect agreement and harmony is produced by the proportionate blending of unlike tones, so also is a state made harmonious by agreement among dissimilar elements, brought about by a fair and reasonable blending together of the upper, middle, and lower classes, just as if they were musical tones. What the musicians call harmony in song is concord in a state, the strongest and best bond of permanent union in any commonwealth; and such concord can never be brought about without the aid of justice.[13]

Throughout his general remarks on the mixed constitution Cicero is thinking of the Roman Republic, with the consuls as the regal power, the senate as the aristocratic power, and the tribunes and popular assemblies as the democratic power. Each checks and balances the other, although the specifics of this arrangement are not spelled out in the detailed fashion of Polybius. But when Cicero identifies the Roman mixture with the best form of state he certainly does not have in mind the Republic of his own day:

Thus, before our own time, the customs of our ancestors produced excellent men, and eminent men preserved our ancient customs and the institutions of their forefathers. But though the republic, when it came to us, was like a beautiful painting, whose colours, however, were already fading with age, our own time not only has neglected to freshen it by renewing the original colours, but has not even taken the trouble to preserve its configuration and, so to speak, its general outlines. For what is now left of the "ancient customs" on which he [Ennius] said "the commonwealth of Rome" was "founded firm"? They have been, as we see, so completely buried in oblivion that they are not only no longer practised, but are already unknown. And what shall I say of the men? For the loss of our customs is due to our lack of men, and for this great evil we must not only give an account, but must even defend ourselves in every way possible, as if we were accused of capital crime. For it is through our own faults, not by any accident, that we retain only the form of the commonwealth, but have long since lost its substance.[14]

Cicero looks back to a golden age in the last century before the Gracchi, whose call for social reform, he thinks, split the Republic into "two parts," the *optimates* and the *populares,* and commenced the troubles that have brought Rome to such a sorry condition. Before this time the Roman constitution followed nature's course, developing over the ages by the wisdom of many eminent individuals and adjusting itself to meet the flux of circumstance.[15] His position is that this sacred ancestral constitution, the apotheosis of *mos maiorum,* safeguarded and advanced by such worthies as Scipio and the other participants in the dialogue of the *Republic,* has been impeded in its natural growth by the actors and events since those halcyon days.

Cicero treats the mixed constitution in the *Republic* and the *Laws,* each of which will be discussed in turn. In the *Republic* he intends to follow Cato's precedent of going back to "the origin of the Roman People," tracing the life history of the Roman state, following the course of nature from its birth through its growth, maturity, and eventual emergence in the ideal form.[16] This recreation of the "constitutional history" of the Roman state and the identification of the acme of its evolution and hence the ideal is the task Cicero sets himself in Book II, which, apart from the first book, is the only nearly complete surviving section of the work. In his constitutional history Cicero hopes to reveal the fundamental political principles for evaluating other states and especially the degenerate structure of rule under which he and his countrymen are living.

The Roman state in its past condition of perfection, according to Cicero, is the ideal because of its mixed nature. He never, however, describes the ideal Roman state simply as a mixture, but, rather, as "moderate and balanced," "well-regulated," a "fair balance," or an "equal mixture."[17] The two characteristics of Cicero's definition of the ideal are absolutely essential. A state can be a mixture and still fall short of the ideal, because of the lack of proper balance of the parts. A mixture of the three simple types of constitution—monarchy, aristocracy, and democracy—is not necessarily a balanced combination. Cicero, then, proposes to identify the balanced quality of the Roman mixture and consequently to reveal the essence of the ideal constitution.

In his search for the nature of the balanced mixture of Rome, Cicero begins his constitutional history with the legendary foundation of the city in 753 by Romulus and continues through the reigns of the traditional seven kings, the abolition of the monarchy, and its replacement by an aristocracy, to the middle of the fifth century, when the Twelve Tables are promulgated and the oligarchy of the decemvirs is overthrown. Cicero terminates his story at this point, apparently with the implication that by that time the ideal constitution had been realized and continued at least for two and a half centuries. The details of his recapitulation of the legendary tale of Roman development need not detain us, nor his discussion of the various contributions of Roman heroes to the greatness of the state. But in the search for the meaning of a balanced mixture, a number of his remarks demand attention. By the reign of the sixth king, Servius Tullius (578–535) and before the tyranny of the seventh, Tarquin the Proud (534–510), Cicero writes, the Roman state, like both Sparta and Carthage at the time, is clearly a mixture of monarchy, aristocracy, and democracy. Yet each of the three states is obviously a monarchy, dominated by a king.[18] So while at this early date Rome and others are mixtures, the mixture is not a balanced one, a preponderance being given to the monarchical element, and hence the state is still subject to corruption, testified to in Rome by the degeneration of monarchy into tyranny under the seventh king, Tarquin the Proud. After his overthrow in 509 by a conspiracy of nobles led by Junius Brutus, the senate, according to Cicero, dominates the mixture. The consulate is instituted as the "monarchical" element, and while the people are free, they have a minimal political role, senatorial approval being necessary for all acts of the popular assembly. In comparison to the mixture under the kings ending with Servius Tullius, the mixture is now seemingly more balanced but still imperfect. It is only after the plebeians assert their rights with the selection of popular tribunes in 494 to offset the monarchical power of the consulate, and with the abolition of debt bondage, that the mixture of the Roman state approaches a perfect balance.[19] The process is a long one, however, the balance of the mixture evidently not being perfected until the publication of the Twelve Tables and, after the mid-fifth century, the overthrow of the oligarchy of the decemvirs.

Clarification of Cicero's conception of a balanced mixture requires still further analysis not only of Book II but also of some of his other views scattered throughout the *Republic*. We are still not in a position to determine precisely what he means by a full or equal balance except that it entails a mixture in which each of the three elements has a role in government. Does this signify that each of the elements possesses a parity of powers? Probably not, given what we know about Cicero's views on numerical equality. An important clue to the resolution of the problem is given in Book II in the comment about the achievement of a balanced mixture by the state when the tribunes of the people are instituted in 494. In that passage he says that fundamental constitutional change cannot be prevented "unless there is in the state a fair [*aequabilis*] balance of rights, duties and functions, so that the magistrates have enough power [*potestatis*], the counsels of the eminent citizens [*in principum consilio*] enough influence [*auctoritatis*], and the people [*populo*] enough liberty [*libertatis*]."[20] From this we understand that all the people, the *populus,* including magistrates and senators, should have *libertas,* largely freedom to vote, but only a portion of the people, the magistrates and senators, will possess power and authority. In other words, a balanced or fair mixture for Cicero is one in which there is no parity of powers among the three elements, but a monopoly of the crucial decision-making functions in the monarchical and aristocratic elements, aided and supported by the popular component. He thinks, moreover, of the monarchical component—the consulate—as fundamentally a creature of the aristocratic senate.

The judgment is confirmed by what Cicero says in different contexts in Book I. There, first in a speech by Scipio, Cicero demands rhetorically whether true liberty in the state can possibly mean the same for all citizens

> even in states where everyone is ostensibly free? I mean states in which the people vote, elect commanders and officials, are canvassed for their votes, and have bills proposed to them, but really grant only what they would have to grant even if they were unwilling to do so, and are asked to give to others what they do not possess themselves. For they have no share in the governing power, in the deliberative function, or in the courts, over which selected judges preside, for those privileges are granted on the basis of birth or wealth. [21]

Here he apparently is thinking of the "well-regulated mixture" of Rome to which he refers, [22] in contrast to the active participation of all citizens in democracies like Rhodes and Athens, which he next mentions. Continuing the discussion somewhat later, he holds that even among free peoples, probably thinking of these same Rhodians and Athenians, distinctions in rank and office are made and special powers are granted to certain individuals. To do otherwise would, he insists, be inequitable: "For when equal honour is given to the highest and the lowest—for men of both types must exist in every nation—then this very 'fairness' is most unfair; but this cannot happen in states ruled by their best citizens."[23]

Although these two passages are meant to be defenses of the simple form of aristocratic constitution, they can be interpreted as expressions of Cicero's own objections to parity and preference for proportionate equality, and his belief that the ideal Roman equal or balanced mixture is one of proportion, not number. In applying this universal precept to a special case, he does not hesitate to state frankly: "And truly in civil dissension, when the good [*boni*] are worth more than the many [*multi*], I think the citizens should be weighed, not counted."[24] Cicero's conception of the ideal constitution, therefore, can perhaps be interpreted as a balance, like the balance of a scale—the scale of true justice—with the "weightier" minority of wealth and good birth equal to the numerical majority of the poor.

Of particular relevance to the priority given by Cicero to "weight" over "number" in his notion of the "equal balance" of the mixture of the ideal state is the treatment in his constitutional history of the sixth king, Servius Tullius. He is praised for having "a better understanding of the government of a state" than the other kings.[25] Cicero is referring to his division of the citizens into five propertied classes (*classes*), and the separation of the youth from the elders. The division is instituted, Cicero tells us, so that the well-to-do landed proprietors (*locuples*) will have a greater number of votes than the poor in the centuriate assembly. Servius is commended for thus putting into practice a principle that Cicero believes should always prevail in a state, namely, "that the greatest number should not have the greatest power"; by Servius's prudent arrangement the *locuples* would control the assembly, while "a large majority of the citizens would neither be deprived of the suffrage, for that would be tyrannical, nor be given too much power, for that would be dangerous."[26] In his legislation Servius calls the *locuples* money-givers (*assiduos*) because they subvent the expenses of the state, and terms the poor, with little or nothing to offer save themselves and their progeny, child-givers (*proletarios*), deriving *proletarius* from *proles,* children. Cicero concludes that "while no one was deprived of the suffrage, the majority of votes was in the hands of those to whom the highest welfare of the state was the most important,"[27] that is, those with the greatest proprietary interest in the state, the *locuples* who subsidize it.

Cicero, then, certainly grounds his idea of the ideal balanced mixture in the *Republic* on the assumptions and principles of the doctrine of the mixed constitution previously outlined. He endorses the typology of the three simple constitutions and their degenerate forms, denounces excess in all things, and is fearful of the corrupting tendencies of power:

For just as an excess of power in the hands of the aristocrats results in the overthrow of an aristocracy, so liberty itself reduces a people who possess it in too great degree to servitude. Thus everything which is in excess—when, for instance, either in the weather, or in the fields, or in men's bodies, conditions have been too favourable—is usually changed into its opposite; and this is especially true in states, where such excess of liberty either in nations or in individuals turns into an excess of servitude.[28]

Cicero's preference for proportionate equality, expressed by his emphasis on weight instead of number in the equal balance of the ideal mixture, also involves the idea of balancing social classes in one all-embracing harmony, similar to a musical harmony of different tones.[29] So this "proportionate blending of unlike tones" is for Cicero the crux of the equal and balanced mixture of the ideal state, one allotting a different role and function to each social class according to its weight and measure, a partnership of unequals, of rich and poor, noble and humble, powerful and powerless. Cicero's objective in prescribing such a harmony is similar to that of the previous theorists of the mixed constitution: the reconciliation of landlord and peasant in order to assure the domination of the former and the compliance of the latter and to withstand any danger of tyrannical rule by either. If his contemporaries would only return to the proportionate balance of social differences constructed by their ancient forebears, Cicero pleads, the Roman state might regain its unity and stability and last forever.[30]

3. *Institutions of the Ideal Mixture*

Cicero's basic conception of the ideal state in the *Republic*—the ancestral mixed constitution of Rome—is further elucidated in the *Laws*. As we have seen, he wrote the work to spell out the principal laws and institutions of the ideal mixture, although the differences between them and those of the existing Roman constitution are minimal. The Roman constitution has, however, veered from its natural course of development, and some of its laws are not true laws in the sense of being just, but the laws of the ideal state will conform to the law of nature. Some of the differences between the ideal and the actual, together with selected portions of his commentary, may be helpful in illuminating his doctrine of the mixed constitution.

Cicero believes that the nature of the ideal state depends essentially on the institutional arrangements for public officials.[31] Chief among them are the senators, and he sees the senate as the core of his recommended system of law and power. The senate should control public policy. The word chosen by Cicero to denote its rule is *dominus,* the "master" of public policy (*publici consilii*).[32] Cicero's choice of *dominus,* with its meaning in Roman law of head of the household and owner of property, aptly reflects the paramountcy he accords to the senate in his ideal constitution. The senate of wealthy landed proprietors not only is in effect the "master" of public policy, but also the "owner" of it, and as a consequence is the "owner" of the state. Citizens should support the supreme role of the senate, dutifully defending and obeying its decisions. Ultimate power (*potestas*), then, should belong to the people, and authority (*auctoritas*) to the senate, a division, Cicero insists, essential to the preservation of "the moderate and harmonious condition of the state" (*moderatus et concors civitatis status*) —the balanced mixture.

In acknowledging the ultimate power of the people, Cicero, of course, is deferring to the sacred constitutional principle of the sovereign *populus,* and not thinking of the popular exercise of power in the actual management of the daily affairs of the Republic. Because of their crucial role in the constitution, senators *"shall be free from dishonour, and shall be a model for the rest of the citizens."*[33] Cicero shares the common ancient conviction that corruption begins in the head of the body politic and spreads downward throughout the body, the result of the tendency in human conduct to imitate what we might call authority figures. Hence, senators should always maintain high personal standards and refrain from immoral and illicit conduct.[34] The senate is to consist of ex-magistrates,[35] the definite tendency of that body after the reforms of Sulla; and the censors are empowered to remove any senator for dishonorable conduct.[36] Cicero does not wish to alter in a fundamental way the current distribution of powers between senate and populace, only to establish a firm legal basis for senatorial power and to extend it to a limited degree. So senatorial decrees receive the status of laws, as had long been the case in practice, but not from a strictly legal standpoint. Minor officials, the quaestors, are legally obligated to obey the directives of the senate, the number of praetors being determined by senatorial de-

cree and popular opinion. In times of peril a dictator without consular direction will be appointed for a maximum of six months
by the senate. However, the emergency powers of the consuls are
evidently to be strengthened without the need of a *senatus con-
sultus ultimum*, the senatorial delegation and confirmation of such
extralegal powers, a subject omitted by Cicero.[37]

Two innovations in regard to the popular assemblies are presented. The first is that all presiding magistrates are legally responsible for any violence or undue disturbance occurring in the
convocations.[38] The second measure, of a more novel character
than the first, has to do with voting: a shrewd combination of the
current use of the secret ballot with the traditional voice vote.[39]
It requires attention because Cicero in his proposal quite clearly
reveals—perhaps more so than any previous thinker—the essence
of the idea of the mixed constitution, and he proves politically
more astute than some of his conservative contemporaries. All
citizens will have the suffrage, thus guaranteeing their *libertas*.
However, Cicero suggests, "let the people have their ballots as a
safeguard of their liberty, but with the provision that these ballots
are to be shown and voluntarily exhibited to any of our best and
most eminent citizens, so that the people may enjoy liberty also
in this very privilege of honourably winning the favour of the
aristocracy."[40] Secret ballots, Cicero maintains, deprive the aristocracy of its authority by keeping them in ignorance of the true
opinions of the voters. He thus hopes to grant "liberty to the
people in such a way as to ensure that the aristocracy shall have
great authority and the opportunity to use it."[41] Consequently,
the people will retain their political freedom, the power of the
aristocracy will be preserved, and the dangers of class conflict
avoided. While the "appearance of liberty" (*libertatis species*) will
be maintained, in actuality the people will be governed by "authority and favour" (*auctoritati aut gratiae*).[42] In other words, the
reality of aristocratic power rests on the network of *amicitiae*
among the nobility themselves, and on the patron–client relationship between members of the gentlemanly classes and lower orders.

Another device, according to Cicero, that paradoxically tends
to keep the people in line is the very institution introduced to
enhance their power, the tribunate. He readily admits that the trib-

unes of the people have in the past been "troublesome," but he feels that some of his friends are misguided in wishing to abolish them, and so he retains them in his ideal constitution.[43] For despite its evils, the people perhaps have less real power under the leadership of the tribunes than without. In fact, contrary to the belief of the people, the power of the tribunes is not equal to that of the senators. While the establishment of the tribunes is a necessary compromise, a sop, Cicero implies, offered by the ancient aristocracy to satisfy the popular clamor for increased participation in government, in reality over the long run a people organized under the tribunes is less dangerous than without them. Conflict between people and nobility, Cicero seems to suggest, is more restrained and moderate when it is institutionalized, brought out into the open, and regulated by mutually agreed procedures. Hence, liberty through the institution of the tribunes was "granted in such a manner that the people were induced by many excellent provisions to yield to the authority of the nobles [*auctoritati principum cederet*]."[44]

Cicero views the mixed constitution as above all else an ingenious mechanism to maintain the dominance of the large noble landholders in an age of mounting popular demand for more liberty and a greater role in government. However, the question immediately arises as to how he thinks a state with such a complex three-headed government can possibly act as a viable and unified whole with solidarity, loyalty, and spirit. What is the basis of the broad social consensus that must be the foundation of aristocratic authority? For one answer we must search behind the formal machinery of government to discover the informal social and political relationships linking and lubricating the system, thereby accounting for the superiority of aristocratic power. One such integrator of the political process and of society as a whole, just touched upon, is simply taken for granted by Cicero and never explained in any detail. It is the politics of influence and favor arising from *amicitiae* and patronage: the first generates power within the upper classes, the second enables aristocratic power to be exercised over the lower classes.

A second answer is the shaping of popular opinion by the civic religious cult. Cicero, with Plato, Aristotle, and Polybius, is a vigorous advocate of the social utility of religion. Like them he

believes that religion legitimizes the acts of government and in-
duces citizens to be respectful of their institutions and deferential
toward their rulers and their policies, thus creating a broad base
of support and enduring loyalty. In short, religion is the absolutely
crucial foundation of civic education and virtue, and hence of the
unity and order of the state. Cicero's reasons for the importance
of religion to the state are worth summarizing. First and foremost,
religion provides the state with authority, thereby enabling it to
command loyalty and obedience from the citizenry.[45] If the state
is held to have been founded by the gods and to have acted with
the approval of the gods, then all it does possesses a divine aura
of legitimacy eliciting the respect and wholehearted support of the
populace. The state, thus, becomes sacred, and any civic disobedience or act against the state is a matter of sacrilege. Another
essential function performed by religion is to foster virtuous conduct, which in turn produces an environment of mutual trust and
cooperation. Citizens who come to believe that the gods are ever-
watchful, taking note of their individual conduct and observing
their transgressions, are more likely to conform carefully to the
community's moral prescriptions, especially if these are thought
to rest ultimately on divine will. Fear of divine punishment and
hope of divine reward help to enforce obligations such as oaths
and treaties and to deter crime and the potential criminal. Nor
would death be feared if there were a promise of a hereafter where
the virtuous would enjoy eternal happiness.[46] Finally, the net social
effect of religion is taming and pacifying a people. It lifts them
out of savagery and barbarism, and is instrumental in fashioning
a harmonious, refined, and civilized way of life.[47] Through religion a peaceful and orderly society can be established, possessing
the morale, vigor, and strength necessary for self-preservation in
a hostile world.

In the account of the development of the Roman state in Book
II of the *Republic,* Cicero emphasizes the religious innovations of
the second king, Numa Pompilius.[48] By creating the "greater auspices," increasing the original number of augurs by two, and ap-
pointing five pontiffs to oversee the religious rites and various
other religious offices, Numa was responsible for the institution
of the Roman civic cult in much the same form in which it continues to exist. His intention was to tame the military passions of

the Romans in order to produce a period of peace and consolidation. Cicero concludes that Numa "died after having established the two elements which most conspicuously contribute to the stability of a state—religion and the spirit of tranquillity [*clementia*]."[49] In the *Laws* Cicero affirms that the establishment of religion is even more important than the magistrates in the creation of a commonwealth.[50] It is no accident that in his recommendations for the ideal constitution he begins with a lengthy discourse on religious institutions, since he fully realizes their significance for the government he subsequently describes. Toward the end of his life he reiterates the "conviction that Romulus by his auspices and Numa by his establishment of our ritual laid the foundation of our state."[51]

The system of religion prescribed by Cicero in *Laws*, Book II, for his ideal polity—differing little from the Roman state—is practically identical with that of Numa as it evolved. The sacredness of the state will be stressed by the erection of shrines to suggest to the people that the gods dwell among them. An augur himself, Cicero assumes that ideally the priesthood should be a monopoly and instrument of the aristocracy as it was in actual Roman practice.[52] In addition to being in charge of all public rites, priests will attend all private services, because "the people's constant need for the advice and authority of the aristocracy helps to hold the state together."[53] Augurs in the ideal state are to be "the highest and most important authority."[54] The act of every magistrate, in order to be valid, is subject to them, and any disobedience to the augurs is to be penalized by death.[55] From a philosophic perspective, Cicero may express some reservations about divination;[56] nevertheless, he has no doubts about its vital social function for the state. In the *Republic* he favors augury and the auspices;[57] and in the *Laws,* he explicitly upholds the art of divination and expresses a conviction of its validity:

For if we admit that gods exist, and that the universe is ruled by their will, that they are mindful of the human race, and that they have the power to give us indications of future events, then I do not see any reason for denying the existence of divination. . . . Nor indeed would our own Romulus have taken the auspices before founding Rome, nor would the name of Attius Navius have been remembered all these years, had not all these people made many prophecies which were in remarkable agreement with the truth.[58]

Another classic question arises. If the aristocracy through the senate actually governs, how are these custodians themselves to be controlled? In Juvenal's classic query: *Quis custodiet ipsos custodes?* What precautions are to be taken to check their conduct, thereby ensuring that in fact they serve as models for the emulation of other citizens? Religion has a vital role in this regard, too. Cicero prescribes simplicity in ritual and wishes to take steps to provide the ancient beliefs with greater ethical substance. His prohibitions against exorbitant financial outlays for funerals and monuments, monetary contributions for religious purposes, the consecration of useful agricultural land, and soft, licentious music in connection with ceremonies are aimed in part at strengthening the upper classes, curtailing their extravagance, and purifying their morals.[59]

Another significant instrument for the control of the aristocratic custodians of the state, and Cicero's major innovation in the ideal constitution of the *Laws,* is the strengthening and refurbishing of a venerable institution: the censorship.[60] The office should be filled permanently, instead of sporadically, as is the current practice. Two censors would be appointed for five-year terms for the performance of a number of traditional functions. They would categorize all citizens by age, family, and wealth into tribes and other divisions, and enroll recruits into the army. Temples, streets, and aqueducts in the city and the public treasury and state revenues would be under their jurisdiction. The morals of the people and the senators are to be subject to their regulation. In addition Cicero assigns a number of duties to the censors—the innovative feature of his stipulation—that would have struck his Roman contemporaries as definite oddities. The censors would supervise the texts of all laws with the purpose of determining their authenticity. Above all, in a novel recommendation, he makes the censors Guardians of the Laws, *nomophylakes,* in the Greek tradition of Plato, Aristotle, and Demetrius of Phalerum.[61] All governmental acts are to be scrutinized for conformity to the law. On leaving office each magistrate will be required to explain and justify his official conduct to the censors, who in turn will submit a report. If the findings of the censors reveal any legal irregularities or violations, the outgoing magistrate will be liable to state prosecution in a regular court.

Perhaps it is not overstating the case to argue that in the *Republic* and *Laws* the development of the doctrine of the mixed constitution in the ancient world attains its apogee. From Cicero's exposition there can be little doubt as to the basic principles and purpose of the doctrine. It is entirely compatible with an authoritarian, elitist, and inegalitarian political society. It represents a partnership of landlord and peasant, in which the latter is a very junior partner. The mixed constitution is a masterful device for stabilizing and conserving lordly domination, while at the same time pacifying the peasantry and maintaining the solidarity of the state as a whole. But as Cicero fully realizes, no political mechanism can be any better than the men who operate it. The solution to Roman difficulties, he thinks, is the regeneration of its operators, not simply the repair of the constitutional machine. Unless the aristocracy returns to its original harmony and unity, recapturing some of its traditional ancestral vigor and virtue, the constitution can never work as it should. If Cicero the statesman fails to weld the aristocracy into a single, public-spirited phalanx, at least Cicero the educator and philosopher can still cling to the hope of reforming the ways of his peers and, especially, of rejuvenating the noble youth on whom the future operation of the mixed constitution so depends. With the benefit of hindsight, we know that the hope was a vain and forlorn one. The rot had set in too deeply for Cicero to remedy, even with all his powers of persuasion.

CHAPTER TEN

The Art of Politics

1. *Nature of Politics*

Cicero is the only important political thinker who devoted a life
to politics and attained the highest governmental office. We might,
therefore, expect that in addition to his discourses on justice, law,
and the state, he might convey in some form to his readers the
wisdom and insight gained in the actual conduct of weighty political affairs. Given his brilliant intellect, superb rhetorical ability,
keen analytic mind, and unrivaled experience as a practicing politician, he surely must have something of value to impart on the
activity to which he was so dedicated. Little or no attention has
been given to the matter. Commentators usually single out Machiavelli, a public official for fourteen years in Renaissance Florence,
for the honor of being the first great political realist, and even the
founder of the modern science of politics. Machiavelli, so the
common interpretation goes, by his forthright compilation of *ar-
cana imperii* in *The Prince,* turns inside out the humanistic "mirror of princes" literary tradition which advises rulers to be morally
virtuous. Since Cicero's *On Duties* was a decisive influence on
this ethical approach to statecraft, he is starkly contrasted to
Machiavelli, almost as Christ to anti-Christ. Yet this sharp distinction between Cicero and Machiavelli blurs if some of the Roman's lesser-known writings—among them his political orations,
forensic speeches, and correspondence—are searched for perceptive thoughts on the nature of political activity. The result is that
Cicero, no less than Machiavelli, comes across as a hard-headed
realist, well versed in the pitfalls of power, the complexities of

manipulation, and the uses of violence. Furthermore, Cicero goes beyond Machiavelli in his concern over questions of economic policy in politics. The Cicero characterized in this chapter, therefore, will sometimes seem strange to those who rely solely on the *Republic, Laws,* and *On Duties* for an understanding of his ideas. He is a master of the practical art of politics who would have had little to learn from Machiavelli about the acquisition, conservation, and increase of power.

In order to highlight the less familiar picture of the shrewd and highly accomplished practitioner of the political craft, let us begin very briefly with the best illustration of the stereotyped Cicero as the supreme political moralizer: his view of the ideal statesman. He distinguishes politics, *res civiles* or *res publica,* and political science or the art of statesmanship, *ratio civilis* or *scientia civilis,* from other branches of knowledge and other skills.[1] Statesmanship is the highest calling, or, as he affirms in the *Republic:* the *procuratio atque administratio rei publicae* is the "supreme art" (*maxima ars*).[2] In the past, he claims, statecraft has produced the highest virtue in some of those who pursue it and has attracted individuals of unsurpassed genius. Cicero's ideal statesman is far removed from the politicians of his own day, who are driven solely by cupidity and *libido dominandi.* The common good is his only object:

For just as the aim of the pilot is a successful voyage, of the physician, health, and of the general, victory, so this director of the state [*moderatori rei publicae*] has as his aim for his fellow-citizens a happy life, fortified by wealth, rich in material resources, great in glory and honoured for virtue. I want him to bring to perfection this achievement, which is the greatest and best possible among men.[3]

Unfortunately, much of what Cicero says about the ideal statesman in the *Republic* has been lost. Nevertheless on the basis of the few remaining passages on the subject and remarks in other works, we are able to catch a glimpse of Cicero's vision. Because he uses the terms *rector* (ruler), *rector rerum publicarum* (ruler or director of public affairs), *moderator rei publicae* (governor of the state), and *princeps civitatis* (leader of the state) to denote the ideal statesman, some commentators argue that Cicero is thinking of a supreme lawgiver and ruler—possibly in anticipation of the principate founded by Augustus—as an integral institutional feature of the ideal state of the *Republic*.[4] If this is indeed his intention, there is no mention of a *rector* in the constitutional provisions of the *Laws*. More than likely, however, Cicero employs the conception in the *Republic* only to designate an idealized general type, a man (or men) of ability, virtue, and dedication like the ancestral heroes, who should dominate the senate and magistracy of the ideal mixed state in order that it may function properly, just as Plato portrays the Guardians of Kallipolis in his *Republic*.

What, then, are the chief characteristics of the ideal statesman?[5] Many of the qualities assigned to him by Cicero seem to be derived from the model of the Stoic sage. The ideal statesman is a man of prudence or practical wisdom.[6] Guided by reason, he is a person of moderation, able to control his passions, for who can govern others if he cannot rule himself? Above all, he is an individual of justice, just in all he says and does because of a full knowledge of justice. A man of honor, integrity, and good faith, he resists bribery and all other kinds of corruption. Always the true lover of glory, he displays manliness, courage, and magnanimity, and he labors with energy and industry.[7] His sole duty consists "of improving and examining himself continually, urging others to imitate him, and furnishing in himself, as it were, a mirror to his fellow-citizens by reason of the supreme excellence of his life and character."[8] Thereby he will win the affection and esteem of his countrymen, two of the prerequisites of great and successful leadership. Quite different from the tyrant ruling by fear, the ideal statesman strives for the security and welfare of the citizens instead of his own aggrandizement.[9] By acting for the common interest, he gains the citizens' confidence and support. His authority, therefore, rests on advantage and usefulness, on affection and esteem, and on magnificence and grandeur; or as Cicero phrases it in explaining the necessary qualities of a consul: "Any career which is to win us the support of the Roman people must have a splendour to impress and a utility to please them."[10] In addition to these attributes, the ideal statesman is an excellent military commander and an able public speaker, and is readily accessible to his fellow citizens. Good luck, of course, is essential, for without the blessing of fortune, all that he is and does will be of no avail.[11]

The actual policies of the ideal statesman evidently differ little from Cicero's own. He stresses the importance of shaping public opinion by example and by proper civic education.[12] On the latter point, Cicero no doubt has in mind the socializing and legitimizing effect of religion, the necessary basis of a harmonious and vigorous state. Through participation and belief in a civic cult, the citizen will develop a keen sense of shame, a much more effective basis for obedience to the law than fear. Besides fostering religion, Cicero's ideal statesman should be particularly concerned with caring for military and deliberative institutions and with maintaining a hierarchical system of orders.

Cicero recalls in 49 the ideal of the *Republic,* contrasting it to the pursuit of power and narrow self-interest by Pompey and Julius Caesar:

Both of the pair have aimed at personal domination, not the happiness and fair fame of the community. Pompey did not abandon Rome because he could not have defended her, nor Italy because he was driven from her shores. His plan from the first has been to ransack every land and sea, to stir up foreign kings, to bring savage races in arms to Italy, to raise enormous armies. . . . Neither sees our happiness as his mark. Both want to reign.[13]

Never the starry-eyed political philosopher, Cicero is a clever and hardheaded politician with his feet firmly planted on the ground, seldom deluding himself as to what goes on and can go on in the harsh and brutal forum of Roman government. In a momentary fit of wistfulness, nostalgia for past times, and anxiety over the catastrophic turn of public affairs, he might in retirement at one of his rural retreats conjure up a dream—as he does in the *Republic*—of what should be the case. Nevertheless, he is more realist and pragmatist than idealist, not overly sanguine about the capabilities of mankind, and poignantly aware that statecraft is the art of the possible.

So from Cicero's vision of the ideal statesman impossible of attainment, we must turn to his different treatment of the practical activity of politics. His position is directly related to his estimation of actual human conduct. He is never the complete pessimist about man that Augustine and Hobbes were to be at much later dates. Men for Cicero are neither completely evil nor totally good. Cicero's outlook is to be expected of a person of his intellect, social position, and political interests: gentlemanly, cultured, and

worldly. The "human race," he writes in the *Laws,* "is clearly
marked in its evil tendencies as well as in its goodness."[14] All men
are attracted by pleasure, and few are not moved by ambition.[15]
By nature, men constitute a single universal commonwealth of
reason and morality. However, because of their "depravity" (*pra-*
vitas), conflict and dissension divide them.[16] Most men, even the
best among them, succumb to the blandishments of power, and
for this reason tyranny is a perpetual threat to civic order.[17] All
things of human contrivance—families, states, laws, and customs
—are "frail and fleeting."[18] Consequently, Cicero suspects and rejects any ideal of perfect virtue such as that profferred by the
Stoics.[19] Virtue is for human beings, and since they are all too
human instead of divine, we must lower our moral sights and
strive for what is morally possible: a "mean" virtue, in the sense
of a mean between extremes. This is an ethical ideal that men like
himself, human beings with all their weaknesses and imperfections, can hope to achieve.

Men of this sort, therefore, have molded the politics of all ages.
For politics consists of the ideas, ideals, motives, and actions of
such men, on the average neither all good nor all evil. Politics is
an activity of the greatest intricacy and complexity, one of contingency and unpredictability, a realm of constant change and flux,
of danger and duplicity: "how potent in politics is opportunity,
how shifting the phases, how incalculable the issues, of events,
how easily swayed are men's predilections, what pitfalls there are
and what insincerity in life."[20] The uncertainty and apparent irrationality of politics are typified by the vagaries of elections as
perceived by Cicero and echoed throughout the ages to our own
day of pollster and psephologist:

Can you think of any strait, any channel, that has the currents and variety
of rough patches and changes of tide strong enough to match the upsets
and the ebb and flow that accompany the workings of elections? The
whole situation is often changed by having to break off for a day or by
night intervening and the merest breath of a rumour sometimes changes
everyone's views. Often, too, for no apparent reason the turn of events
takes you by surprise and at times even the people are amazed at a result
as if it were not itself responsible. Nothing is more fickle than people in
a crowd, nothing harder to discover than how men intend to vote, nothing trickier than the whole way in which elections work. Who thought
that a man of Lucius Philippus' exceptional talents, public service, high

esteem and nobility could be defeated by Marcus Herennius? That a man
of Quintus Catulus' culture, intelligence and integrity could be defeated
by Gnaeus Mallius? That a man of Marcus Scaurus' influence, outstanding
qualities as a citizen and distinction as a senator could be defeated by
Quintus Maximus? All these defeats were unexpected and could not even
be explained when they had occurred. Storms are frequently raised by a
particular constellation, but often break unexpectedly for some obscure
reason that defies explanation. In the same way you may often recognize
in elections the sign responsible for the storm brought on by the voters,
but the cause is often so obscure that it appears to have blown up quite
by chance.[21]

Because of such complexity, uncertainty, and constant flux, politics is fundamentally an activity most effectively conducted by
elders. It entails reason, seasoned judgment, discrimination, and
the prudence acquired from long experience, not the rashness and
lack of foresight of the young: "had it not been for old men no
state would have existed at all."[22] Politics is a lonely enterprise
because it comprises a sphere of endeavor in which men usually
subordinate their friendships to the quest for power; and enmity
toward previous friends results from changes in political attitudes
and opinions. As a consequence of the very high stakes, and the
jealousies and hatreds aroused in the contention for office, if disaster is to be avoided one should become acutely conscious of
whom to trust and not to trust.[23] Holders of public office must
be ever watchful, confiding in others only in proportion to their
trustworthiness, yet at the same time they must not be overly
harsh or suspicious of their subordinates.[24] Obvious sycophants
should never be made intimates by responsible officials and statesmen, nor should those who have proven "deceitful and unstable."[25]

Policy and its execution should always be highly flexible and
adaptable. The contingency and ever-shifting circumstances of
politics confer upon opportunity a major importance. Opportunity should be seized as it presents itself, not in a rash and imprudent fashion. Time and timing are of the essence of politics:
"how much turns on time in politics, and what a difference it
makes to the selfsame policy, whether one is beforehand or belated
in laying it down, taking it in hand, and carrying it into effect."[26]
While decisiveness is the sine qua non of successful political action,
a particular position should never be held in an unwavering and

obstinate manner. We must always be willing to meet change with change, to adjust ourselves to new occurrences and unexpected alterations in any situation. Nor should we adhere to precedent for its own sake. Precedent has always been an invaluable guide to the statesman, but no one should expect from precedent what it cannot yield: how to deal with novel circumstances that have no apparent precedent. The prudent man of action must learn to tack and trim just as in sailing a boat, and, when necessary, run with the wind even if a delay in reaching the destination is thereby incurred.[27] The vital consideration is to reach the port of call safely, and this may not always be managed by setting the most obvious or direct course.

In these recommendations Cicero never entertains the thought of surrender of major political goals. He is thinking solely of the means, of the tactical approach to basic ends. In political tactics, compromise and temporizing, the regrouping of forces and the change of alliances, keeping a low profile when odds are unfavorable, balancing inconveniences, and choosing the lesser evil may all be required for the attainment of the primary objective. Above all, in politics one must act in a rational, calculating way, carefully planning and making preparations. The skillful statesman should behave with the moderation and decorum appropriate to a gentleman, steeling himself to endure misfortunes and reversals and suiting the means to his fundamental objectives. Toward foes and lawbreakers he can never be lenient, but always severe.[28] The severity, however, should invariably be impartial, consistent, and firm: "a wholesome sternness carries the day against the vain show of leniency."[29] Deterrence, not vengeance or retribution, must always be the motive in adopting policies, measures, decisions, and severe punishments. Statesmen should also steep themselves in a knowledge of political science in order to understand, on the basis of history, the principal causes of the decay of states and the remedial measures necessary to stem the tide of decay.[30]

Cicero is fully aware of the importance of the informal political arrangements of influence and favor that bind together the Roman political system, enabling it to function, and in practice he never hesitates to use them. His power and that of his peers depends on these arrangements, and he encourages their full employment for the securing of political ends. The first of these is the *amicitiae*, the networks of friends and associates that give cohesion to the upper classes and provide support to political candidates.[31] Indeed, Cicero's *On Friendship* can in part and with caution be read in this light. There, at least in one passage, if considered in the context of Roman politics, Cicero reveals a willingness to deviate from moral convention for tactical reasons:

and, even if by some chance the wishes of a friend are not altogether honourable and require to be forwarded in matters which involve his life or reputation, we should turn aside from the straight path, provided, however, utter disgrace does not follow; for there are limits to the indulgence which can be allowed to friendship. Nor indeed ought a man either to disregard his reputation, or to consider the goodwill of his countrymen a poor weapon in the battle of life, though to hunt after it with fawning and flattery is disgraceful; as to virtue we must by no means abjure it, for it is attended by regard.[32]

Elsewhere in the same volume he strongly condemns the *amicitiae* of wicked men, such as that between Tiberius Gracchus and Gaius Papirius Carbo, bent on the destruction of the state, and warns *boni viri* to avoid such relationships and to withdraw from such friendships.[33]

The second informal arrangement, *clientela,* that of client and patron, which cemented upper and lower classes and mobilized backing for the political activities of the former, is acknowledged by Cicero to be an exceedingly useful institution. Clientage, however, is not to be confused with corrupt practices such as bribery:

Men of small means are only able to earn favours from our order or pay us back in one way and that is by helping us and following us about when we are candidates for office. It is not possible and it cannot be asked of us senators or of the Roman knights that they should attend for whole days their friends who are candidates. If they come in large numbers to our houses and on occasion accompany us down to the forum, if they condescend to walk with us the length of a public hall, we think that we are receiving great attention and respect. It is the poorer men with the time available who provide the constant attention that is habitually given to men of standing and to those who confer benefits. Do not, then, Cato, take from the lower class this fruit of their attention. Allow the men who hope for everything from us to have something to give us in return. If poor men have nothing but their vote, then, even if they vote, their support is valueless. Finally, as they are always saying, they cannot plead for us, stand surety for us, or invite us to their homes. They ask us for all these favours but think they can only repay us for what they receive from us by personal service.[34]

Seats in the circus and forum and public banquets are one aristocratic method of repaying clients for their services and constitute
an indispensable ancestral custom.[35] We know that Cicero built his
political career on the artful use of the institutions of *amicitia* and
clientela.[36]

No discussion of Cicero's approach to the practical activity of
politics is complete without citing the *Commentariolum Petitionis*
or *Handbook of Electioneering,* of uncertain authorship but customarily ascribed to Cicero's brother, Quintus. It may have been
written sometime in 65–64 for Cicero's guidance in campaigning
for election to the consulate of 63; it bears the dedication, "Quintus to His Brother Marcus." The author concludes with the self-
deprecatory remark: "I thought, not that I knew all this better
than you, but that, considering how busy you are, I could more
easily pull it together into one whole and send it to you in
writing."[37] Whatever the identity of the author, his recommendations do not seem to do an injustice to what we have learned
of the practical political outlook of Cicero, who certainly appears
to share in the basic assumption that the realm of politics is like
a theater with the politician playing a role as appealing as possible
to the audience of electors: "Though nature is strong indeed, yet
an assumed personality can, it seems, overcome the natural self
for an affair of a few months."[38] Canvassing for a magistracy, we
are advised, requires securing the support of friends and the people.[39] The backing of friends in the broadest sense—relatives, intimates, associates, neighbors, acquaintances, clients—should be
sought by kindnesses and observance of obligations. One must
not be overly trusting in seeking their support, however, for "all
things are full of deceit, snares, and treachery."[40] On this score
the ancient saying of Epicharmus is invoked, "that the bone and
sinew of wisdom is: 'Never trust rashly,' " but in canvassing
friends one should also "get to know . . . the methods and types
of your detractors and your opponents. The types are three: first,
those whom you have hurt; second, those who do not like you,
though they have no reason; third, those who are close friends of
your competitors."[41]

The politician's acting ability, his talent for appearing to be
what he is not, is stretched to the full in the attempt to win the
support of the people, for which purpose one must "be deter-

mined that what you lack by nature should be so well simulated
that it seems a natural act."[42] In the first place, the role played by
the candidate "requires a memory for names, an ingratiating manner, constant attendance, generosity, publicity, a fine political image."[43] Although flattery is normally contemptible, in an election
it is "indispensable for a candidate, whose facial expression and
conversation must be modified and adapted to the humour and
the inclination of all whom he meets."[44] The ambitious canvasser
will never hesitate to promise the world to his popular audience,
since they crave "promises made in a lavish and complimentary
way."[45] Although he may pledge his services to everyone, once
elected he should only actually give help "to those in whom he
expected he was making the best investment."[46] Throughout the
campaign he should give special attention to publicizing himself
and his electoral efforts:

see that your whole canvass is a *fine show,* brilliant, resplendent, and
popular, with the utmost display and prestige; and also, if it can be managed at all, that there should be scandalous talk, in character, about the
crimes, lusts, and briberies of your competitors. Above all, it must be
shown in this canvass that high hopes and good opinions are entertained
for your political future.[47]

Do all of this with oratorical luster, the author urges, and on a
related note he completes his memorandum:

Further, as the worst vice of this city is to forget moral worth when
bribery enters in, know yourself—I mean, understand that you, of all
people, can put the fear of prosecution and its dangers into your competitors. Let them know that they are under your watchful observation;
they will be terrified . . . by your application, your authority and power
as an orator.[48]

Whether Quintus wrote the *Handbook* or not matters little, because it apparently reflects the opinions of Cicero and his peers.
They would have had little to glean about political mechanics from
our own sophisticated campaign managers.

2. *Violence as a Political Instrument*

Violence was one of the principal instruments at the disposal of
the political actor of the age.[49] Far from defending the rule of law
at all costs or abhorring violence, Cicero, living in extremely violent times, seldom hesitates to recommend its use when neces-

sary, to employ it himself, or to praise others compelled to resort to it. He was obviously no stranger to violence. As consul in 63 he forcibly suppressed the Catilinarian conspiracy, was responsible for the summary execution without trial of the conspirators, and has long been remembered and praised by libertarians as one of the most vigorous opponents of tyranny and dedicated advocates of tyrannicide. But violence contrary to the law, he believes, should be a political instrument only under certain conditions. Violence is legitimate for the sake of self-defense and survival when a breakdown of law and order occurs. Life in a society that has deteriorated into a jungle requires following the law of the jungle. If the security of the state is at stake, then resort to violence may be necessary. Extralegal force, however, should be employed only if a distinct possibility of success exists, if the odds are not sufficiently against one as to make defeat inevitable and result in a greater evil. If the choice is between the use of violence and the destruction of the state, then the lesser of the two evils must prevail. From Cicero's standpoint, of course, the security of the state is the sovereign political and social value, to which all other ideals and actions must give way. Finally, Cicero thinks, no less than Machiavelli, that violence should always be instrumental. The use of violence must never be escalated into an end in itself, which is the way of unprincipled tyranny, but should always be restricted to self-defense and the preservation of the state when no other alternative is possible.

Cicero sometimes gives the impression of strong opposition to violence of any kind. The ideal constitution of the *Laws* prohibits violence (*vis*) in public meetings.[50] His comment on the provision is: "Nothing is more destructive to governments, nothing is in such complete opposition to justice and law, nothing is less suitable for civilized men, than the use of violence in a state which has a fixed and definite constitution."[51] In *On Duties,* while considering war, he mentions two ways of resolving disputes: one by discussion, the way of man; the other by force, a characteristic of beasts. Men should resort to war only when discussion is no longer possible, and even then only in self-defense.[52] During Caesar's dictatorship Cicero writes justifying his own acquiescence:

For that same Plato, whose teaching I earnestly endeavour to follow, gives us this injunction—"to assert yourself in politics only so far as you can justify your measures to your fellow-citizens; for it is as wrong to use violence to your country as to one of your parents." And indeed he declares that the reason why he did not take part in public affairs was that, finding the people of Athens now almost in a state of dotage, and seeing that they could be ruled neither by argument nor by anything but force, while he despaired of their being persuaded, he did not deem it lawful that they should be forced.[53]

In one protest against the use of force, Cicero distinguishes between two kinds of violence. Most commonly violence is defined as the infliction of force upon a person, doing him damage or bodily harm. Cicero, however, in an eloquent plea in 69 on behalf of a plaintiff, Aulus Caecina, refers to another type of violence. Caecina claims that his property is being surrounded by an armed band sent by the defendant, thereby threatening him with physical harm if he attempts to exercise his legal right of possession. Whatever the merits of the case, the important point is Cicero's argument that the defendant's threat has terrorized Caecina and is no less violence than if bodily harm had actually been inflicted:

force [*vis*] which touches our persons or our lives is not the only form of force: much more serious is the force which removes a man from a definite position or situation by exposing him to the danger of death and striking terror into his mind. Thus there are many cases of wounded men whose minds refuse to give way, though their bodies are weakened, and who do not abandon the position they are resolved to defend; others, on the contrary, are driven back although unscathed; which proves that a greater degree of force is brought to bear upon the man whose mind is terror-stricken than on the man whose body is wounded.[54]

Cicero then applies these generalizations to the specific situation of his client who has been prevented from occupying his legal property by the threat of force instead of its actual use: "anything constitutes force which, by threat of danger, either compels us to leave or prevents us from reaching any place."[55] Psychic violence, for Cicero, therefore, is a more potent means of control and manipulation than physical violence. We recognize it as one of the chief traits of the Roman political arena and the stuff of tyranny. All government, of course, in part rests on psychic violence, but not to the extent and in the extreme form of a tyrannical regime. The tyrant constantly terrorizes his subjects, not so much by what he actually does as by the persistent and overwhelming threat of what he might do to those failing to bend to his will, and he eventually comes to live in terror of those whom he terrorizes.

From Cicero's writings, however, it is apparent that he does not oppose, under specific conditions, the use of violence either by the state or by private citizens. Occasionally, he even appears to relish violence. For example, he writes to Atticus, praising the consul Dolabella for his massacre of Caesarian rioters in 44 and his destruction of a monument erected in Caesar's honor in the Forum:

> This affair really gives people something to think about! Over the rock with them, on to the cross with them, away with the pillar, contract for paving the site! Why, it's Homeric! He seems to me to have quashed that affectation of regret for Caesar which was spreading from day to day. I was afraid it might become a danger to our tyrannicides if it took root.[56]

Two days later, Cicero congratulates Dolabella, pointing out that his "extreme of penal rigour has brought not merely no odium but actual popularity, delighting the lower orders as well as all honest folk."[57]

Nevertheless, although Cicero may be carried away at times by the idea of the forcible suppression of those whom he considers dangerous to the welfare of the state, his attitude toward violence is not entirely capricious or without logic. His position rests on the assumption that the safety of the state takes precedence over all other considerations.[58] When its security is threatened, those with supreme executive power should, if required, employ extraordinary measures to put down the danger. So in the case of the Catilinarian conspiracy, Cicero as consul obtained from the senate a *senatus consultum ultimum* or decree of emergency that gave him the authority to take any requisite steps, unlimited by law, to crush the threat.[59] Under the decree the senate temporarily assumed sovereign power (normally residing in the *populus*) and conferred on him its implementation. Hence, he arrested the conspirators in December of 63. The senate, at Cicero's request, voted the death penalty; and the culprits were summarily executed without benefit of trial, under normal circumstances a legal violation of the right of all citizens. In this case it was the senate, at the urging of Cicero as consul, that defined the threat, passed the decree of emergency, and used its constitutional power to take the appropriate extralegal measures to meet the danger.

For Cicero, in his perilous times, the security of the state is always jeopardized by any widespread protest from below or popular disturbance for social reform: abolition of debts, land reform, and so forth. The foremost threat to the state and the status quo originates in this internal source.[60] The definition of what constitutes a serious danger to the security of the state and hence to the mixed constitution, thereby requiring the suspension of due process and the rule of law and necessitating the use of violence, is for Cicero the sacred responsibility of the *viri boni,* the good men or best citizens, the *optimates,* notables like himself, the well-to-do landholders who rule the Roman polity and have its true interests at heart. They are not so much a law unto themselves as servants of a supreme law to which all must bow: the survival and well-being of the moderate and balanced mixed constitution with all it implies for power relationships in Roman society. The *viri boni* are the trustees of the *mos maiorum.*

What should happen when law and order break down, when the legal system and such critical institutions as the consulate and senate become impotent? Who then is to define the threat to state security? Who then is to employ violence, to crush the threat? Cicero's answer is the same, the *boni.* They are, he implies, the self-appointed guardians of the welfare of the ancestral state and mixed constitution. When law and order disintegrate, the *boni* have the duty and right to employ violence against the disturbers of the peace, usually from below, in order to protect themselves and restore the state to harmony. Under normal circumstances the *boni* are obligated

to resist the crimes of reckless men, men who would overthrow the state, by means of the laws and courts of law; if the laws had no force and there were no courts of law, if the state were shackled by violence and crushed by a conspiracy of desperadoes, then life and liberty must be defended by a protecting force. To understand this is a sign of wisdom, to act accordingly, of courage: both to understand and to act, a sign of perfect and consummate merit.[61]

For Cicero no middle ground between law and violence is possible. In comparing society before the state and a civilized life under government, he writes:

Now, between life thus refined and humanized, and that life of savagery, nothing marks the difference so clearly as law and violence [*ius atque vis*]. Whichever of the two we are unwilling to use, we must use the other. If we would have violence abolished, law must prevail, that is, the administration of justice, on which the law wholly depends; if we dislike the administration of justice, or if there is none, force must rule [*vis dominetur necesse est*].[62]

If law becomes ineffectual and violence prevails, then, since we are no longer able to rely upon law, force must be met with force.

Traditionally, Cicero argues, when violence rules and constitutional procedures have broken down, private citizens of Rome have taken the law into their own hands in order to save the state. One of his favorite examples is that of P. Cornelius Scipio Serapio. In 133, while the consul Publius Mucius did nothing, Serapio rallied a crowd of senators and their clients to defend the safety of the state and killed the tribune Tiberius Gracchus, whose seditious program of land reform was inciting anarchy. Another instance cited by Cicero is the assassination of Spurius Maelius in 440 by Gaius Servilius Ahala, a commander under the dictator Cincinnatus.[63] The rich, plebeian corn-dealer Maelius sought, according to Cicero, to foment revolution and seize power by selling corn at a low price to the people. Cicero laments the loss of the ancient virtue that enabled the heroes of the past to save their country: "Gone, gone for ever is that valour that used to be found in this Republic and caused brave men to suppress a citizen traitor with keener punishment than the most bitter foe."[64]

Not himself a party to the conspiracy against Julius Caesar that led to his assassination, Cicero nevertheless was a friend of Brutus and later glorified his act.[65] Caesar, after all, was tyrant and *popularis* whose power rested on the rabble and who was the mastermind behind a previous divisive and inflammatory proposal for agrarian reform. Like Tiberius Gracchus before him, Caesar is just one more confirmation of Cicero's precept that the real menace to the security of Rome is from below and should be ruthlessly crushed. Later he justifies another act of violence committed by Brutus, by the right "which Jupiter himself has sanctioned, that all things salutary for the state should be held lawful and right; for law is nothing else but a principle of right derived from the will of the gods, commanding what is honest, forbidding the contrary."[66] In a sudden and pressing emergency, when higher authority cannot be consulted, the state official has a right to violate the rule of law for the sake of the safety of the state: "Be a Senate unto yourself, and follow whatever path is indicated by your consideration for the public welfare."[67]

As we have seen, Cicero places two limitations on the use of violence by private citizens for the sake of the security of the state, limitations which apparently also apply to the actions of government. Violence should only be used when one has sufficient actual armed might to ensure some likelihood of success. Again, violence should not be employed if the probable result is the increase of danger to the security of the state by splitting it into hostile and irreconcilable camps.[68] In both cases, the wise and prudent policy is to temporize and bargain for time, and perhaps even dissociate oneself from the regime and retire from the political arena, ready to return under different and more favorable circumstances. In sum, Cicero believes that violence is a legitimate political instrument, if employed by the propertied and well-to-do to ensure what from the standpoint of their interests is defined as the security of state and constitution and not to place them in greater jeopardy, and if violence so used is a practicable alternative to other means. Consequently, violence from above is sometimes but not always rightful, whereas violence from below is without exception an evil.

Cicero's much-acclaimed defense and justification of tyrannicide is a special instance of his general views on violence in politics. He is quite unequivocal about the remedy for tyrants:

all that pestilent and abominable race should be exterminated from human society. And this may be done by proper measures; for, as certain members are amputated, if they show signs themselves of being bloodless and virtually lifeless and thus jeopardize the health of the other parts of the body, so those fierce and savage monsters in human form should be cut off from what may be called the common body of humanity.[69]

Of all acts conducive to winning glory, none is more noble than tyrannicide. If murder is morally wrong, what for Cicero makes tyrannicide such a glorious deed, in fact one in which morality and utility are identical? The difference between murder and tyrannicide, both acts of the utmost violence, lies for Cicero in the difference in intention and circumstance.[70] Ordinarily, taking the life of another or stealing from a fellow human being is immoral because these acts are committed solely out of self-interest and as such violate the common interest. Consequently, they contravene the law of nature. But the murder of a tyrant is a matter of the common interest and the security of the state, not a private affair motivated by self-interest. Since tyranny is destructive of the state and the common interest, anyone who terminates the life of a tyrant puts an end to injustice, thereby saving the state and restoring the common interest. Because the state (in a just form) should be the object of our greatest love and loyalty, those who thus rescue it from destruction act in a way at once moral and expedient and perform the most signal service to mankind. In effect, then, anyone who disregards the common interest, whether tyrant or would-be tyrant—for example, a leader like Clodius or Caesar who spearheads a movement of popular protest for social reform—places himself at war with the rest of society and can be legitimately treated as an enemy.

The key in determining those to whom violence can and cannot rightfully be applied is the idea of the common interest and the safety of the state. Cicero in effect claims that he and those like him can correctly define the common interest for the dominant propertied classes, and hence for the state as a whole. The specification of what regime constitutes a tyranny is ultimately theirs, the prerogative of the *boni*. All governments or aspirants to government that actually violate or threaten the interests of the propertied classes, thereby endangering the common interest and the security of the state, are by definition tyrannical. Violence used by the propertied classes and their supporters for the removal or death of such tyrants and would-be tyrants is just and proper. Cicero, therefore, obviously excludes from the category of tyranny any government such as that of the conservative senatorial oligarchs, for so long the rulers of the vast majority in an autocratic, inhumane, and exploitative fashion. Cicero's distinctions in respect to tyranny and violence resemble in a way John Locke's notions of "rebellion" and "revolution."[71] Rebellion for Locke, it is arguable, is essentially any use of force from below against the dominant propertied interests and their government. Revolution, on the other hand, is force employed by the dominant propertied classes against government persistently violating their interests. Revolution is morally justifiable, rebellion is not. In the final analysis, justice—the moral duties to preserve and protect lives and property, to keep promises, and to act generously—is for both Cicero and Locke in the interests of the stronger, the dominant landholders. Cicero's perspective on violence in politics, generally speaking, anticipates the attitude in the following centuries of the more enlightened members of the lordly class and the governments that served them.

3. Major Ends of Statecraft

So far the focus has been on politics as means. But what of the ends of politics, as Cicero sees them? The preservation of the state, he maintains, should be the chief goal of statecraft. Protection of the state signifies two things to him. It is used, first of all, in a narrow, short-term sense. Every precaution must be taken to establish and maintain law and order, to prevent sedition and civic disturbances, and to guard against hostile external threats.[72] In addition, security of the state denotes a broader, long-term goal of strengthening and conserving the mixed constitution. The harmony, well-being, and survival of the state, for Cicero, depend to an important extent on the existence and effectiveness of the mixed constitution, an instrument far superior to any other type of constitution for safeguarding the state. Since Rome possesses a mixed constitution, although one seriously weakened, the statesman should take measures to restore and foster its moderate and balanced nature. So the statesman whose primary aim is the security of the state must strive to preserve it as a going day-to-day concern and adopt a strategy that rejuvenates the moderation and balance of the mixture. Security of the state in the first sense is always the condition for it in the second sense, and must receive priority, but with the ultimate health of the mixture in mind.

Cicero thinks, as we have seen, that a properly mixed constitution consists of a *concordia* of social orders, devised, however, to guarantee the political domination of the aristocratic landholding minority.[73] The basic purpose of the Roman statesman, therefore, should be the attainment and preservation of this kind of harmony and unity. In the two decades separating his consulate from his death in 43, Cicero frequently employs as a political slogan to designate this special sort of concord the word *otium*, in a variety of combinations.[74] He, in fact, may possibly have been the first to use *otium* in the political arena to stand for the internal peace and tranquillity of the state without civic dissension. Commonly, *otium* had the highly personal meaning of individual quiet, repose, and leisure, a freedom from public duties. *Otium,* the political slogan devised by Cicero, refers not to any kind of political order but to the preservation of the status quo, the mixed constitution undisturbed by strife and popular reform.

During his consulship he promises this kind of order and attempts to further it by ruthlessly suppressing the Catilinarian conspiracy and by vigorously opposing the agrarian reforms proposed by Rullus. *Otium* is still his political watchword even when he no longer has a leading role in the Republic. The crux of his conception of *otium* is *dignitas,* which means *libertas* for all, with authority for the large propertyholders in a hierarchical social system. So in his strictures against the agrarian proposals of Rullus in 63, which Cicero believes would destroy the *otium* he so cherishes and consequently the unity on which the state rests, he exclaims: "For what is so welcome to the people as peace [*pax*] . . . ? What is so welcome to the people as liberty [*libertas*] . . . ? What is so welcome to the people as repose [*otium*] . . . especially when accompanied by authority and dignity [*imperio ac dignitate*]?"[75] In arguing against the Rullan measures, he appeals directly to the interests of the senators, clearly revealing what he has in mind by *otium:*

But if, conscript fathers, you promise me your zeal in upholding the common dignity [*communem dignitatem*], I will certainly fulfill the most ardent wish of the republic, that the authority [*auctoritas*] of this order, which existed in the time of our ancestors, may now, after a long interval, be seen to be restored to the state.[76]

The year after his return from exile and restoration, in the *Defence of Sestius* in 56, Cicero stresses the conventional distinction between two general political persuasions in the ruling class, the *optimates* and *populares,* and coins the political slogan *cum dignitate otium.* Neither *populares* nor *optimates* should be mistakenly identified with organized political parties or unified groups.[77] They were instead loose and fluctuating collections of notables sharing to a greater or lesser degree certain common interests and attitudes. *Populares* exhibited even less coherence than the *optimates* occasionally did. For Cicero, the Gracchi, Marius, Saturninus, Catiline, Clodius, and Caesar typify the *populares*. They are mischief-makers, demagogues, subverters of the established order with designs for the capture of state power; while defenders of the existing constitutional order like himself are the *optimates*. *Populares* stand for the rights of assembly and tribunate, opposition to senatorial authority, and economic reforms; *optimates*, for the conservation of the mixed constitution.

In the *Defence of Sestius* Cicero contends that *populares* pursue a policy designed to win favor with the multitude; and in contrast the *optimates* act in the interests of the best citizens (*boni*), that is, the well-to-do propertied classes. *Populares* are opposed by Cicero to both senate and *boni*.[78] From the time of his consulate to his death, Cicero characterizes *populares*—in the *Defence of Sestius* and in other forensic and senatorial speeches—by a distinctive rhetorical formula, unique in late republican political discourse.[79] Among the key words he employs are *furor, perditus, audax*, and *latro*. *Populares* are depicted as mentally deranged, morally lost, and insolently reckless criminals and incendiarists whose illicit use of force terrorizes all good citizens, threatens law and order, and endangers the propertied.

The real troublemakers among the *populares*, but by no means synonymous with them, are the *audaces*, the "destroyers of the state" (*eversorum rei publicae*).[80] *Audax* used positively means daring and courageous; used negatively, audacious, rash, reckless, foolhardy. Cicero capitalizes on the pejorative sense, often contrasting *boni* to *audaces*, the mad dogs of the *populares*, dangerous radicals whose reckless machinations threaten to undermine and destroy the state. Clodius, the "raving and audacious tribune of the commons" (*tribunum pl. furiosum et audacem*),[81] personifies the evil for Cicero, and among the others are Verres, Antony, Piso, Catiline, and Caesar. From the standpoint of Cicero and the *boni* they are desperadoes whose every act is a heinous crime. The felonious *audaces* incite the masses to civil discord, using illicit means such as bribery to corrupt and mobilize them for treacherous undertakings.[82] In general, *populares* undermine the whole structure of authority on which the Roman state rests.

Optimates, in contrast, believe in the supremacy of the senate. Magistrates should be subordinate to the senate, which in turn should be supported by the equestrian order. However, *optimates* should always protect the interests and liberty of the masses. Cicero, for tendentious reasons, expands the conventional meaning of *optimates* to include not only notables but also their supporters from all stations.[83] His description of the Catilinarian conspirators provides some indication of his view of the social composition of *populares* and their supporters. At the top are discontented, ambitious members of the upper orders, *populares,* many of whom are in financial straits or whose quest for high honor and office has been thwarted. Below them are their supporters, the many hard-pressed smallholders, the urban rabble, and the criminal element. Catilinarians are the *audacissimi* ("the most reckless").[84] In contrast to *populares,* portrayed by Cicero as mercenary gangs of bandits and insurrectionists, *optimates* are presented as honorable, upright, loyal, sensible, law-abiding citizens: the natural custodians of the state. They consist of a *consensus bonorum,* a union of "good" or "honest" men, the financially solvent and propertied of all classes, including not only the landholders of the senatorial and equestrian orders and the decurions, but also men of business of all kinds including freedmen, who monopolized small business enterprise in Rome.[85]

In a notable passage Cicero explains the nature of the *optimates* and their main political goal:

All are *Optimates* who are neither criminal nor vicious in disposition, nor made revolutionaries, nor embarrassed by home troubles. It follows, then, that those who are upright, sound in mind, and easy in circumstances [*bene de rebus domesticis*] are those whom you have called a "Breed." Those who serve the wishes, the interests and principles of these men in the government of the state are called the supporters of the *Optimates* and are themselves reckoned as the most influential of the *Optimates,* the most eminent citizens, and leaders of the state. What then is the mark set before those who guide the helm of state, upon which they ought to keep their eyes and towards which they ought to direct their course? It is that which is far the best and the most desirable for all who are sound and good and prosperous [*beatis*]; it is *cum dignitate otium.* Those who desire this are all reckoned as *Optimates,* those who achieve it as the foremost men and saviours of the state. For just as it is unfitting for men to be so carried away by the honour of public office that they are indifferent to peace, so too it is unfitting for them to welcome a peace [*otium*] which is inconsistent with honour [*dignitate*].[86]

In using the word *optimates,* denoting both the "best" and the "aristocrats," Cicero again shows his political acumen, for he is appealing not only to the true nobility but to those who identify their interests with the blue-blooded landholders and who esteem their own social status even though it is based on wealth rather than family. Cicero is certainly thinking of an alliance of the prosperous and propertied, for in two places he mentions the *optimates* in these terms: as those who are *bene de rebus domesticis* and those who are *beatis,* both denoting the well-to-do.

Cicero's use of *cum dignitate otium* further substantiates this interpretation of his political outlook. Literally translated, the slogan means tranquillity or peace with honor or worthiness. Ever possessing a shrewd political eye, Cicero may have selected the slogan because of its variety of meanings, its susceptibility to differing definition, depending on the context.[87] It suggests more than is apparent on the surface: a private life of honorable retirement, as well as a harmonious state. If the referent is the latter, then the implication of *dignitas* is not any political order, but a very specific kind. For these reasons classicists paraphrase the slogan freely in order to capture Cicero's true political connotation, and all with roughly similar results, for example: "peace for all and distinction for some"; "tranquillity of all and the dignity of the 'best' "; "peace and quietness for the masses, political prestige, influence and worthiness for the 'Best Men' "; "absence of domestic strife" with "satisfaction of legitimate ambition"; "freedom from disturbance [*otium*], and respect for the government and its members, who themselves deserve respect"; "an ordered state in which men were valued according to their rank in a hierarchical social structure."[88] The *optimates* of the past who faithfully followed the ideal of *cum dignitate otium* are singled out by Cicero. They are all unrelenting foes of the *populares,* staunch defenders of aristocratic privilege and senatorial domination: M. Aemilius Scaurus (cos. 115), Q. Caecilius Metellus Numidicus (cos. 109), and Q. Lutatius Catulus (cos. 78).[89] That Cicero intends the slogan to symbolize a hierarchical social order dominated by the propertied is also testified to by his enumeration of the institutional foundations of *cum dignitate otium,* those that *optimates* should revere, strengthen, and preserve: religion and religious observances, magistral powers (*potestates*), senatorial authority (*auc-*

toritas), the laws and legal jurisdiction, *mos maiorum*, good faith and credit, public finance (*aerarium*), and so forth.[90] In short, Cicero thinks of himself and the *optimates* as defenders of the Roman mixed constitution and restorers of its original moderation and balance, inspired and guided by ancestral custom, *mos maiorum*. A decade after writing the *Defence of Sestius*, devoting himself in retirement to his literary pursuits, Cicero recalls that he was the spokesman of an "honorable peace" (*honestam otium*) over the use of violence. When, however, the union of good citizens (*consensus bonorum*) that he promoted became weaker than the employers of force (Caesar and his followers), then he was willing to accept peace on any condition, for the sake of preserving the state.[91]

The practical means of securing *cum dignitate otium* and consequently the mixed constitutional order are suggested by Cicero. The first is the creation of a *concordia ordinum*, the forging of an alliance between the senatorial and equestrian orders, to be his rallying cry to the upper classes against Catiline and his fellow conspirators:

Why should I mention the Roman knights at this point? They may yield to you the first place in rank and councils of state but they rival you in patriotism. After many years' strife this day and this cause renews their harmonious alliance with your order and reunites them with you. If we maintain for ever in the Republic this union that we have cemented in my consulship, I assure you that hereafter no civil and domestic strife will touch any part of the state.[92]

The mere words *concordia ordinum*, however, scarcely suggest the full nature of Cicero's perspicacity in choosing the political slogan.[93] For evidently he had in mind, now that the franchise had been extended to all Italians, the creation of a united front of the two orders in the whole peninsula, not simply in Rome itself. Furthermore, after the Italian enfranchisement and Sulla's doubling of senatorial membership, enmity between the two orders was gradually dissipating. With the increasing recruitment of senators from the Italian equestrian order and their growing homogeneity and convergence of interests, both engaging in business and reaping the spoils of empire, a new and firm foundation for their unity existed. Shrewdly perceiving these profound changes

in the substance of the ruling class, Cicero was apparently prepared to capitalize on them politically.

He describes those of every rank and station who cooperated
with and supported his *concordia ordinum*. This is, indeed, the
second way of securing *cum dignitate otium*, through a *consensus
bonorum*, a union of like-minded men from both the upper and
lower orders, one cutting across all classes, but provided with
leaders from the upper classes.[94] The two ways of underwriting
cum dignitate otium proposed by Cicero interestingly parallel the
two informal networks of relationship that enabled the Roman
political system to function, *amicitiae* providing the cement for
the upper orders and *clientelae* furnishing the cohesion between
the upper and lower social levels and assuring the domination of
the notables over the people.

But what happens, in Cicero's calculation, if the pursuit of these
major political objectives so dear to him should place the very
security and well-being of the state in jeopardy and threaten to
destroy it? Then, he seems to be saying, is the time for a strategic
retreat, a disengagement and withdrawal of forces, to bide time
until circumstances are again favorable. We have already seen that
his ultimate political objective is a moderate and balanced mixed
constitution, to be achieved through *cum dignitate otium* founded
on *concordia ordinum* and *consensus bonorum*. What happens if these
supports of his fundamental policy objectives are weakened, when
the alliance of senators and equestrians disintegrates and a broad
basis of support among the lower orders disappears, when the
optimates are in disunity, overwhelmed by the superior forces of
the *populares?* To resist them with force would be a heroic but
foolhardy gesture, for a disastrous and bloody defeat would inevitably follow in a struggle that might hazard the very existence of
the state. It would be at this point that Cicero would acknowledge
the priority of the claims of the security of the state and would
surrender the struggle for his ideal political ends. But we are led
to believe that this would be only an expediential measure, part
of the tactics of temporizing, of choosing the lesser evil, not a
complete abdication of responsibility or rejection of principle.
When the time is ripe, when the opposition is in turn weakened,
and when forces can be mustered that can render victory possible
without destroying the state, then is the appropriate moment to
strike back.

4. Rudiments of Economic Policy

An integral part of Cicero's policy in warding off the *populares*
and in defending the mixed constitution is an "economic program" for government. He seems to be the first classic political
theorist to consider the matter and make concrete economic recommendations.[95] His correspondence, speeches, and treatises indicate that he gave more than passing attention to the subject. In
general, his economic policies are characterized by an emphasis
on the value of safeguarding private property and on individual
initiative and enterprise, and by a virtual rejection of state intervention in the economic life of the Republic. While it would be
rash to universalize his prescriptions, he seems to think that his
economic policies are essential to the health and well-being of any
great state.

Since the basic purpose of the state is to protect private property, Cicero believes government has a special responsibility to
secure the rightful possessions of all from violations by magistrates
and fellow citizens.[96] He insists on the duty of the magistrate to
ensure that everyone possesses what is his own and that neither
state nor citizen infringes upon the property rights of anyone. Law
and justice should be applied equitably so that the possessions of
the poor are safe and the wealthy hold what is rightfully theirs.

Cicero's economic policy gives top priority to the interests of
the wealthy. They in turn found it to their advantage to support
him when he was in office, for, as he contends: "Nature in the
first place makes good citizens, in the next Fortune helps them;
for it is the interest of all good men that the state should be safe;
but it is in those that are fortunate that this is more apparent."[97]
In the highly acquisitive and individualistic society of Rome on
the eve of Caesar's dictatorship, he found the propertied in town
and country primarily concerned with their holdings, investments,
and profits.[98] So in government he did everything possible to serve
their needs and promote their welfare. Special attention is always
given to the *publicani*, those, largely of the equestrian order, who
farmed the taxes and held governmental contracts for building
roads and public works and provisioning the armies: "For if we
have always held that our revenues are the sinews of the commonwealth, then we shall assuredly be right in saying that the

class which farms those revenues is the mainstay of the other classes."[99] He keeps an eye on the profits of the *publicani*, supports bankers and businessmen, and in Cilicia is careful to curry the favor of tax farmers.[100] Pains are taken to secure the holdings and investments of Romans abroad and in the provinces.[101] Cicero is aware of the economic interdependence of finance and credit throughout the Empire, and that any loss of property or fortune in Rome or in the provinces adversely affects every other part. Small wonder that with all these prudent measures he says in 60 that his "army" consists of the "well-to-do."[102]

Among Cicero's favorite specific policies designed to win the allegiance of this "army" are administrative thrift, opposition to property taxes, and strengthening public credit. Government should be conducted with the utmost economy and public expenditure reduced to a minimum, following the principle enunciated in the *Republic* that "frugality" is "the best revenue both for private families and for states."[103] He prides himself on the financial parsimony of his tenure as governor of Cilicia and the elimination of graft:

I have produced some astonishing results. A great number of communities have been entirely cleared of debt, many others substantially relieved. All have come to life again with the acquisition of home rule under their own laws and courts. I have enabled them to free themselves wholly or partially from debt in two ways. First no expense whatsoever has been incurred during my term as governor—and when I say "no expense" I am not speaking in hyperbole, I mean literally none, not a penny. You would hardly believe how much that has helped to drag the communities out of the mire. Then there is another thing. The natives themselves were responsible for an astonishing number of peculations in the communities, committed by their own magistrates. I personally investigated those who had held office in the last ten years. They admitted it quite frankly. So without any open disgrace they put back the money with their own hands into the various public purses. The civic bodies for their part, which had paid the tax-farmers nothing in this present quinquennium, have now without any moaning paid the arrears of the previous quinquennium as well. So I am a prime favourite with the tax-farmers. "Grateful gentry" you may say. I have experienced their gratitude.[104]

Since his early post as quaestor in Sicily and the prosecution of Verres for corruption in that province, Cicero was particularly sensitive to these problems. He also resisted the assessment of property taxes. His insistence that they must not be levied except in extraordinary circumstances seems to imply that the consent of the propertied would be necessary. On one occasion, when the treasury was empty and money was needed for the payment of troops, he rather grudgingly admits that the imposition of a property tax might be the only alternative.[105] Throughout his political career he underscores the importance of maintaining the credit of government and condemns any erosion of that credit.[106] Governmental credit must always be guaranteed and payment of debts strictly enforced by law, and they should neither be cancelled nor reduced. He is also firmly against the public remission of urban rents instituted by Caesar in 48–47.[107]

A fundamental axiom of Cicero's policy recommendations is that no action should be taken by the state that helps one element of society to the economic detriment of other segments. In practice this means he is opposed to any leveling measure, such as agrarian reforms he thinks might disadvantage the rich for the sake of aiding the poor. He sternly objects to large-scale grain doles like that of Gaius Gracchus. Not only would they exhaust the treasury, but they would encourage the lower classes to forsake industry for idleness. He approves, however, of the much more moderate dole instituted by Marcus Octavius, one that in his view is financially feasible and necessary for the welfare of the lower orders.[108]

Cicero in general is convinced that charity should be private and voluntary. The wealthy, of course, must guard and advance their own interests. But in addition they are under a moral obligation to utilize a portion of their riches for the public good and to help needy individuals, as long as such support does not harm the state. The common interest is served by subsidizing public construction and staging games and festivals. Charity to individuals is best promoted through the system of private patronage, instituted, according to tradition, by Romulus.[109] Cicero affirms that the ancient patricians "made it their practice to aid individual citizens most liberally in their private difficulties by action, advice, and financial support."[110] Liberality of patron to client is part of ancient custom, which should continue and not be criticized or discouraged.[111]

Cicero refuses to tolerate any scheme of agrarian reform entailing the extensive redistribution and equalization of holdings on the vast areas of *ager publicus,* or public land, largely acquired through conquest by Roman legions. Agrarian legislation, he reasons, violates the very essence of government, whose chief object is the protection of private property. Agrarian reform "robs one man to enrich another."[112] These laws usually entailed depriving the well-to-do of many of their holdings of public land and allotting it to the poor, equalizing and limiting the size of the holdings, buying up private land to be used for public distribution, and cancellation of the debts of the holders. Policies of this kind, from Cicero's standpoint, weaken the foundation of the state, disrupt the essential *otium,* foment dissension among the orders, and subvert equity:

And yet, when it comes to measures so ruinous to public welfare, they do not gain even that popularity which they anticipate. For he who has been robbed of his property is their enemy; he to whom it has been turned over actually pretends that he had no wish to take it; and most of all, when his debts are cancelled, the debtor conceals his joy, for fear that he may be thought to have been insolvent; whereas the victim of the wrong both remembers it and shows his resentment openly. Thus even though they to whom property has been wrongfully awarded be more in number than they from whom it has been unjustly taken, they do not for that reason have more influence; for in such matters influence is measured not by numbers but by weight. And how is it fair that a man who never had any property should take possession of lands that had been occupied for many years or even generations, and that he who had them before should lose possession of them?[113]

Redistribution for Cicero is an indisputable violation of the law of nature.[114]

Some of his more specific criticisms have a political import or are related to his other postulates of good government. The dispossession of long-term tenants not only deprives them of their legitimate holdings sanctioned by convention and custom, but also lessens their support of the state.[115] Cicero here seems to be speculating about the weakening of the cause of the *optimates* and the corresponding growth of the *populares.* Furthermore, the credit and good faith of the state—the foundation of a sound economy and vigorous government—are threatened by the cancellation of debts, which invariably accompanies schemes for land reform. Because of the enormous sums needed for the compensation invariably required by such schemes, the treasury would be drained, a situation that again would threaten state credit.[116] Finally, he fears a system of administration of the reforms such as the board of ten commissioners of the Rullan proposals.[117] A body of this kind would have inordinate power over the lives and possessions of many citizens and might prove to be a dangerous rival of duly constituted state authority, with a constituency hostile to everything for which the senatorial oligarchy and *boni* stand. In other words, Cicero seems to see an incipient tyranny with a broad mass support arising from the administrative apparatus itself.

Cicero admits that he is not opposed to every agrarian law. After all it is no offense to praise the Gracchi, who accomplished many notable things. However, his objections to the reforms of Tiberius Gracchus in 133 and Rullus in 63 were common knowledge. Even the moderate measures of Flavius in 60 are criticized. Had the Rullan legislation, in his opinion, been of use to the Roman plebeians, he would have supported it.[118] These pronouncements are obviously of a political nature meant to soften the blow of his opposition. As a substitute for the Rullan scheme, he offers his countrymen "peace, tranquillity, and quiet" (*pacem, tranquillitatem, otium*). He warns them that under the resettlement plans of the law they would simply be exchanging their urban pleasures, together with their influence, liberty, votes, and dignity, for the swamps and desolate wasteland of Apulia.[119]

As one might expect of a consummate practitioner, Cicero can be illuminating and suggestive on his craft, on the nature of politics, political means, and the relationship of means to ends. In this, he could have been—if he actually was not—the teacher of Machiavelli, as he was definitely the mentor of Edmund Burke. Harold Laski's encomium to Burke could well apply to Cicero, that "Burke has endured as the permanent manual of political wisdom without which statesmen are as sailors on an uncharted sea,"[120] except for the fact that this would be a Cicero virtually unknown and unremembered. The Cicero who has endured throughout the ages is the supreme political moralist, not the masterful politician. Nevertheless, on the question of ends, the enduring Cicero is a distinct disappointment. In the name of natural justice and moral equality he persists in a policy—since the day of his persuasive rhetoric, to become an entrenched conservative program—of preservation of the propertied status quo, regeneration of time-honored gentlemanly values, restoration of the ancestral constitution, and economic prescriptions to the advantage of the rich and the detriment of the poor. At the same time, he fails utterly to grasp the futility and bankruptcy of his recommendations. Shrewd politician though he is, he seems to have little understanding of the root of the troubles afflicting and destroying the Republic; and, of course, he is not alone in his failure. Perhaps precisely because of his mastery of his craft, because he was too personally embroiled in the conflicts of his day, too deeply involved in the manipulative mechanics of the existing governmental system, he was unable to perceive clearly its fragility and self-destructive impetus.

Conclusion

The preceding pages have attempted to describe in some detail Cicero's social and political ideas and their contribution to the history of the subject. From this standpoint his legacy can be most economically summarized as consisting of a conception of natural law and justice; a theory of the state to which a notion of private property is central; a doctrine of constitutionalism entailing limited and responsible government through a mixed constitution, and a justification of tyrannicide; and an emphasis on politics as means. To a greater or lesser degree, the elements reflect a pronounced and unprecedented individualism. Although arising in response to the troubles of the late Republic and offering invaluable testimony to the nature of the Roman ruling class, his social and political thought is primarily significant to us because of the ways in which it strikingly anticipated and profoundly influenced the early modern intellect.

Perhaps more than in the case of any other ancient or even modern thinker, his outlook typifies a particular approach to civic affairs: the *conservative mentality*. Its way of perceiving the social and political world, so familiar as to be taken for granted, is as old as the beginnings of European systematic speculation. A few of the components are to be found in Plato and Aristotle, but Cicero's articulation of the position is archetypal. Fundamental to Cicero's conservatism is his idealization of the ancestral constitution and ancestral way of life, the *mos maiorum,* fashioned by previous generations. It is the sacred archetype of social truth and civic virtue, an awesome monad of morality and utility from which we deviate at our own peril. Our social and moral duty is to safeguard and adapt such a priceless inheritance to present circumstances, and ready it for passage to posterity. Since we hold the gift in trust both to past and present, our mission is to preserve it by doing nothing basically to alter the state or to upset the status quo, and by steering a course of moderation and caution. Stress is always placed on means, on devising by trial and error the most effective procedures to secure the end, which is always the given, a treasured donation from the past to be used for our well-being. The chief purpose of the state is its own preservation and the protection of the lives and properties of its citizens. Traditional tried-and-true values are to be faithfully observed: loyalty to family, friends, and country; and the security and enhancement of private property, contract, and commercial intercourse as the foundations of civilized life. Priority is given to liberty over equality; but liberty, not to be confused with license, signifies doing what the law permits in accord with one's social station; and although all are considered to be morally equal, some are socially and politically more equal than others. Democracy and democratic institutions, consequently, are suspect. The majority are fitted only to labor and to serve; the minority, to benefit from their labor, to receive their services, and to manage the concerns of state and society; in practice, a distinction between propertyless and propertied. Since the coexistence of the propertyless many and the propertied few is inevitable, the division of society into poor and rich, laboring and leisured, servants and masters, ruled and rulers is the natural order of things.

The fact that government, however, is best left to the propertied minority does not mean that it can be allowed to become arbitrary and tyrannical in its actions, for this would threaten the lives and possessions not only of the laboring many, but also of the leisured few, whose interests the state primarily guards. Government, therefore, should be so organized as to act within the framework of law and due process and to be answerable for its conduct to the governed. In a word, constitutionalism is the solution. It can best promote limited, predictable, and responsible rule by means of an institutional mixture that grants all citizens, poor or rich, humble or exalted, some voice in deliberations on common matters, while assuring the prerogative of the propertied to make ultimate political decisions. Finally, in order to guarantee and strengthen the prevailing balance of social and political power, reform will be minimal, governmental expenses will be pared to the bone, public credit will be prudently upheld, and the disadvantage of the propertied for the sake of aiding the poor will be strenuously avoided. Initiatives in society must largely originate in the private instead of the public sector, whether they are in regard to charity, education, or the economy. Those of the lower social orders who are deserving will improve their lot through their own effort and merit. Albeit in more varied and sophisticated form, our own world today is marked by a resurgence of belief in many of the ingredients of this conservative mentality that Cicero did so much to articulate and promote.

The fact that Cicero can be called the father of the idea of constitutionalism should remind us of an important feature of its earliest formulations. While today constitutionalism has to a pronounced degree been democratized, this should not blind us to its conservative and oligarchic origins. Before the advent of modern political democracy, constitutionalism in theory and practice was aimed at the protection of the propertied status quo, not the mass of people living under government. Full consciousness of the necessity of constitutionalism and the elaboration of its doctrine seem to have appeared in the past among the more enlightened members of a ruling class on the verge of self-destruction. In the beginning, at any rate, the doctrine often emerged at a time when the very survival of the ruling class was in question. The fundamental principles of government embodied by constitutionalism were for the conservation of a ruling class threatened by internecine strife and disruption. The initial purpose of the doctrine and its implementation, then, was usually not the improvement of the situation of the majority, but the consolidation and strengthening of the ruling class vis-à-vis subordinate classes, by thwarting any segment of either from establishing a tyrannical regime subversive of the interests of the propertied as a whole.

Since Cicero, the twin pillars of conservative constitutional doctrine have often been the ideas of liberty and equality, of a special, mutually sustaining kind, each helping in a different way to preserve the existing structure of government. In such a context, neither liberty nor equality is intended to have democratic implications. The concept of liberty, so conceived, instead of signifying the equal absence of constraints on the actions of everyone becomes a means of supporting a conservative and oligarchic constitutionalism. By contrast, in a modern political democracy, constitutionalism tends to be a function of libertarianism. For Cicero and constitutionalists of his breed, however, liberty and the rights it involves are differential, not a matter of parity. All should possess some liberty, but the ruling minority should have more rights and hence greater freedom than the many. The liberty granted to all is basically the right of every qualified citizen to vote. Suffrage, in this instance, is designed not so much to check the power of the whole ruling class in the interests of the citizen majority as to obstruct any portion of the ruling class from governing in an unrestrained and arbitrary way, which would be to the detriment of the ruling class *in toto*. All qualified citizens have the right to vote; nevertheless, not all are equally free to hold public office, which remains a preserve for members of the ruling class.

Again since Cicero, most conservative constitutionalists have professed a belief in the moral equality of all, at the same time accepting in practice the existence of widespread social and political inequalities. Equality to conservative constitutionalists, like their notion of liberty, is basically of a differential nature, but its goal in respect to the maintenance of the constitution is thought of somewhat differently from the liberty that serves to curb the more obstreperous and ambitious power-holders in the interests of the whole ruling class. Differential equality, as seen by conservative constitutionalists, assigns to each citizen a social station carrying with it specific rights and duties. Some citizens—the ruling minority—have more rights and fewer duties than do members of the majority. The latter are not to trespass beyond the limits of the freedom and obligation imposed by their rank. Unlike differential liberty, which in the eyes of conservative constitutionalists should obstruct tyranny from above, differential equality functions to restrain tyranny from below or "mob rule," their name for democracy. The institution of both liberty and equality, in these restricted senses of the concepts, should aid in ensuring the domination of a united ruling class.

Cicero is quite clearly a spokesman for the supreme control of the Roman state by his own class, but like other great social and political thinkers, he is not solely an ideologist or simpleminded apologist for the existing ruling order. He is highly critical of its divisive internal struggle for power and riches. When fragmentation is endangering the ruling class, Cicero calls for its unity and harmony. He wishes to revitalize it, to restore its firm direction of the state, presenting a solid front to the lower classes. Cicero is a child of his times whose life symbolizes the transformation of the ruling class following the enfranchisement of Italy and the Sullan enlargement of the senate. Like many of his fellow senators, Cicero was an equestrian, a new man much of whose income came from non-agrarian sources, as was increasingly true of the *nobilitas* themselves. In an age when the interests and social origins of senators and equestrians were converging, Cicero was one of the foremost exponents of the growing individualism of the changing aristocracy. He justifies a way of life that more and more emphasized private property, business investment, and the accumulation of riches, although he takes to task the excesses to which many of his peers were prone.

The very slogans chosen by Cicero to advance his political fortunes—*concordia ordinum, consensus bonorum, cum dignitate otium* —in a way mirror the changes occurring in the ruling class. "Concord of the orders" was a feasible rallying call because of the new homogeneity of the ruling class. It was also a plea to end the factional strife cutting across the two orders. Cicero was seeking to mobilize the Italian aristocracy of decurions and equestrians as well as senators. So it was with his idea of a "consensus of good men," a consensus not confined solely to the aristocracy but one that would bring "well-intentioned" urban and rural citizens of every rank into his fold. In a sense all of Italy had become Cicero's constituency. His third electoral battle-cry, *cum dignitate otium,* was artfully contrived to heal a festering sore of the ruling class. Their fragmentation, resulting from an individualistic pursuit of power and riches, was often in the name of *dignitas,* for the purpose of redressing, maintaining, or forwarding the personal standing and honor of a notable. In adopting the slogan, Cicero in effect was urging his combative peers to end their mutual recriminations and individualistic quest for *dignitas* to the peril of all, and instead to find honor and standing in the new harmony of a united Italian ruling class and their clients.

Cicero, perhaps better than any of his contemporaries, represents by his politics and expression of political views the process of change within the ruling class. The trouble, however, was that his proposals for solving the problem did not match his awareness of it. Ruling-class solidarity, he believes, can best be achieved by a refurbished mixed constitution in the image of the previous age, by a return to the ancestral constitution whose natural course of growth, he is convinced, had been disrupted by the machinations of the Gracchi and successive *populares*. Only by such a revival, Cicero insists, can the ruling class reassert its rightful domination, revive its hegemony, and stem the dreaded threat of tyranny from above and below. Once internal peace and order are reestablished, every citizen according to his rank will be able to preserve and forward his *dignitas,* thereby fulfilling the promise of *cum dignitate otium.*

The shortcomings of Cicero's panacea are obvious, for too much happened in his century to allow the clock simply to be turned back. The illnesses of Roman society and state were too long-standing and severe for such a cure. He places too much reliance on the balm of structural mechanics and on the resuscitation of senatorial domination at a time when the ruling class is severely fractured. A fatal blind spot in his social and political speculations is a failure to give attention to the thorny question of Roman imperial expansion. He never ponders seriously the urgent problems of empire, for the far-flung realm of countless subjects and the temptations it offered notables for self-aggrandizement were crucial factors in the atomization of the ruling class and the breakdown of law and order. Moreover, he has no answer to the vital need for basic social reform, except obstinate, imprudent opposition to it. Roman success had apparently made things too easy. Why should a Roman notable worry about the grievous difficulties of the peasants or the grave plight of the urban masses when there was a massive slave-labor force and an increasingly professionalized army? Yet reliance on slavery and military professionalization helped to accelerate the divisive individualism against which Cicero protested.

A glaring deficiency of Cicero's diagnosis and prognosis is his choice of political heroes and ideals from among the arch-conservatives who held power before the transformation of the ruling class touched off by the Social War and Sullan reforms, and before the Empire became an emporium for the exercise of senatorial avarice. Dignitaries selected by Cicero from the past for emulation, such as Scipio Aemilianus, Laelius and his own mentors, Scaurus, Lucius Licinius Crassus, and the Scaevolae, were hardly appropriate guides for his time. In their day the ruling class tended to be more heterogeneous than homogeneous, but still much more of a hierarchy under senatorial vigilance. So by the age of Cicero, when the peasantry was no longer a threat to be feared and when a more homogeneous and egalitarian aristocracy had fragmented into individualistic strife over power and riches and the pillaging of the provinces, his plea for senatorial domination has a somewhat hollow and anachronistic ring. Furthermore, the adamant resistance of Cicero's conservative heroes to the social measures of the Gracchi and their successors was hardly the model to follow in his efforts to revitalize the state and unify the aristocracy. Cicero's worthies from the past failed to come to terms with the crucial question of social reform. Since their day, too much capital had been made out of the matter by unscrupulous politicians, and the ever-growing excesses of an atomized ruling class had for too long ground down the lower orders. If the Republic was to be preserved, social reform could no longer be erased from the agenda of the most serious political issues.

Yet Cicero must be given his due. He does not confine his solution of the troubles of the late Republic solely to tinkering with the mechanics of the governmental system, to a return to a golden age of the past, and to the obstruction of social reform. Forced to retire from politics, he takes on the herculean task of educating his peers. In keeping with his basic view that social and political ills arise from the irrationality of human beings, he seeks in his last writings to enlighten his contemporaries, to purify their psyches by revealing to them their false beliefs and by persuading them to follow the principles of rational conduct and civic virtue that he so convincingly expounds. As usually happens in comparable circumstances, however, even from one of such prodigious energy and masterly eloquence such exhortation was fruitless. Moreover, and this is perhaps the crux of the problem, he could never sufficiently transcend the social, moral, and intellectual environment of which he was so much a part in order to view matters from a detached perspective. Aside from his questionable assumption concerning the source of the troubles, the enlightener himself needed enlightenment. The rational values, attitudes, and ideals, which he promoted in such an accomplished manner, were little more than a refined and intellectualized abstraction of the spirit of the times, the spirit that was inextricably bound up with the disorders of the day. So, for instance, while taking exception to the divisive individualism of the ruling class and its excesses, he possibly contributed to their war of all against all by presenting them with a rationalization for social, political, and moral individualism. His cure, in fact, was symptomatic of the disease.

Cicero, then, philosophically sophisticated and as politically astute as he was inventive, perceived something of the malady of the ruling class but never really understood its causes, and consequently was unable to prescribe an effective therapy. The afflictions of his class could not be treated in a vacuum, as he seemed determined to do, isolated from other fundamental structural infirmities of the Roman state. If Cicero, however, was incapable of the dispassionate and self-denying reflection necessary for the task, so were his distinguished contemporaries. Makers of history seldom are its most discerning students.

Notes

1 For the details of Cicero's intellectual influence, my treatment has relied on the following: R. R. Bolgar, ed., *The Classical Heritage and Its Beneficiaries* (Cambridge, England: Cambridge University Press, 1954); idem, ed., *Classical Influences on Western Thought, A.D. 1650–1870* (Cambridge, England: Cambridge University Press, 1979); M. L. Clarke, *Classical Education in Britain, 1500–1900* (Cambridge, England: Cambridge University Press, 1959); T. A. Dorey, ed., *Cicero* (New York: Basic Books, 1965); A. E. Douglas, *Cicero* (Oxford: Clarendon Press, 1968); Peter Gay, *The Enlightenment: An Interpretation.* Vol. 1: *The Rise of Modern Paganism* (New York: Knopf, 1966); Gilbert Highet, *The Classical Tradition: Greek and Roman Influences on Western Literature* (London: Oxford University Press, 1949); W. K. Lacey, *Cicero and the End of the Roman Republic* (London: Hodder and Stoughton, 1978), chap. 10; Elizabeth Rawson, *Cicero: A Portrait* (London: Allen Lane, 1975), chap. 17; T. Zielinski, *Cicero im Wandel der Jahrhunderte* (Leipzig: Teubner, 1908).

   Gay's many references to Cicero and the thinkers of the Enlightenment are invaluable, as are the essays by M. L. Clarke, A. E. Douglas, and R. G. M. Nisbet in the Dorey volume.

2 According to Leslie J. Walker, trans. and ed., *The Discourses of Niccolò Machiavelli* (London: Routledge and Kegan Paul, 1950), vol. 2, pp. 277–79.

3 Machiavelli's *The Prince* represents in many ways an inversion of Ciceronian humanism. See Quentin Skinner, *Machiaevelli* (Oxford: Oxford University Press, 1981), pp. 35–37, 40, 43–47, 54.

4 The descriptive term is that of Nannerl O. Keohane, *Philosophy*

and the State in France: The Renaissance to the Enlightenment (Princeton, N.J.: Princeton University Press, 1980), p. 84. On Cicero and Bodin, see the introduction of Kenneth McRae to his edition of Jean Bodin, *The Six Bookes of a Commonweale*, trans. Richard Knolles (Cambridge, Mass.: Harvard University Press, 1962), pp. A27, A30; M. M. Goldsmith, *Hobbes's Science of Politics* (New York: Columbia University Press, 1966), p. 147 and n. 38.

For the influence of Cicero on a "lesser intellect," see the account of Jean de Bourg, Archiepiscopal judge of the town of Vienne and delegate (as was Bodin) to the Estates General in 1576 at Blois, in Emmanuel Le Roy Ladurie, *Carnival in Romans*, trans. Mary Feeney (New York: Braziller, 1979), chap. 3. Ladurie, p. 65, calls him "a provincial Jean Bodin."

5 Clarence DeWitt Thorpe, *The Aesthetic Theory of Thomas Hobbes, with Special Reference to His Contribution to the Psychological Approach in English Literary Criticism* (Ann Arbor: University of Michigan Press, 1940), esp. pp. 28, 34–35. In addition to Cicero, Hobbes mentions Lucian and Justus Lipsius.

6 For Harrington's many references to Cicero, see J. G. A. Pocock, ed., *The Political Works of James Harrington* (Cambridge, England: Cambridge University Press, 1977). On the commonwealth tradition, see Caroline Robbins, *The Eighteenth-Century Commonwealthman: Studies in the Transmission, Development and Circumstance of English Liberal Thought from the Restoration of Charles II until the War with the Thirteen Colonies* (Cambridge, Mass.: Harvard University Press, 1961). For Locke and Cicero, see my book, *The Politics of Locke's Philosophy: A Social Study of "An Essay Concerning Human Understanding"* (Berkeley and Los Angeles: University of California Press, 1983), pp. 29–30; also Robert Denoon Cumming, *Human Nature and History: A Study of the Development of Liberal Political Thought* (Chicago: University of Chicago Press, 1969), vol. 2, pp. 133–37, 146–47; Raymond Polin, *La Politique Morale de John Locke* (Paris: Presses Universitaires de France, 1960), for example, pp. 12, 29, 34, 45, 74, 91, 121.

7 For the influence of Cicero on the youthful Montesquieu, see Robert Shackleton, *Montesquieu: A Critical Biography* (London: Oxford University Press, 1961), pp. 20, 69–71. For Rosseau's criticism of Cicero, see, for example, *Social Contract*, IV, iv; the quoted term is in *Discours sur les Sciences et les Arts*, in *Oeuvres Complètes* (Pléiade), vol. 3, p. 29.

8 Conyers Middleton (1708–1770) was a deist and friend of prominent real whigs, although not himself politically active. His stress on the popular aspects of the Roman state and on Cicero's libertarianism alarmed his more conservative English contemporaries. See Robbins, *The Eighteenth-Century Commonwealthman*, pp. 19, 291–93; and the *Dictionary of National Biography*. Macaulay had a high opinion of Middleton and a low opinion of his treatment of Cicero. See T. B. Macaulay, "Lord Bacon" (*Edinburgh Review*, 1837), in his *Critical, Historical, and Miscellaneous Essays and Poems* (Philadelphia: Porter and Coates, 1879), vol. 2, p. 145.

9 B. T. Wilkins, *The Problem of Burke's Political Philosophy* (Oxford: Clarendon Press, 1967), p. 43. On Hume and Cicero, see Ernest Campbell Mossner, *The Life of David Hume* (Austin: University of Texas Press, 1954), pp. 52, 64–65; John B. Stewart, *The Moral and Political Philosophy of David Hume* (New York: Columbia University Press, 1963), pp. 354 n. 9, 356 n. 29. Smith in the *Wealth of Nations* uses Cicero largely as a factual source, more than any other ancient. See *An Inquiry into the Nature and Causes of the Wealth of Nations* (Oxford: Clarendon Press, 1976), vol. 1, pp. 111, 166, 236; vol. 2, pp. 683–84, 876.

10 Meyer Reinhold, "Eighteenth-Century American Political Thought," in Bolgar, ed., *Classical Influences*, p. 232.

11 "Notebooks on Epicurean Philosophy" (1839) in Karl Marx and Friedrich Engels, *Collected Works* (New York: International Publishers, 1975–), vol. 1, p. 472. See the many references to Cicero in *The Ethnological Notebooks of Karl Marx*, trans. and ed. Lawrence Krader (2d ed. Assen: Van Gorcum, 1974).

12 Highet, *Classical Tradition*, p. 323.

13 R. G. M. Nisbet, "The Speeches," in Dorey, ed., *Cicero*, p. 77; J. P. V. D. Balsdon, "Cicero the Man," in ibid., p. 205.

14 Quoted in W. W. Willoughby, *The Political Theories of the Ancient World* (New York: Macmillan, 1903), p. 274.

15 Mulford Q. Sibley, *Political Ideas and Ideologies: A History of Political Thought* (New York: Harper and Row, 1970), p. 125.

16 Friedrich Cauer, *Ciceros politisches Denken: Ein Versuch* (Berlin: Wiedmann, 1903).

17 Cicero, *On the Commonwealth,* trans. and ed. G. H. Sabine and S. B. Smith (Columbus: Ohio State University Press, 1929), pp. 1–102. The reprint in 1976 was published by Bobbs-Merrill in the Library of Liberal Arts. Note should also be taken of the able recent essay by John B. Morrall, "Cicero as a Political Thinker," *History Today* 33 (March 1982): 33–37.

18 Sabine and Smith, eds., *On the Commonwealth,* p. 99.

19 Ernest Barker, trans. and ed., *From Alexander to Constantine: Passages and Documents Illustrating the History of Social and Political Ideas, 336 B.C.–A.D. 337* (Oxford: Clarendon Press, 1956), pp. 185–204; Huntington Cairns, *Legal Philosophy from Plato to Hegel* (Baltimore: Johns Hopkins Press, 1949), pp. 127–62; R. W. Carlyle and A. J. Carlyle, *A History of Mediaeval Thought in the West,* vol. 1 (London: Blackwood, 1903), pp. 1–18; George Catlin, *The Story of the Political Philosophers* (1st ed. New York: McGraw-Hill, 1939), pp. 119–21; F. W. Coker, *Readings in Political Philosophy* (rev. ed. New York: Macmillan, 1938), pp. 129–52; T. I. Cook, *History of Political Philosophy: From Plato to Burke* (New York: Prentice-Hall, 1937), pp. 143–49; Cumming, *Human Nature and History,* vol. 1, chaps. 7–9; vol. 2, pp. 3, 11–13, 17–20, 63–70, 133–37, 330–31; W. A. Dunning, *A History of Political Theories* (New York: Macmillan, 1935), vol. 1, pp. 118–25; M. B. Foster, ed., *Masters of Political Thought* (Boston: Houghton, Mifflin, 1941), vol. 1, pp. 179–95; R. G. Gettell, *History of Political Thought* (New York: Appleton-Century-Crofts, 1924), pp. 74–76; Andrew Hacker, *Political Theory: Philosophy, Ideology, Science* (New York: Macmillan, 1961); J. H. Hallowell, *Main Currents in Modern Political Thought* (New York: Holt, 1950), p. 18; M. Judd Harmon, *Political Thought from Plato to the Present* (New York: McGraw-Hill, 1964), pp. 84–86; J. E. Holton, "Marcus Tullius Cicero," in Leo Strauss and Joseph Cropsey, eds., *History of Political Philosophy* (2d ed. Chicago: Rand McNally, 1972), pp. 130–50; C. H. McIlwain, *The Growth of Political Thought in the West: From the Greeks to the End of the Middle Ages* (New York: Macmillan, 1932), pp. 114–18; Christopher Morris, *Western Political Thought* (London: Longmans, 1967), vol. 1, pp. 140–65; George H. Sabine, *A History of Political Theory* (3d ed. New York: Holt, Rinehart, and Winston, 1961), pp. 61–67; Sabine and Smith, eds., *On the Commonwealth,* pp. 1–102; Sibley, *Political Ideas and Ideologies,* pp. 125–30; Frederick Watkins, *The Political Tradition of the West: A Study in the Development of Modern Liberalism* (Cambridge, Mass.: Harvard University Press, 1948); Willoughby, *Political Theories of the Ancient World,* pp. 274–89; J. L. Wiser, *Political Philosophy:*

A History of the Search for Order (Englewood Cliffs, N.J.: Prentice-Hall, 1983), pp. 74, 77, 79, 93, 101, 122; Sheldon S. Wolin, *Politics and Vision: Continuity and Innovation in Western Political Thought* (Boston: Little, Brown, 1960), pp. 86–91. The two who omit all mention of Cicero are Hacker and Watkins.

20 Sibley, *Political Ideas,* covers the issue of private property. Barker, ed., *From Alexander to Constantine,* quotes the relevant passages from *On Duties* but does not discuss them. Morris, *Western Political Thought,* and Wolin, *Politics and Vision,* briefly mention property. Charles Norris Cochrane recognizes Cicero for stressing the important role of the state in protecting private property: *Christianity and Classical Culture: A Study of Thought and Action from Augustus to Augustine* (rev. ed. New York: Oxford University Press, 1944), pp. 45–46. Cumming's perceptive treatment of Cicero in *Human Nature and History* is clearly an important exception to most commentaries, and it is one to which I am indebted throughout this book, although we may not always be in agreement.

    Barker, ed., *From Alexander to Constantine;* Sibley, *Political Ideas;* and Willoughby, *Political Theories,* discuss *On Duties;* Willoughby alone deals with the issue of tyrannicide.

21 Sabine and Smith, eds., *On the Commonwealth* (and Sabine on his own in 1937, in the first edition of his *History of Political Theory*) certainly treat the doctrine of the mixed constitution but seemingly fail to perceive its full implications.

22 *The International Encyclopedia,* although containing no article on Cicero, treats some of his views under other entries such as "Natural Law," "Authority."

23 Sabine's conclusion in the 1930 *Encyclopedia,* vol. 3–4, p. 469, in regard to Cicero's political thought: "Its main historical importance lay in the fact that it transmitted the stoic theory of natural law to the church fathers and thus to mediaeval political theorists. In this way the belief that justice, right, equality and fair dealing should underlie positive law became a commonplace in European political philosophy."

24 Carlyle and Carlyle, *Mediaeval Thought,* vol. 1, p. 2.

25 C. H. McIlwain, *Growth of Political Thought,* p. 117; Sabine, *Political Theory* (1937), p. 165.

CHAPTER TWO

1 Polybius, *The Histories* I, 1 (Loeb Classical Library translation).
  Also see I, 2; VI, 1.

2 This chapter is intended to introduce the general reader to the
  context of late republican society so necessary to an understanding
  of Cicero's social and political ideas. I have relied heavily on the
  following works, using freely the ideas, facts, and figures presented by the authors, usually without further acknowledgment:
  E. Badian, *Foreign Clientelae (264–70 B.C.)* (Oxford: Clarendon
  Press, 1958); idem, *Publicans and Sinners: Private Enterprise in
  the Service of the Roman Republic, with a Critical Bibliography*
  (rev. ed. Ithaca, N.Y.: Cornell University Press, 1983); idem, *Roman Imperialism in the Late Republic* (2d ed. Oxford: Blackwell,
  1968); P. A. Brunt, *Italian Manpower, 225 B.C.–A.D. 14* (Oxford: Clarendon Press, 1971); idem, "The Roman Mob," *Past and
  Present* 35 (1966): 3–27; idem, *Social Conflicts in the Roman Republic* (London: Chatto and Windus, 1971); M. I. Finley, *The Ancient Economy* (Berkeley and Los Angeles: University of California Press, 1973); idem, *Politics in the Ancient World* (Cambridge,
  England: Cambridge University Press, 1983); Matthias Gelzer, *The
  Roman Nobility,* trans. Robin Seager (Oxford: Blackwell, 1969);
  Erich S. Gruen, *The Last Generation of the Roman Republic*
  (Berkeley and Los Angeles: University of California Press, 1974);
  Keith Hopkins, *Conquerors and Slaves,* vol. 1 *of Sociological
  Studies in Roman History* (Cambridge, England: Cambridge Uni-
  versity Press, 1978); H. F. Jolowicz and Barry Nicholas, *Historical
  Introduction to the Study of Roman Law* (3d ed. Cambridge, En-
  gland: Cambridge University Press, 1972); Wolfgang Kunkel, *An
  Introduction to Roman Legal and Constitutional History,* trans.
  J. M. Kelly (2d ed. Oxford: Clarendon Press, 1973); Andrew Lin-
  tott, *Violence in Republican Rome* (Oxford: Clarendon Press,
  1968); Ramsay MacMullen, *Roman Social Relations, 50 B.C. to
  A.D. 284* (New Haven: Yale University Press, 1974); Claude Ni-
  colet, *The World of the Citizen in Republican Rome,* trans. P. S.
  Falla (Berkeley and Los Angeles: University of California Press,
  1980); G. E. M. de Ste. Croix, *The Class Struggle in the Ancient
  Greek World: From the Archaic Age to the Arab Conquests* (Ithaca,
  N.Y.: Cornell University Press, 1981); Robin Seager, ed., *The
  Crisis of the Roman Republic* (Cambridge, England: Heffer, 1969);
  A. N. Sherwin-White, *The Roman Citizenship* (2d ed. Oxford:
  Clarendon Press, 1973); Ronald Syme, *The Roman Revolution*
  (Oxford: Oxford University Press, 1960); L. R. Taylor, *Party Pol-
  itics in the Age of Caesar* (Berkeley and Los Angeles: University
  of California Press, 1949); Susan Treggiari, *Roman Freedmen*

During the Late Republic (Oxford: Clarendon Press, 1969); T. P.
Wiseman, *New Men in the Roman Senate, 139 B.C.–A.D. 14*
(London: Oxford University Press, 1971).
   Articles in the *Oxford Classical Dictionary* have also proved
valuable. Those new to late Republican history might best begin
with three useful textbooks: Mary Beard and Michael Crawford,
Rome in the Late Republic: Problems and Interpretations (London:
Duckworth, 1985); Michael Crawford, *The Roman Republic*
(London: Fontana/Collins, 1978); H. H. Scullard, *From the Grac-
chi to Nero: A History of Rome from 133 B.C. to A.D. 68* (5th
ed. London: Methuen, 1982).

3 The figures in this paragraph are derived from Hopkins, *Conquerors and Slaves,* chap. 1.

4 Throughout the following discussion of social structure, *class* is
basically employed in a Marxist sense. Class is a grouping of human beings who perform similar functions in the total economic
process of production, distribution, and exchange. In the social division of labor entailed by any economic system, some individuals
have positions of domination by virtue of their control of the instruments of production (land, workshops, factories), whereas
others—the direct economic producers—have subordinate roles,
laboring for their livelihood under the former and largely in their
interest. All class structures are systems of exploitation with the
controllers of the means of production or their agents appropriating, in the form of rents, fees, tributes, taxes, and profits, the surplus labor of the subordinate workers. For a treatment of the idea
of class and its application to an analysis of precapitalist society,
see Ellen Meiksins Wood and Neal Wood, *Class Ideology and Ancient Political Theory: Socrates, Plato, and Aristotle in Social
Context* (New York: Oxford University Press, 1978), chap. 2;
Neal Wood, *The Politics of Locke's Philosophy: A Social Study
of "An Essay Concerning Human Understanding"* (Berkeley and
Los Angeles: University of California Press, 1983), chap. 1.
   Although the view of class above is similar to that of Ste.
Croix, *Class Struggle in the Ancient World,* esp. pp. 31–69, his
application of the concept to the analysis of ancient Greek and Roman history differs from my own. For the rejection of the concept
of class as being applicable to a study of ancient society, see Finley, *Ancient Economy,* chap. 2.

5 Hopkins, *Conquerors and Slaves,* pp. 7, 15.

6 Finley, *Ancient Economy,* p. 105.

7 On the concept of *slave society,* see M. I. Finley, "Slavery," *The International Encyclopedia of the Social Sciences* (New York: Macmillan and The Free Press, 1968), vol. 14, pp. 307–13; and Hopkins, *Conquerors and Slaves,* pp. 99–102.

8 Hopkins, *Conquerors and Slaves,* pp. 7–8.

9 Rodney Hilton, *Bond Men Made Free: Medieval Peasant Movements and the English Rising of 1381* (London: Temple Smith, 1973), p. 10. For a reassessment of the role of agrarian slavery in ancient Athens, see Ellen Meiksins Wood, "Agricultural Slavery in Classical Athens," *American Journal of Ancient History* 8 (1983): 1–47.

10 Polybius, *The Histories* VI.

11 G. W. Trompf, *The Idea of Historical Recurrence in Western Thought: From Antiquity to the Reformation* (Berkeley and Los Angeles: University of California Press, 1979), p. 46.

12 See Chapter Nine for a discussion of the doctrine of the mixed constitution and Cicero's conception of it.

13 Polybius, *The Histories* VI, 17, 51.

14 Trompf, *Historical Recurrence,* p. 55.

15 Polybius, *The Histories* VI, 50–52.

16 The curule was the official seat of some higher magistrates: dictator, consul, praetor, censor, curule aedile.

17 Since 202 B.C. the office of dictator had not been used in the traditional sense, and after Sulla elections of censors were irregular.

18 Gelzer, *Roman Nobility,* p. 4.

19 Jolowicz and Nicholas, *Historical Introduction,* p. 46.

20 Syme, *Roman Revolution,* p. 15.

21 For Cicero's views on *amicitia* and *clientela* see Chapter Ten.

22 Gelzer, *Roman Nobility,* p. 137 and n. 615.

23　One notable exception is the persuasively argued thesis of Gruen, *Last Generation of the Roman Republic.*

24　Thinkers and scholars have long remarked upon the unrestrained and highly individualistic competition and conflict among Roman notables. Hegel commented on their greed and rapaciousness in a memorable passage in *Philosophy of History,* trans. J. Sibree (New York: Collier, 1912), p. 397. Gelzer in his classic treatment, *Roman Nobility,* pp. 136–37, pondered the remarkable upsurge of ambition and avarice.

25　Badian, *Roman Imperialism,* p. 87.

26　Gruen, *Last Generation of the Roman Republic,* p. 497.

27　A point made in Elizabeth Rawson, *Cicero: A Portrait* (London: Allen Lane, 1975), p. 146.

28　These ratios are based on a minimal annual wage of 500 H.S. as against Cicero's estimate that at least 600,000 H.S. per annum were required for a gentlemanly life of luxury, and 10 million H.S., which represents 5 percent annual interest on the fortune of 200 million H.S. of Marcus Licinius Crassus, reputedly the wealthiest person of the period, although Caesar and Pompey were probably far richer. See Richard Duncan-Jones, *The Economy of the Roman Empire: Quantitative Studies* (corrected ed. Cambridge, England: Cambridge University Press, 1977), pp. 4–5.

29　MacMullen, *Roman Social Relations,* p. 38.

30　See the summary in E. J. Jonkers, *Social and Economic Commentary on Cicero's "De Lege Agraria Orationes Tres"* (Leiden: Brill, 1963), pp. 1–6.

31　Gruen, *Last Generation of the Roman Republic,* pp. 500–501, 505–6.

32　Lintott, *Violence in Republican Rome,* pp. 178–79.

33　On the critical factor of conflict within the ruling class in later historical periods, see the valuable treatment by George Comninel, *Rethinking the French Revolution,* to be published in 1987 by Verso Books, London.

34　Badian, *Publicans and Sinners,* pp. 64–66.

35 On this basic change see especially Badian, *Roman Imperialism,*pp. 60–64, 79–89; also Wiseman, *New Men in the Roman Senate,* pp. 6–8.

36 Brunt, *Social Conflicts,* p. 73.

37 Badian, *Roman Imperialism,* p. 92.

CHAPTER THREE

1 Elizabeth Rawson, *Intellectual Life in the Late Roman Republic* (London: Duckworth, 1985), pp. 3–4.

2 For the details of Cicero's life, readers should consult the following standard works upon which I have relied for my summary: Stanley F. Bonner, *Education in Ancient Rome: From the Elder Cato to the Younger Pliny* (Berkeley and Los Angeles: University of California Press, 1977), esp. chap. 7; T. A. Dorey, ed., *Cicero* (New York: Basic Books, 1965); A. E. Douglas, *Cicero* (Oxford: Clarendon Press, 1968); Matthias Gelzer, *Cicero: Ein biographischer Versuch* (Wiesbaden: Franz Steiner, 1969); W. K. Lacey, *Cicero and the End of the Roman Republic* (London: Hodder and Stoughton, 1978); Thomas N. Mitchell, *Cicero: The Ascending Years* (New Haven: Yale University Press, 1979); Elizabeth Rawson, *Cicero: A Portrait* (London: Allen Lane, 1975); idem, *Intellectual Life;* D. R. Shackleton Bailey, *Cicero* (London: Duckworth, 1971); R. E. Smith, *Cicero: The Statesman* (Cambridge, England: Cambridge University Press, 1966); David Stockton, *Cicero: A Political Biography* (London: Oxford University Press, 1971).
   Cicero's correspondence, of course, is indispensable. Of interest is Plutarch's *Life of Cicero.* J. V. P. D. Balsdon's article in the *Oxford Classical Dictionary* is an excellent summary of Cicero's life and works, as is Marcia L. Colish's treatment in *The Stoic Tradition from Antiquity to the Early Middle Ages.* Vol. 1: *Stoicism in Classical Latin Literature* (Leiden: Brill, 1985), pp. 61–65. Also see Chapter Six.

3 For fragments of the poetry, see *Div.* I, 13–15, 17–22, 106; *Off.* I, 77.

4 J. D. Minyard, *Lucretius and the Late Republic: An Essay in Roman Intellectual History* (Leiden: Brill, 1985), pp. 72–73.

5 *De Or.* II, 1–4.

6 *De Or.* I, 214; *Verr.* I, 52.

7 Rawson, *Intellectual Life,* p. 227.

8 *De Or.* I, 214; *Verr.* I, 52; *Sest.* 101.

9 Mitchell, *Cicero,* p. 41.

10 On *mos maiorum,* see Minyard, *Lucretius,* pp. 5–12, 29–32.

11 Rawson, *Intellectual Life,* p. 6.

12 *Fam.* XIII, i, 2; *Fin.* I, 16.

13 *Acad.* II, 115; *Att.* 40 (II.20) 6.

14 *Brut.* 309.

15 Rawson, *Intellectual Life,* p. 290.

16 *Att.* 89 (IV.16) 3; *Fam.* I, ix, 12, 18; *Q.F.* I, i, 29.

17 See Section 2 of this chapter.

18 T. P. Wiseman, *New Men in the Roman Senate, 139 B.C.–A.D. 14* (London: Oxford University Press, 1971), pp. 6–7.

19 According to E. J. Jonkers, *Social and Economic Commentary on Cicero's "De Lege Agraria Orationes Tres"* (Leiden: Brill, 1963), pp. 147–48.

20 Erich S. Gruen, *The Last Generation of the Roman Republic* (Berkeley and Los Angeles: University of California Press, 1974), pp. 420–26.

21 Mitchell, *Cicero,* pp. 239–40.

22 *Off.* I, 77.

23 *Fam.* IV, xiii, 2. Cicero is writing to a partisan of Pompey and a former supporter during the Catilinarian conspiracy, the learned P. Nigidius Figulus.

24 *Fam.* XI, xxvii, 5. The reference seems to be to *Acad., Fin.,* and possibly *Tusc.* In 47, Caesar informed Matius in Rome of his defeat of Pharnaces II at Zela in the universally remembered line

veni, vidi, vici. See Matthias Gelzer, *Caesar: Politician and States-man*, trans. Peter Needham (Oxford: Blackwell, 1969), p. 260.

25 *Div.* II, i–ii.

26 *Arch.* 16.

27 *Att.* 36 (II.16) 3.

28 *N.D.* I, 7–9; *Div.* II, 4–7; *Off.* II, 3–6.

29 *Tusc.* V, 5.

30 *Off.* III, 2–3; *Fam.* IX, viii, 2.

31 For Cicero's view of philosophy: *Off.* II, 6; *N.D.* I, 7–9; *Tusc.* I, 119; V, 57–67; *Fam.* IV, iii, 3–4; V, xiii, 1; xxi, 2; IX, iii, 2.

32 Among the numerous passages in Cicero's works on Academic skepticism, the most helpful summaries of his philosophic position are *Off.* II, 7–8; *Acad.* I, 45–46; II, 99–104.

33 *N.D.* I, 12. Cf. *Acad.* II, 19.

34 *Tusc.* I, 17.

35 *Tusc.* II, 5.

36 *Acad.* Fragments, 2d ed., Fragments of Uncertain Context, 19 (Loeb Classical Library), p. 461.

37 *N.D.* I, 84.

38 What follows on Cicero's attitude to religion is indebted to Col-ish, *Stoic Tradition*, vol. 1, pp. 31–35, 109–26; R. M. Ogilvie, *The Romans and Their Gods* (London: Chatto and Windus, 1969); Rawson, *Intellectual Life*, chap. 20; Alan Wardman, *Religion and Statecraft Among the Romans* (London: Granada, 1982), chap. 2.

39 *Rep.* II, 16–17, 26–27; *Leg.* II, 21, 30–34.

40 See, for example, *Div.* II, 28, 43, 70–71, 148–49.

41 For the nature of the rhetorical formula, see Guy Achard, *Pra-tique, Rhétorique, et Idéologie Politique dans les Discours "Opti-*

mates" de Cicéron (Leiden: Brill, 1981), and Chapter Ten of this book.

42 Rawson, *Intellectual Life,* p. 216.

43 *Div.* II, 1–5, for his comments on the writing and intended audience of his philosophic works. Cf. the fragmentary quote from the poet Lucilius used by Cicero in *Rep.* Fragments of Book I (Loeb Classical Library), p. 109.

44 Minyard, *Lucretius,* esp. pp. 75–76. For a similar view, although not as explicit or systematic, see Charles Norris Cochrane, *Christianity and Classical Culture: A Study of Thought and Action from Augustus to Augustine* (rev. ed. New York: Oxford University Press, 1944), pp. 35–42.

45 For Cicero's defense of the active political life, apparently directed against the Epicureans, see Chapter Seven of this book.

46 *Q.F.* II, xiv, 1.

47 *Q.F.* III, v and vi, 1: *de optimo statu civitatis et de optimo cive.*

48 *Am.* 14, for a reference to Scipio's discussion of the state just a few days before his death in 129.

49 *Fam.* VIII, i, 5; *Att.* 105 (V.12) 2.

50 *Rep.* I, 13.

51 *Rep.* I, 14, 68.

52 *Rep.* I, 31.

53 *Am.* 14.

54 *Am.* 69; *Rep.* I, 34.

55 See M. I. Finley, *Politics in the Ancient World* (Cambridge, England: Cambridge University Press, 1983), p. 127.

56 *Rep.* I, 12–13, 38.

57 *Rep.* I, 33–34, 70; II, 3, 22, 30, 33, 53, 65–66; *Leg.* I, 15; II, 23; III, 12.

58 *Rep.* I, 36.

59 *Rep.* II, 21–22.

60 *Rep.* I, 34, 36; II, 22, 52, 66.

61 *Rep.* II, 3, 22, 53.

62 *Fam.* IX, ii, 5.

63 *Leg.* I, 15.

64 *Leg.* I, 17.

65 *Leg.* II, 18.

66 C. W. Keyes, "Original Elements in Cicero's Ideal Constitution," *American Journal of Philology* 42 (1921): 309–10.

67 *Leg.* II, 23; III, 12.

68 A. E. Douglas, "Cicero the Philosopher," in Dorey, ed., *Cicero*, p. 149.

69 *Att.* 417 (XV.13a) 2.

70 *Off.* I, 6.

71 *Att.* 420 (XVI.11) 4; *Off.* III, 34.

72 See Shackleton Bailey's commentary, *Cicero's Letters to Atticus*, vol. 6, pp. 301–2.

73 *Off.* III, 34.

74 *Att.* 420 (XVI.11) 4, Puteoli, Nov. 5, 44; 425 (XVI.14) 3, Arpinum, Nov. 12(?), 44, the penultimate extant letter to Atticus.

CHAPTER FOUR

1 *Leg.* II, 8.

2 For a brief discussion of this matter, see Marcia L. Colish, *The*

Stoic Tradition from Antiquity to the Early Middle Ages (Leiden: Brill, 1985), vol. 1, pp. 33–34.

3 *Inv.* II, 65, 160; *Leg.* I, 30, 43.

4 *Rep.* III, 33. While these words are spoken by Laelius and not by Scipio, commentators accept them as representing Cicero's own view on the subject. Colish, *Stoic Tradition,* vol. 1, p. 96, writes: "Cicero develops the Stoic doctrine of natural law well beyond the point to which the Stoics themselves had taken it." On this passage she remarks, p. 97: "we see expressed for the first time in the Latin language the Stoic conception of a universal and eternal law of nature, identified with God and right reason and superimposed on the laws and institutions of Rome, treated as the norm of their legitimacy."

5 *Inv.* II, 65–68, 162.

6 *Leg.* I, 19. Cicero adds that this "is the crowd's definition of law." Statute law, according to *Inv.* 162, "is what is contained in a written document which is published for the people to observe."

7 *Inv.* II, 162.

8 *Inv.* II, 162.

9 *Leg.* I, 19; II, 12–13.

10 *Leg.* II, 13.

11 *Top.* 90.

12 *Inv.* II, 65–66, 161.

13 *Leg.* I, 19–23.

14 *Rep.* III, 13–23.

15 *Rep.* III, 24, and cf. *Off.* II, 39–40; St. Augustine, *Civ. Dei* IV, iv.

16 *Rep.* III, 24.

17 *N.D.* II, 124–29; *Off.* I, 11.

18 *Inv.* II, 160.

19 Passages in *Off.* particularly relevant to his conception of justice are I, 15, 20–49, 153–59; II, 38–43.

20 *Rep.* I, 39.

21 *Off.* II, 40.

22 *Leg.* I, 33.

23 *Off.* III, 26.

24 A summary of the various points made by Cicero in *Off.*, esp. I, 15, 20, 23, 42–45.

25 On Cicero's conception of proportionate equality, see esp. *Rep.* I, 43, 53, 69; II, 39–40, 56–57; *Leg.* III, 24–25, 28, 38–39.

26 *Off.* I, 153–59.

27 *Off.* I, 20; III, 28.

28 *Off.* I, 159.

29 *Off.* I, 160.

30 *N.D.* II, 78–79, 133, 147–58; *Leg.* I, 22–25.

31 Bruno Snell, *The Discovery of the Mind: The Greek Origins of European Thought,* trans. T. G. Rosenmeyer (New York: Harper Torchbooks, 1960), p. 254. See his chap. 11 for a discussion of *humanitas*.

32 For example, W. Den Boer, *Private Morality in Greece and Rome: Some Historical Aspects* (Leiden: Brill, 1979), pp. 78–82, 89–92; A. R. Hands, *Charities and Social Aid in Greece and Rome* (London: Thames and Hudson, 1968), pp. 86–88. On Cicero's notion of *societas generis humani,* see esp. *Off.* I, 50–52.

33 Whether slaves are considered by Cicero to be members of this universal community, i.e., human beings, is a moot point among scholars. *Off.* I, 41, indicates that slaves, despite their inferior status, are human and should be treated as such. On the other hand, Den Boer, *Private Morality,* pp. 89–92, makes a case against such an interpretation of Cicero.

34 *N.D.* II, 133, 154–62; *Leg.* I, 25.

35 *N.D.* II, 133–46; *Leg.* I, 26–27.

36 *Leg.* I, 26.

37 *N.D.* II, 150–52; *Off.* II, 12–15; *Leg.* I, 26.

38 *N.D.* II, 148.

39 *Leg.* I, 26, 30; *Off.* I, 11–14; *N.D.* II, 147–49, 153.

40 *Leg.* I, 27–35; *Rep.* III, 3; *Am.* 19–27; *Off.* I, 50, 158; II, 12–16; III, 69.

41 *Leg.* I, 28.

42 *Off.* I, 158; *Am.* 26–27.

43 *Att.* 125 (VII.2) 4, Brundisium, Nov. 25(?), 50 B.C.

44 *Off.* I, 12.

45 *Off.* II, 12–16.

46 *Off.* III, 69; *Am.* 19.

47 *Leg.* I, 25.

48 *Tusc.* II, 47–48, 51–53; IV, 10–14; *Off.* I, 101; *Rep.* I, 60.

49 *Rep.* I, 60; *Tusc.* II, 47–48.

50 *Off.* I, 13–14.

51 *Off.* I, 12.

52 *Tusc.* II, 43.

53 *Leg.* I, 43.

54 On these two *personae,* see *Off.* I, 107–25. Colish, *Stoic Tradition,* vol. 1, p. 147, refers to this treatment "as a virtual translation of Panaetius' rules of casuistry into Latin."

55 *Off.* I, 107.

56 *Off.* I, 110.

57 *Off.* I, 59.

58 On the individualism of Cicero's thought, see Robert Denoon Cumming, *Human Nature and History: A Study of the Development of Liberal Political Thought* (Chicago: University of Chicago Press, 1969), vol. 2, part 4 in general, and esp. pp. 3, 11, 13, 17, 20, 25, 64–65, 331.

59 *Off.* III, 13–17; *Am.* 20–21.

60 *Am.* 21; *Leg.* I, 30.

61 *Leg.* I, 31.

62 *Tusc.* II, 47; III, 12.

63 *Rep.* II, 67.

64 *Leg.* Fragment (Loeb Classical Library), p. 519.

65 *Off.* II, 16.

66 *Arch.* 26–30.

67 *N.D.* III, 66–78.

68 *Leg.* I, 31–32.

69 *Tusc.* IV, 10–14.

70 *Tusc.* IV, 22.

71 *Leg.* I, 29, 33.

72 *Tusc.* IV, 65, 82–83; V, 39.

73 *Tusc.* II, 53.

74 *Tusc.* IV, 83–84; also see III, 13.

75 See Chapter Five of this book for a discussion of the idea.

CHAPTER FIVE

1 Esp. *Leg.* I, 23. On the question of slaves as members of the universal commonwealth, see n. 33 in Chapter Four of this book.

2 See Chapter Four of this book for a discussion of the human *personae*.

3 *Leg.* I, 30.

4 See Chapter Three of this book.

5 See Chapter Three and Chapter Ten of this book.

6 *Sen.* 33.

7 *Sen.* 5.

8 Marcia L. Colish, *The Stoic Tradition from Antiquity to the Early Middle Ages* (Leiden: Brill, 1985), vol. 1, p. 102.

9 *Rep.* I, 53, also 49.

10 *Rep.* I, 51. Cicero is apparently in agreement, although aristocracy is being defended by Scipio. Also note the speech of Laelius, III, 37, defending Roman imperialism and slavery as the rule of the naturally superior. It is not clear whether this sentiment is Cicero's own, although in response to Laelius's general remarks, III, 42, "Scipio, whose delight went beyond that of the rest, was almost carried away with enthusiasm."

11 Relevant for his doctrine of proportionate equality: *Rep.* I, 43, 53, 69; II, 39–40, 56–57; *Leg.* III, 24–25, 28, 38–39. The principle of proportionate or geometrical equality, in contrast to numerical or arithmetical equality, is central to the conceptions of justice in Plato's *Laws* 757a–d, and of distributive justice in Aristotle: see his *Nicomachean Ethics* 1130b–31b, and *Politics* 1280a–82b, 1293a–96b, 1301a–2a, 1317b–18a. Their respective ideas of the mixed constitution rest upon this principle, as does Cicero's.

12 *Rep.* I, 43, 69.

13 See Chapter Nine of this book for the mixed constitution.

14 See Chapter Four of this book.

15 *Leg.* I, 29–33.

16 *Leg.* Fragment 2 (Loeb Classical Library), p. 519.

17 *Leg. Agr.* II, 3–4; *Verr.* II, v, 180–82; *Mur.* 16–17. Also see T. P.

Wiseman, *New Men in the Roman Senate, 139 B.C.–A.D. 14*
(London: Oxford University Press, 1971), "The Ideology of *Novitas*," pp. 107–16.

18 *Mur.* 17; *Sest.* 137.

19 *Balb.* 18–19.

20 *Verr.* II, v, 180–82.

21 *Sulla* 23.

22 For reference to these heroes, see esp. *Sulla* 23; *Mur.* 16–17.

23 *Rep.* I, 1.

24 *Mur.* 16–17, and editor's note (Loeb Classical Library).

25 *Off.* I, 115–16.

26 *Rep.* I, 10.

27 *Off.* I, 116.

28 Aristotle, *Politics* 1328a–29a. Plato, *Statesman* 281d–e, 287b–90e, makes a somewhat similar distinction between "contributory" and "productive" arts.

29 *Cat.* II, 18; *Verr.* II, iv, 46; v, 15, 154.

30 *Tusc.* V, 15, 29; *Fin.* III, 51; *Leg. Agr.* I, 22; *Dom.* 58, 89. P. A. Brunt, *Social Conflicts in the Roman Republic* (London: Chatto and Windus, 1971), p. 128: "Cicero . . . came near regarding poverty as a crime."

31 *Mur.* 36; *Att.* 16 (I.16) 11.

32 *Rosc. Am.* 120.

33 *Flacc.* 18–19.

34 *Rep.* II, 24; *Orator* 161, 172; *Phil.* X, 22; *Off.* I, 129.

35 *Off.* I, 150–51. Classicists usually treat these passages as being concerned broadly with "occupations." For example, J. P. V. D.

Balsdon, *Life and Leisure in Ancient Rome* (2d rev. ed. London: Bodley Head, 1974), pp. 131–32; Colish, *Stoic Tradition*, vol. 1, pp. 147–48; M. I. Finley, *The Ancient Economy* (Berkeley and Los Angeles: University of California Press, 1973), pp. 41–44; Elizabeth Rawson, *Intellectual Life in the Late Roman Republic* (London: Duckworth, 1985), p. 84. Strictly speaking, however, Cicero's concern is with different forms of money-making.

36   *Off.* I, 151. Cicero takes this for granted instead of being explicit: Balsdon, *Life and Leisure*, p. 132; Rawson, *Intellectual Life*, p. 84.

37   In the passage in *Off.* cited in n. 35 above, only farming and large-scale commerce are mentioned. Cicero also refers to war, politics, law, oratory, and philosophy in *Off.* I, 115–16; *Mur.* 30. Naturally, the gentleman should receive no wages for these pursuits.

38   *Tusc.* II, 35.

39   *Off.* II, 46.

40   *Tusc.* V, 8–9. Also see Diogenes Laertius, *Lives of Eminent Philosophers* VIII, 8.

41   *Tusc.* V, 9.

42   *N.D.* II, 150–52; *Off.* II, 12–15. See Chapter Four of this book.

43   *N.D.* II, 150.

44   *N.D.* II, 152.

45   *Off.* II, 14.

46   The following description of Cicero's ideal of the gentleman is from *Off.* I.

47   Cicero's views on generosity are in *Off.* I, 42–60; II, 52–89; also see Chapter Four of this book. Cf. Aristotle, *Nicomachean Ethics* 1119b–22a.

48   *Off.* II, 54; *Tusc.* IV, 56.

49   A. R. Hands, *Charities and Social Aid in Greece and Rome* (London: Thames and Hudson, 1968), p. 31. Also see his remarks on Cicero and generosity, pp. 47, 64, 74, 82.

50 For magnanimity, *Off.* I, 63–92. Cf. Aristotle, *Nicomachean Ethics* 1123a–25a.

51 For *decorum, Off.* I, 93–151. Again, Cicero appears to be following the Stoicism of Panaetius and, like him, makes *decorum* central to *temperantia.* See Colish, *Stoic Tradition,* vol. 1, p. 147.

52 *Off.* I, 96.

53 *Off.* I, 111.

54 *Off.* I, 129–30. For this notion of womanish traits, also see *Mur.* 27; *Fam.* XVI, xxvii, 1.

55 A point made in *Cael.* 28–29, 42–43.

56 This aesthetic dimension of true gentlemanly conduct also characterizes Plato's ideal for the Guardian class in Kallipolis. See *Republic* 400a–403c, 411c–12a, 486d, 535a.

57 On glory, in addition to *Off.,* see *Tusc.* III, 3–4; *Fam.* II, iv, 2.

58 *Tusc.* III, 3–4.

CHAPTER SIX

1 Of particular use in what follows in this section has been Elizabeth Rawson, "The Ciceronian Aristocracy and Its Properties," *Studies in Roman Property,* ed. M. I. Finley (Cambridge, England: Cambridge University Press, 1976), pp. 85–102. Her views, however, should be supplemented and modified by the comments of Susan Treggiari, "Sentiment and Property: Some Roman Attitudes," *Theories of Property: Aristotle to the Present,* ed. Anthony Parel and Thomas Flanagan (Waterloo, Ont.: Wilfrid Laurier University Press, 1979), pp. 53–85. Also of use on the subject are several recent biographical studies: W. K. Lacey, *Cicero and the End of the Roman Republic* (London: Hodder and Stoughton, 1978); Thomas N. Mitchell, *Cicero: The Ascending Years* (New Haven: Yale University Press, 1979); Elizabeth Rawson, *Cicero: A Portrait* (London: Allen Lane, 1975); D. R. Shackleton Bailey, *Cicero* (London: Duckworth, 1971).

2 M. I. Finley, *The Ancient Economy* (Berkeley and Los Angeles: University of California Press, 1973), p. 53; *Att.* 19 (I.19) 4.

3 *Att.,* 116 (VI.2) 5; 115 (VI.1) 16.

4 For example, *Fam.* XIII, xxvi, xliii, xlv, liii, lvi. On Cicero's atti-
tude to commerce see the detailed study by John H. D'Arms,
Commerce and Social Standing in Ancient Rome (Cambridge,
Mass.: Harvard University Press, 1981), chaps. 2–3.

5 Mitchell, *Cicero,* pp. 100–105.

6 *Fam.* XIII, xi, 1.

7 *Att.* 426 (XVI.15) 6.

8 *Att.* 414 (XVI.6) 2. Mitchell, *Cicero,* p. 103, suggests possible
reasons for the purchase of some of these properties.

9 *Off.* II, 87. The translation has not survived.

10 *Att.* 300 (XIII.29) 1–2. Chrysippus is the architect.

11 *Fam.* VII, xxiii, 2. Also see *Att.* 4 (I.8) 2.

12 *Att.* 73 (IV.1) 3.

13 *Dom.* 146.

14 *Phil.* II, 40.

15 *Att.* 211 (XI.1) 2; *Fam.* V, xx, 9. Cicero believes this to be a fair
and legitimate profit for one in a position to acquire far more. In
comparison to the exorbitant spoils of provincial office gained by
many of his contemporaries, it was a relatively modest amount.

16 *Fam.* XVI, xviii, 2.

17 For the details see Bruce W. Frier, *Landlords and Tenants in Imperial Rome* (Princeton, N.J.: Princeton University Press, 1980),
pp. 23–24, 30, 34–36, 179 and n. 12. Also see P. A. Brunt, "The
Roman Mob," *Past and Present* 35 (1966): 13.

18 *Att.* 363 (XIV.9) 1; 364 (XIV.10) 3; 365 (XIV.11) 2. Z. Yavetz,
"The Living Conditions of the Urban Plebs in Republican Rome,"
Latomus 17 (1958): 510 n. 3, states that the word *taberna* in the
quotation given below should be translated "tenement" rather than
"workshop."

19 *Att.* 409 (XVI.1) 5.

20 *Att.* 363 (XIV.9) 1. Chrysippus was the architect. The comment of Yavetz, "Living Conditions," p. 510, is relevant: "Cicero thought he would have to invest good money in the matter, but with the help of Vestorius (who was not only a banker, but used also to instruct workers how to build and make plans for buildings) he finds a way to turn loss into profit. If we add this story to the descriptions supplied by Vitruvius . . . then the picture we get is complete: the landlord, the architect, the banker, all work hand in hand, with the aim of economizing on the cost of living quarters, and the inhabitants of the insulae had to put up with the results."

21 *Att.* 365 (XIV.11) 2.

22 *Off.* I, 11–12, 21, 22, 51.

23 *Off.* III, 21–24.

24 *Off.* III, 54–67.

25 *Top.* 90.

26 *Off.* I, 15, 20, 23, 42–45.

27 *Off.* II, 73, 76–87; III, 21–23; *Leg. Agr.* II, 10–16, 71, 102; *Sest.* 103; and *Rep.* I, 49; *Leg.* II, 59; *Fin.* III, 67.

28 *Rep.* I, 27–28; *Off.* I, 106. See Chapter Five of this book.

29 For the Stoic attitude toward property see Ludwig Edelstein, *The Meaning of Stoicism* (Cambridge, Mass.: Harvard University Press, 1966), p. 79.

30 *Rep.* I, 27–28; *Off.* II, 71, 77; *Phil.* I, 29; *Par. St.* 33–41.

31 *Par. St.* 50–52.

32 *Fin.* III, 67.

33 *Off.* I, 20, 25, 92; II, 64, 87.

34 *Off.* III, 42. Thomas Hobbes, *The Elements of Law Natural and Politic,* ed. Ferdinand Tonnies, Introduction by M. M. Goldsmith (2d ed. London: Cass, 1969), pp. 47–48.

35 For a brief discussion of Locke's possible intellectual debt to Cicero, see my book, *The Politics of Locke's Philosophy: A Social Study of "An Essay Concerning Human Understanding"* (Berkeley and Los Angeles: University of California Press, 1983), chap. 2.

36 On Cicero's individualism see Robert Denoon Cumming, *Human Nature and History: A Study of the Development of Liberal Political Thought* (Chicago: University of Chicago Press, 1969), vol. 2, part 4 in general and esp. pp. 3, 11, 13, 17, 20, 25, 64–65, 331.

37 Donald Earl, *The Moral and Political Tradition of Rome* (Ithaca, N.Y.: Cornell University Press, 1967), p. 41: "The old Stoics were concerned with the individual, not the state. Panaetius placed the individual in the framework of the state: no ideal state either, but the actual Roman Republic which was justified by being based on the universal law of human society."

38 See Chapter Two of this book.

39 C. B. Macpherson, *The Political Theory of Possessive Individualism: Hobbes to Locke* (Oxford: Clarendon Press, 1962).

40 On this aspect of Hobbes, see my "Thomas Hobbes and the Crisis of the English Aristocracy," *History of Political Thought* 1 (1980): 437–52. On the other hand, Locke's outlook was intimately related to emergent capitalism in late Stuart England. See my *Politics of Locke's Philosophy,* and my *John Locke and Agrarian Capitalism* (Berkeley and Los Angeles: University of California Press, 1984).

41 *Leg.* II, 3–6.

42 *Att.* 104 (V.11) 1; *Fam.* II, xi, 1.

43 For example, *Rep.* II, 24; *Phil.* X, 22.

44 See *Att.* 26 (II.6), for a picture of a bored Cicero whiling away the time in the countryside. Cicero suggests that he fishes.

45 *N.D.* II, 150–52; *Off.* II, 12–15. See Chapter Five of this book.

46 *N.D.* II, 152.

47 *Off.* I, 151.

48 *Rep.* II, 5–9.

49 *Off.* I, 150–51.

50 *Verr.* II, iii, 27.

51 *Verr.* II, ii, 149.

52 *Verr.* II, ii, 7.

53 *Flacc.* 71.

54 *Off.* III, 77.

55 *Rosc. Am.* 50–51; *Sen.* 55–56, 60.

56 *Sest.* 72.

57 *Rosc. Am.* 50.

58 *Sen.* 59.

59 *Sen.* 51–60.

60 *Rosc. Am.* 75. On *audacia,* see C. Wirszubski, *"Audaces:* A Study in Political Phraseology," *Journal of Roman Studies* 51 (1961): 12–22, and Chapter Eight and Chapter Ten of this study.

61 Virgil, *Georgics* II, 458–68 (Loeb Classical Library translation).

CHAPTER SEVEN

1 A generalization suggested by remarks in Robert Denoon Cumming, *Human Nature and History: A Study of the Development of Liberal Political Thought* (Chicago: University of Chicago Press, 1969), vol. 1, pp. 172–73, 207.

2 *Fam.* II, xv, 3.

3 *Fam.* VII, xxviii, 3; X, xii, 5.

4 *Tusc.* I, 90.

5 *Fam.* X, xii, 5. For what follows see *Rep.* I, 2, 3, 12; III, 5; VI, 13, 29.

6 *Rep.* I, 8. Cf. Plato, *Crito* 51a–e.

7 *Rep.* I, 4–11. That Cicero was directing the *Republic* primarily against the Epicurean Lucretius is a thesis propounded in J. D. Minyard, *Lucretius and the Late Republic: An Essay in Roman Intellectual History* (Leiden: Brill, 1985), pp. 72–76. See Chapter Three of this book.

8 *Rep.* III, 5–6.

9 *Rep.* III, 7.

10 *Rep.* III, 7.

11 *Rep.* I, 2.

12 *Off.* I, 70–73.

13 *Rep.* I, 13.

14 *Leg.* III, 14. Other references to Demetrius are *Leg.* II, 66; *Rep.* II, 2; *Off.* I, 3; *Fin.* V, 54.

15 For a brief discussion of Demetrius and his political significance, see Ellen Meiksins Wood and Neal Wood, *Class Ideology and Ancient Political Theory: Socrates, Plato, and Aristotle in Social Context* (New York: Oxford University Press, 1978), pp. 249–53.

16 Among the first postwar critics of the use of the concept of the state in political science are T. I. Cook, "The Methods of Political Science, Chiefly in the United States," in *Contemporary Political Science: A Survey of Methods, Research and Teaching* (Paris: UNESCO, 1950), p. 82; David Easton, *The Political System: An Inquiry into the State of Political Science* (New York: Knopf, 1953), esp. pp. 106–15. Also see Easton's recent article "The Political System Besieged by the State," *Political Theory* 9 (1981): 303–25.

17 Morton H. Fried, *The Evolution of Political Society: An Essay in Political Anthropology* (New York: Random House, 1967), pp. 229–30.

18 It is not my purpose here to examine the complex question of the material and intellectual preconditions of the early modern conception of the state. One recent attempt to do this is Quentin Skinner, *The Foundations of Modern Political Thought* (Cambridge,

England: Cambridge University Press, 1978), esp. vol. 1, pp. ix–xi; vol. 2, pp. 349–58. Unfortunately, Skinner does not deal extensively with the social and economic factors—conflict between lord and peasant, the decline of feudalism, the emergence of agrarian and mercantile capitalism, population and urban growth, and so forth—so central to the material preconditions. For valuable discussions of them, see Perry Anderson, *Lineages of the Absolutist State* (London: New Left Books, 1974), esp. pp. 15–42; and the ground-breaking essays of Robert Brenner: "Agrarian Class Structure and Economic Development in Pre-Industrial Europe," *Past and Present* 70 (1976): 30–75; "The Origins of Capitalist Development: A Critique of Neo-Smithian Marxism," *New Left Review* 104 (1977): 25–42; "The Agrarian Roots of European Capitalism," *Past and Present* 97 (1982): 16–113. The *Past and Present* articles, together with the numerous responses, have been collected in a volume edited by T. H. Aston and C. H. E. Philpin, *The Brenner Debate: Agrarian Class Structure and Economic Development in Pre-Industrial Europe* (Cambridge, England: Cambridge University Press, 1985).

19 Esther Bréguet, in a recent critical edition of *Rep.* in French translation, renders *res publica* as *république* and *civitas* as *cité*. See her *Cicéron, "La République"* (Paris: Société d'Edition "les Belles Lettres," 1980), 2 vols. *Commonwealth* is the translation of *res publica* used by G. H. Sabine and S. B. Smith in their edition of *Rep.: On the Commonwealth* (Columbus: Ohio State University Press, 1929), reprinted by the Bobbs-Merrill Library of Liberal Arts in 1976. Sabine and Smith translate the *res* of *res publica* as "affair," as does F. E. Adcock in *Roman Political Ideas and Practice* (Ann Arbor: University of Michigan Press, 1964), p. 10.

20 Wolfgang Kunkel, *An Introduction to Roman and Legal Constitutional History,* trans. J. M. Kelly (2d ed. Oxford: Clarendon Press, 1973), p. 9.

21 See Alan Watson, *Roman Private Law Around 200 B.C.* (Edinburgh: Edinburgh University Press, 1971), pp. 59–60.

22 Matthias Gelzer, *The Roman Nobility,* trans. Robin Seager (Oxford: Blackwell, 1969), p. 137 and n. 615.

23 For instance, *Leg.* II, 12; *Par. St.* 27.

24 *Rep.* I, 12, 33, 36, 38.

25 *Rep.* I, 39, 41, 43, 48.

26 *Rep.* I, 39: *sed coetus multitudinis iuris consensu et utilitatis communione sociatus.*

27 *Rep.* I, 49; *Cluen.* 146–47.

28 *Rep.* II, 69–70; V, 1–2; *Leg.* II, 12–13.

29 For example, *Off.* II, 2, 23–29; III, 83–85.

30 *Par. St.* 27. Here Cicero is speaking of Rome and Clodius during his own exile in 58.

31 *Inv.* I, 2; *Rep.* I, 40.

32 *Rep.* I, 41.

33 *Rep.* I, 39; *Off.* I, 50–53, 158; II, 73. Walbank makes the important point that in *Rep.* I, 39, by attributing the primary cause of the state to human sociability Cicero does not exclude the Epicurean weakness (*imbecillitas*) as a cause, if a less important one. See F. W. Walbank, *Polybius* (Berkeley and Los Angeles: University of California Press, 1972), p. 139. Walbank's contention is borne out by what Cicero says about the state and property (see Section 3 of this chapter), and in *Off.* II, 41–42, he maintains that in the beginning the multitude instituted monarchy to protect themselves against the strong.

34 *Rep.* I, 1–2.

35 *Off.* I, 54.

36 *Rep.* I, 41–42.

37 *Inv.* II, 168–69.

38 *Leg.* II, 11.

39 *Leg.* III, 8.

40 *Off.* II, 15, 41–42.

41 See esp. *Off.* III, 34–35.

42 For a discussion of these duties see Chapter Four of this book.

43 The whole of Plato's *Republic* and *Laws* warrant this conclusion.

Also see his *Protagoras* 319b–d; *Statesman* 281d–e, 287b–290e. Of direct relevance to the point is Aristotle's distinction between "parts" and "conditions" of the ideal *polis* in *Politics* 1328a–29a.

44 This is derived primarily from the Plato of the *Laws*.

45 *Caec.* 70, 73–75.

46 *Top.* II, 9. Cf. *Dom.* 33.

47 *Off.* II, 73.

48 *Off.* II, 78.

49 One of the most recent commentators to recognize and emphasize this significant characteristic of Cicero's political thought is G. E. M. de Ste. Croix, in *The Class Struggle in the Ancient Greek World: From the Archaic Age to the Arab Conquests* (Ithaca, N.Y.: Cornell University Press, 1981), p. 426: "No surviving Greek writer is quite as explicit about the overriding importance of property rights as Cicero, the earliest known to me in a long line of thinkers, extending into modern times, who have seen the protection of private property rights as the prime function of the state."

50 Here I am using *civitas*, as Cicero often did, rather than *res publica*, in order to stress the state as a complex of institutions.

51 *Rep.* I, 47; *Leg.* III, 5.

52 For example, *Rep.* I, 2; *Off.* I, 85.

53 For example, *Rep.* I, 47; III, 37; and throughout *Leg.*

54 *Leg.* III, 2; *Cluen.* 146–47.

55 *Leg.* III, 2.

56 *Leg.* III, 2; *Off.* I, 85; *Dom.* 33.

57 *Off.* I, 85.

58 *Verr.* II, v, 35. On the theater of politics see *Off.* I, 124; *Q.F.* I, i, 42, 46; and the following discussion and that in re electioneering in Chapter Ten of this book.

59 On *tutela* see J. A. Crook, *Law and Life of Rome* (Ithaca, N.Y.: Cornell University Press, 1967), pp. 113–16; H. F. Jolowicz and Barry Nicholas, *Historical Introduction to the Study of Roman Law* (3d ed. Cambridge, England: Cambridge University Press, 1972), pp. 121–22, 239–40; Watson, *Roman Private Law,* chap. 4.

60 *Off.* I, 124.

61 *Off.* III, 70; *Rosc. Am.* 111–15; *Mur.* 70–77—on *fides* and these relationships see Gelzer, *Roman Nobility,* esp. pp. 62–69; *Off.* I, 23.

62 *Off.* I, 15, 26.

63 *Off.* I, 11–12, 50–58.

64 See Chapter Four of this book.

65 See Chapter Six of this book.

66 *Quir.* 4.

67 *Leg.* II, 5.

68 *Leg.* II, 5.

69 *Off.* I, 160.

70 *Off.* I, 159.

71 One is tempted to mention another "society" which served Cicero and other Romans as a source of knowledge and truth and a foundation of ethics: *mos maiorum* or ancestral custom, the "society of ancestors." This was more of a genuine society than the *societas hominum,* a concrete cultural and historical entity, albeit idealized and mythologized by the Romans. Exactly how Cicero conceived of its relationship to the universal commonwealth of reason is not at all obvious. It seems, however, that from his standpoint Roman ancestral custom embodies the moral law of the *cosmopolis.* For *mos maiorum,* see Minyard, *Lucretius,* pp. 5–12.

72 J. W. Jones, *The Law and Legal Theory of the Greeks: An Introduction* (Oxford: Clarendon Press, 1956), pp. 116–19, 120–22, 271.

73 See Chapters Eight and Ten of this book for a discussion of tyranny and tyrannicide.

CHAPTER EIGHT

1 *Rep.* II, 2.

2 *Rep.* II, 30.

3 *Rep.* I, 41–42.

4 *Leg.* III, 12.

5 For example, *Rep.* I, 65, 68; III, 43.

6 *Rep.* II, 47; cf. I, 44.

7 *Rep.* III, 44.

8 *Rep.* III, 45.

9 Writing in Greek, *Att.* 173 (IX.4) 2, Cicero in treating tyranny uses the Greek *tyrannia* and *tyrannos* instead of *despotēs* and its variants.

10 *Rep.* III, 43–45.

11 *Rep.* I, 69; II, 41–42.

12 *Rep.* I, 42–44, 47, 54, 68; III, 47–48. Massalia, an ancient Greek aristocracy occupying the site of modern Marseilles and famed for its stability, was captured by Julius Caesar in 49. For a discussion of Massalia and the ancient sources, see G. E. M. de Ste. Croix, *The Class Struggle in the Ancient Greek World: From the Archaic Age to the Arab Conquests* (Ithaca, N.Y.: Cornell University Press, 1981), pp. 535–36.

13 *Rep.* I, 42; III, 47.

14 *Rep.* I, 43–44, 47, 54–55, 65, 69; III, 47.

15 *Rep.* I, 47–69.

16 *Rep.* I, 51.

17 See Chapter Five of this book.

18 *Rep.* I, 28, 44–45, 65–69; II, 46, 63; III, 43. At I, 65–68, Cicero quotes in a rather free rendition Plato's famous description of how mob rule arising out of democracy eventuates in tyranny. See Plato, *Republic* 562c–563e.

19 *Rep.* I, 43, 65–69.

20 Excellent guides to Cicero on *libertas, aequabilitas, dignitas,* and *auctoritas* are J. P. V. D. Balsdon, *"Auctoritas, Dignitas, Otium,"* *Classical Quarterly* n.s. 10 (Continuous 54) (1960): 43–50; Thomas N. Mitchell, *Cicero: The Ascending Years* (New Haven: Yale University Press, 1979), 198–200; Ste. Croix, *Class Struggle,* pp. 368–70; Ronald Syme, *The Roman Revolution* (Oxford: Oxford University Press, 1960), chap. 11; C. Wirszubski, *Libertas as a Political Idea at Rome During the Late Republic and Early Principate* (Cambridge, England: Cambridge University Press, 1950), pp. 1–96.

21 *Rep.* I, 43.

22 *Rep.* I, 53.

23 *Rep.* I, 69.

24 Balsdon, *"Auctoritas, Dignitas, Otium,"* p. 45: "In politics a man's *dignitas* was his good name." See Chapter Two of this book and p. 223, n. 26.

25 *Inv.* II, 160.

26 *Inv.* II, 166.

27 See Chapter Three of this book and, on the idea of proportionate equality, Chapter Four and Chapter Five.

28 *Quir.* 4–5, 21, 25.

29 *Phil.* I, 34.

30 *Rep.* I, 69.

31 *Inv.* II, 166.

32 *Rep.* I, 65–69.

33 This paragraph closely follows the treatment in Ste. Croix, *Class Struggle,* pp. 367–70. Also of value on this point is Syme, *Roman Revolution,* pp. 153–55.

34 Syme, *Roman Revolution,* p. 155.

35 *Leg.* II, 42. Cf. *Dom.* 131.

36 *Fam.* IV, xiv, 1; *M.B.* XVII (I.17) 4–6, Brutus to Atticus, June, 43 B.C.; Ste. Croix, *Class Struggle,* p. 370.

37 *Sest.* 141; *Rep.* I, 5; *Flacc.* 9–12, 16–17, 57, 71; *Leg.* III, 26; *Sen.* 63–64; *Verr.* II, ii, 7.

38 *Flacc.* 16.

39 *Flacc.* 17–18.

40 *Flacc.* 19.

41 *Flacc.* 15.

42 For example, *Flacc.* 9–12, 62–63.

43 Lucius Valerius Flaccus, who came of a distinguished family and, as praetor in 63, aided Cicero against Catiline, was appointed governor of the province of Asia in 62. He was charged with extortion in the conduct of that office but was acquitted, although evidence against him seems overwhelming.

44 *Rep.* I, 34.

45 For the theory of *anacyclosis,* see Polybius, *The Histories* VI, 4–9. Among the most useful treatments of *anacyclosis* on which I rely for the following summary are G. W. Trompf, *The Idea of Historical Recurrence in Western Thought: From Antiquity to the Reformation* (Berkeley and Los Angeles: University of California Press, 1979), chaps. 1–2; F. W. Walbank, *A Historical Commentary on Polybius* (Oxford: Clarendon Press, 1957), vol. 1; idem, *Polybius* (Berkeley and Los Angeles: University of California Press, 1972), chap. 5.

46 This seems to be the suggestion in Polybius, *The Histories* VI, 57.

47 *Rep.* I, 44.

48 *Rep.* II, 45.

49 *Rep.* I, 68. Polybius does not seem to place such emphasis on liberty.

50 *Rep.* I, 68.

51 *Rep.* II, esp. 45–63.

52 Trompf, *Historical Recurrence,* p. 181.

53 *Rep.* I, 43–44; IV, 11.

54 *Rep.* I, 65; II, 47.

55 *Rep.* II, 48.

56 *Rep.* II, 51.

57 *Off.* I, 26.

58 *Off.* II, 23–25; III, 84–85.

59 *Off.* II, 23.

60 *Caec.* 42–47. See Chapter Ten of this book.

61 *Rep.* V, 1–2.

62 *Att.* 93 (IV.19) 1–2.

63 *Att.* 152 (VIII.2) 4.

64 *Div.* II, 6–7.

65 *Att.* 173 (IX.4) 2. Cicero is writing in Greek of "tyranny" and "tyrant"; hence they are used instead of Shackleton Bailey's terms in translation, "despotism" and "despot."

66 See Chapter Ten of this book.

CHAPTER NINE

1 Despite the importance of the conception of the mixed constitution, the comprehensive treatise on the subject remains to be writ-

ten. Of importance are Z. S. Fink, *The Classical Republicans:
An Essay in the Recovery of a Pattern of Thought in Seventeenth-Century England* (2d ed. Evanston, Ill.: Northwestern University Press, 1962), chap. 1; Kurt von Fritz, *The Theory of the
Mixed Constitution in Antiquity: A Critical Analysis of Polybius'
Political Ideas* (New York: Columbia University Press, 1954);
Glenn R. Morrow, *Plato's Cretan City: A Historical Interpretation of the "Laws"* (Princeton, N.J.: Princeton University Press,
1960), chaps. 5, 10; G. W. Trompf, *The Idea of Historical Recurrence in Western Thought: From Antiquity to the Reformation*
(Berkeley and Los Angeles: University of California Press, 1979),
chaps. 1–2; F. W. Walbank, *A Historical Commentary on Polybius* (Oxford: Clarendon Press, 1957), vol. 1; idem, *Polybius*
(Berkeley and Los Angeles: University of California Press, 1972),
chap. 5.

Also see G. J. D. Aalders, *Political Thought in Hellenistic
Times* (Amsterdam: Hakkert, 1975), pp. 105–12; Andrew Lintott,
*Violence, Civil Strife and Revolution in the Classical City, 750–
330 B.C.* (London: Croom Helm, 1982), chap. 7; G. E. M. de
Ste. Croix, *The Class Struggle in the Ancient Greek World: From
the Archaic Age to the Arab Conquests* (Ithaca, N.Y.: Cornell
University Press, 1981), pp. 74–76; Ellen Meiksins Wood and
Neal Wood, *Class Ideology and Ancient Political Theory: Socra-
tes, Plato, and Aristotle in Social Context* (New York: Oxford
University Press, 1978), pp. 237–49.

2 Herodotus, *The Persian Wars* III, 80–82; Plato, *Statesman* 291a–
92a, 301a–3b; Aristotle, *Politics,* esp. 1278b–80a.

3 Thucydides, *The Peloponnesian War* VIII, 97; Plato, *Laws* 712b–
13a; Aristotle, *Politics* 1269a–73b, 1293a–96b, 1302a, 1318b–19a,
1320b. Plato's specific discussion of the mixed constitution for
Magnesia is scattered throughout Books III–VI of the *Laws.*

4 Diogenes Laertius, *Lives of Eminent Philosophers* VII, 131. Zeno,
the founder of the school, and its third head, Chrysippus, are
mentioned.

5 Polybius's views on the mixed constitution are in *The Histories*
VI.

6 Solon, *Elegies* 5; also see 4, and *Iambi* 37 (Loeb Classical Library
translation). A useful guide to the question of the "middle way" is
Chester G. Starr, *The Economic and Social Growth of Early
Greece, 800–500 B.C.* (New York: Oxford University Press,
1977), pp. 124–28, 178–79, 234–35 nn. 18–20.

7 Theognis, *Elegiac Poems* 335; also see 219–20, 331–32 (Loeb Classical Library translation). On the Athenian social ideal see K. J. Dover, *Greek Popular Morality in the Time of Plato and Aristotle* (Oxford: Blackwell, 1974), pp. 112–13, 173.

8 Plato, *Laws* 691c–d, 713c–14a, 875a–d.

9 Plato, *Laws* 757a–e; Aristotle, *Nicomachean Ethics* 1130b–31b; *Politics,* esp. 1280a–81a, 1282b–83a, 1293b–94b, 1301a–2a, 1317b. Also see Chapter Four and Chapter Nine of this book.

10 *Rep.* I, 42, 45, 69–70; II, 41–42, 57. In *Rep.* II, 42, Cicero refers to the Roman state with its mixed constitution as the "most splendid conceivable," and in II, 66, as "the greatest state of all." Cf. *Leg.* II, 23.

11 *Rep.* I, 69.

12 *Rep.* I, 69; II, 57.

13 *Rep.* II, 69.

14 *Rep.* V, 2.

15 *Rep.* I, 31; II, 2–3, 29–30, 65–66. Nevertheless, as we shall see, Cicero never intends that the Roman state should return to this golden age in any literal constitutional sense, although he believes that his fellow citizens should recapture the virtue and spirit of their forebears. See C. W. Keyes, "Original Elements in Cicero's Ideal Constitution," *American Journal of Philology* 42 (1921): 310, 322–23.

16 *Rep.* II, 3, 30.

17 *Rep.* I, 45, 69; II, 41, 57, 65, 69.

18 *Rep.* II, 42, 43.

19 *Rep.* II, 56–59.

20 *Rep.* II, 57.

21 *Rep.* I, 47.

22 *Rep.* I, 45.

23 *Rep.* I, 53.

24 *Rep.* VI, 1. Cf. *Off.* II, 79.

25 *Rep.* II, 37.

26 *Rep.* II, 39.

27 *Rep.* II, 40.

28 *Rep.* I, 68.

29 *Rep.* II, 69.

30 *Rep.* III, 41.

31 *Leg.* III, 5.

32 *Leg.* III, 28.

33 *Leg.* III, 28.

34 *Leg.* III, 30–32.

35 *Leg.* III, 10, 28. A law of the ideal state.

36 *Leg.* III, 7.

37 *Leg.* III, 6, 8–10.

38 *Leg.* III, 11, 42.

39 *Leg.* III, 10, 33–39.

40 *Leg.* III, 39.

41 *Leg.* III, 38.

42 *Leg.* III, 39.

43 *Leg.* III, 44, and 19–25.

44 *Leg.* III, 25.

45 *Leg.* II, 15–16.

46 *Sen.* 66.

47 *Leg.* II, 36.

48 *Rep.* II, 26–27; V, 3.

49 *Rep.* II, 27.

50 *Leg.* II, 69.

51 *N.D.* III, 5.

52 *Leg.* II, 26, 310

53 *Leg.* II, 30.

54 *Leg.* II, 31.

55 *Leg.* II, 31, 21.

56 See Chapter Three of this book and *Div.* II, 28, 43, 70, 148; *N.D.*
    II, 60–72; III, 53–60.

57 *Rep.* II, 16–17, 26–27.

58 *Leg.* II, 32–33.

59 *Leg.* II, 19, 22, 24–25, 28, 38–39, 40–41, 45, 59–68.

60 *Leg.* III, 7, 46–47.

61 See Wood and Wood, *Class Ideology,* p. 252.

CHAPTER TEN

1 *Rep.* I, 34; *Fam.* II, vii, 2; *Inv.* I, 6.

2 See Chapter Seven of this book; *Rep.* I, 35.

3 *Rep.* V, 8.

4 *Rep.* V, 6, 8, 9. For a discussion of this interpretation see W. W.
   How, "Cicero's Ideal in his *De Republica,*" *Journal of Roman
   Studies* 19 (1929): 24–42; G. H. Sabine and S. B. Smith, Introduc-

tion to their edition of Cicero, *On the Commonwealth* (Columbus: Ohio State University Press, 1929), pp. 93–98. My own view is closer to that of How, pp. 39–42.

5 See *Rep.* II, 67–69; V, 3–11; VI, 1, 16, 26, 29. The following description of the ideal statesman is, as indicated, based mainly but not exclusively on *Rep.*

6 *Rep.* II, 67; V, 3–5; VI, 1, 16, 29.

7 *Off.* II, 75; *Rep.* V, 9.

8 *Rep.* II, 69.

9 *Off.* II, 20–38; *Rep.* V, 8; *Att.* 161 (VIII.11) 1–2.

10 *Mur.* 23

11 *Mur.* 22–24; *Man.* 41, 47–48.

12 *Rep.* II, 69; V, 6.

13 *Att.* 161 (VII.11) 2. Cicero precedes this statement by quoting *Rep.* V, 8, on the ideal statesman.

14 *Leg.* I, 31.

15 *Leg.* I, 31; *Arch.* 26.

16 *Leg.*, Fragment 2 (Loeb Classical Library), p. 519.

17 For example, *Rep.* I, 52, 68; II, 47–48; *Leg.* I, 32–33; *Amic.* 63.

18 *Amic.* 102.

19 *Off.* III, 13–17; *Amic.* 20–21; *Leg.* I, 30.

20 *Fam.* II, vii, 2.

21 *Mur.* 35–36. Philippus was defeated by Herennius in the consular election for 93; Catulus, by Mallius for 105; Scaurus, by Quintus Maximus Eburnus for 116.

22 *Sen.* 67.

23 *Amic.* 63–64; *Fam.* I, vii, 9.

24 *Q.F.* I, i, 11, 14. Actually this lengthy letter, written at the end of 60 by Cicero to his brother, Quintus, then propraetor of Asia, amounts to a short treatise on the proper conduct of a provincial governor. In his commentary, D. R. Shackleton Bailey describes the letter as "a tract, *commentariolum de provincia administranda,* doubtless intended for wider circulation." See his edition of *Cicero: Epistulae ad Quintum Fratrem et M. Brutum* (Cambridge, England: Cambridge University Press, 1980), p. 147. For the stress on watchfulness, also see *M.B.* I (II.1) 2.

25 *Q.F.* I, i, 15–16.

26 *M.B.* I (II.1) 1.

27 *Man.* 60; *Orator* 169; *Fam.* I, ix, 21; *Balb.* 61.

28 *Fam.* I, vii, 9; *Off.* I, 141; *Q.F.* I, i, 20; *M.B.* VI (I.2) 5; XXIV (I.15) 10.

29 *M.B.* VI (I.2) 5.

30 *M.B.* XXIV (I.15) 10; *Rep.* II, 45.

31 On the whole question of *amicitia,* see P. A. Brunt, " 'Amicitia' in the Late Roman Republic," *Proceedings of the Cambridge Philological Society* n.s. 11 (o.s. 191) (1965): 1–20. Brunt believes that the existence of political *amicitiae* in the sense of "long lasting," "powerful, cohesive factions" (pp. 16–17) has been exaggerated. He concludes: "The range of *amicitia* is vast. From the constant intimacy and goodwill of virtuous or at least of like-minded men to the courtesy that etiquette normally enjoined on gentlemen, it covers every degree of genuinely or overtly amicable relation. Within this spectrum purely political connexions have their place, but one whose all-importance must not be assumed. They were often fragile, and ties of private friendship could transcend their bounds" (p. 20).

32 *Amic.* 61.

33 *Amic.* 41–43.

34 *Mur.* 70–71. The reference to Cato is to the prosecutor of the case, the great-grandson of Cato the Censor. Still one of the best treatments of *clientela* is in the classic work by Matthias Gelzer, first published in 1912: *The Roman Nobility,* trans. Robin Seager (Oxford: Blackwell, 1969), esp. pp. 62–86.

35 *Mur.* 72–77.

36 See Thomas N. Mitchell, *Cicero: The Ascending Years* (New Haven: Yale University Press, 1979), passim.

37 *Com. Pet.* 58.

38 *Com. Pet.* 1. On Cicero's conception of politics as theater see Chapter Seven of this book, and *Q.F.* I, i, 42, 46.

39 *Com. Pet.* 16–17.

40 *Com. Pet.* 39.

41 *Com. Pet.* 40.

42 *Com. Pet.* 42.

43 *Com. Pet.* 41.

44 *Com. Pet.* 42.

45 *Com. Pet.* 44.

46 *Com. Pet.* 47.

47 *Com. Pet.* 52–53.

48 *Com. Pet.* 55.

49 An excellent treatment of the violence of the age and of Cicero's views on the use of violence is Andrew Lintott, *Violence in Republican Rome* (Oxford: Clarendon Press, 1968).

50 *Leg.* III, 11.

51 *Leg.* III, 42.

52 *Off.* I, 34.

53 *Fam.* I, ix, 18. The references are to Plato, *Crito* 51c, and *Epistle* V, 322a–b.

54 *Caec.* 42. For details of the case see Bruce W. Frier, *The Rise of the Roman Jurists: Studies in Cicero's "Pro Caecina"* (Princeton, N.J.: Princeton University Press, 1985).

55 *Caec.* 46.

56 *Att.* 369 (XIV.15) 1.

57 *Att.* 371A (XIV.17A) 7.

58 *Leg.* III, 8; *Rab.* 3; *Phil.* XI, 28; *Cat.* I, 2–4; *Fam.* X, xvi, 2; XII, vii, 2.

59 See Mitchell, *Cicero,* pp. 210–13.

60 *Leg. Agr.* I, 26; III, 8; *Rab.* 33. For what follows, see Mitchell, *Cicero,* pp. 66–67.

61 *Sest.* 86; cf. *Fam.* XI, vii, 2; XII, vii, 2.

62 *Sest.* 92.

63 *Cat.* I, 2–4, 28; *Dom.* 91; *Tusc.* IV, 51. On Cicero's opinion of the Gracchi see Robert J. Murray, "Cicero and the Gracchi," *Transactions and Proceedings of the American Philological Society* 97 (1966): 291–98. Although Cicero occasionally praises the Gracchi, his "general attitude toward Gracchan politics is one of clear disapproval" (p. 297).

64 *Cat.* I, 3.

65 *Off.* III, 19, 32, 82–83.

66 *Phil.* XI, 28.

67 *Fam.* X, xvi, 2; cf. *Fam.* XII, vii, 2.

68 *Dom.* 91. Cf. Mitchell, *Cicero,* pp. 86–87.

69 *Off.* III, 32.

70 *Off.* III, 19–32.

71 Locke, *Second Treatise of Government,* chaps. 18–19; *First Treatise of Government,* §§ 79, 121. My position on Locke in what follows differs from that of Richard Ashcraft, *Revolutionary Politics and Locke's "Two Treatises of Government"* (Princeton, N.J.: Princeton University Press, 1986), esp. chap. 11.

72 See n. 58 of this chapter.

73 *Rep.* II, 69. See Chapter Nine of this book.

74 On *otium*, see J. P. V. D. Balsdon, *"Auctoritas, Dignitas, Otium,"* *Classical Quarterly*, n.s. 10 (continuous 54) (1960): 43–50; Mitchell, *Cicero*, pp. 198–204; C. Wirszubski, *Libertas as a Political Idea at Rome During the Late Republic and Early Principate* (Cambridge, England: Cambridge University Press, 1950), pp. 92–94; idem, "Cicero's *Cum Dignitate Otium:* A Reconsideration," *Journal of Roman Studies* 44 (1954): 1–13.

75 *Leg. Agr.* II, 9; also 71, 102, and *Rab.* 33–34.

76 *Leg. Agr.* I, 27.

77 On *populares* and *optimates*, see Robin Seager, "Cicero and the Word *Popularis*," *Classical Quarterly* n.s. 22, (continuous 66) (1972): 328–38.

78 *Sest.* 96. On *boni* and *populares*, see Seager, "Cicero and the Word *Popularis*," pp. 329–30; C. Wirszubski, *"Audaces:* A Study in Political Phraseology," *Journal of Roman Studies* 51 (1961): esp. pp. 13–14.

79 See the excellent study by Guy Achard, *Pratique, Rhétorique, et Idéologie Politique dans les Discours "Optimates" de Cicéron* (Leiden: Brill, 1981). Much of the anti-Circumcellion vocabulary of St. Augustine, a close student of Cicero, is strikingly reminiscent of his rhetorical abuse of *populares*. See my essays, *"Populares* and *Circumcelliones:* The Vocabulary of 'Fallen Man' in Cicero and St. Augustine," *History of Political Thought* 7 (1986): 33–51; "African Peasant Terrorism and Augustine's Political Thought," *History from Below: Studies in Popular Protest and Popular Ideology in Honour of George Rudé*, ed. Frederick Krantz (Montreal: Concordia University, 1985), pp. 279–99.

80 *Sest.* 86. In the following I am relying on Wirszubski, *"Audaces,"* pp. 12–22. Also see Achard, *Pratique, Rhétorique*, pp. 247–48.

81 *Sest.* 20.

82 *Sest.* 139.

83 *Sest.* 97, 136–38.

84 *Cat.* II, 18–23; III, 27.

85 *Sest.* 97.

86 *Sest.* 97–98.

87 Wirszubski, "Cicero's *Cum Dignitate Otium*," p. 7.

88 Respectively: Wirszubski, *Libertas*, p. 94; idem, "Cicero's *Cum Dignitate Otium*," p. 9; R. Gardner, "The Purpose of the *Pro Sestio*," in his Loeb Classical Library translation of *Pro Sestio* (1958), pp. 303–4; F. E. Adcock, *Roman Political Ideas and Practice* (Ann Arbor: University of Michigan Press, 1964), p. 65; Balsdon, "*Auctoritas, Dignitas, Otium*," p. 49; P. A. Brunt, *Social Conflicts in the Roman Republic* (London: Chatto and Windus, 1971), p. 124.

89 *Sest.* 100–102.

90 *Sest.* 98.

91 *Fam.* V, xxi, 2.

92 *Cat.* IV, 15; also see 22 and *Sest.* 137. *Att.* 17 (I.17) 9–10; 21 (II.1) 7–8.

93 See the discussion in Chapter Two of this book and the following: E. Badian, *Publicans and Sinners: Private Enterprise in the Service of the Roman Republic, with a Critical Bibliography* (rev. ed. Ithaca, N.Y.: Cornell University Press, 1983), pp. 64–65, 102–5; idem, *Roman Imperialism in the Late Republic* (2d ed. Oxford: Blackwell, 1968), pp. 60–64; T. P. Wiseman, *New Men in the Roman Senate, 139 B.C.–A.D. 14* (London: Oxford University Press, 1971), pp. 6–7.

94 *Cat.* IV, 15–17; *Fam.* xxi, 2. Cf. *Att.* 130 (VII.7) 5; *Sest.* 97–98.

95 For an able summary of Cicero's economic position, see Mitchell, *Cicero*, pp. 200–205. Cicero's interest in practical economic policy can be accounted for by the fact that he was an active politician in an age of intense upper-class competition for wealth and power, the accumulation of immense fortunes, and the increasing impoverishment and unrest of the masses. We are aware of his views on the subject because they are expressed not only in his treatises but also in a full range of speeches and correspondence that have fortunately survived, unlike those of others before him. They may have had an equal interest, but no evidence exists for it on the basis of their extant writings. However, it should be stressed that

Cicero made no contribution to systematic economic analysis or theory. On this score, see the evaluation of Joseph A. Schumpeter, *History of Economic Analysis,* ed. E. B. Schumpeter (New York: Oxford University Press, 1954), p. 67. Aristotle made an important early contribution to economic theory, although he devoted far less attention in his writings than Cicero to governmental economic policy. On the other hand, Machiavelli, who like Cicero was active in government and whose extensive private papers have also survived, expressed little or no concern with either practical economic policy or systematic analysis. Bodin was probably the first major political theorist to make a genuine contribution to both fields, and as a consequence might be called the first political economist.

96 *Off.* II, 73–74, 84–85. See Chapter Seven of this book.

97 *Phil.* XIII, 16.

98 *Att.* 163 (VIII.13) 1–2.

99 *Man.* 17.

100 *Har. Resp.* 60; *Leg. Agr.* I, 22–27; II, 1–16, 102. *Att.* 19 (I.19) 4; 115 (V.1) 16; 117 (VI.3) 3.

101 *Man.* 18–19; *Verr.* II, ii, 6–7.

102 *Att.* 19 (I.19) 4.

103 *Rep.* IV, 7.

104 *Att.* 116 (VI.2) 4–5; also 114 (V.21) 5; 115 (VI.1) 2; 117 (VI.3) 3.

105 *Off.* II, 74; *Fam.* XII, xxx, 4.

106 *Leg. Agr.* I, 23; II, 8; *Man.* 19; *Sest.* 98; *Fam.* IV, i, 2; *Att.* 232 (XI.23) 3.

107 *Off.* II, 78–79, 83–84; III, 70. See P. A. Brunt, "The Roman Mob," *Past and Present* 35 (1966): 13; Bruce W. Frier, *Landlords and Tenants in Imperial Rome* (Princeton, N.J.: Princeton University Press, 1980), p. 163 and n. 239.

108 *Off.* II, 72; *Sest.* 103.

109 *Off.* I, 92; II, 72; *Rep.* II, 16.

110 *Rep.* II, 60.

111 *Mur.* 71.

112 Esp. *Off.* II, 78–85.

113 *Off.* II, 79.

114 *Off.* III, 21–23.

115 *Off.* II, 78; *Sest.* 103.

116 *Leg. Agr.* I, 23; II, 8, 10; *Sest.* 103.

117 *Leg. Agr.* II, 15–16.

118 *Leg. Agr.* II, 10, but cf. with antipathy to the Gracchi expressed in *Sest.* 103; *Off.* I, 109; II, 43, 80; *Att.* 19 (I.19) 4.

119 *Leg. Agr.* II, 12, 71, 102.

120 Harold J. Laski, *Political Thought in England from Locke to Bentham* (New York: Henry Holt, 1920), p. 223.

Select Bibliography

Many of the items listed below have been cited; some have not; and a number of cited items have not been included. The criteria of selection range from the indispensable to the helpful, those works that either directly or indirectly, or by way of background or particular insight, have in varying degrees proved useful in writing the book.

PRIMARY SOURCES

Aristotle. *Nicomachean Ethics,* trans. and ed. Martin Oswald. Indianapolis: Bobbs-Merrill, Library of Liberal Arts, 1962.
———. *Politics,* trans. and ed. Ernest Barker. Oxford: Clarendon Press, 1948.
St. Augustine. *City of God.* Loeb Classical Library. 7 vols.
Barker, Ernest, trans. and ed. *From Alexander to Constantine: Passages and Documents Illustrating the History of Social and Political Ideas, 336 B.C.–A.D. 337.* Oxford: Clarendon Press, 1956.
Cicero. *On the Commonwealth,* trans. and ed. G. H. Sabine and S. B. Smith. Originally published Columbus: Ohio State University Press, 1929; reprint Indianapolis: Bobbs-Merrill, Library of Liberal Arts, 1976. English translation of *De Re Publica,* with lengthy introductory essay.
———. *Epistulae ad Familiares,* ed. D. R. Shackleton Bailey. Cambridge, England: Cambridge University Press, 1977. 2 vols. Latin text with commentary.

Select Bibliography

264   *Select Bibliography*

————. *Epistulae ad Quintum Fratrem et M. Brutum,* ed. D. R. Shackleton Bailey. Cambridge, England: Cambridge University Press, 1980. Latin text with commentary.

————. *Letters to Atticus,* trans. and ed. D. R. Shackleton Bailey. Cambridge, England: Cambridge University Press, 1965–1970. 7 vols. Latin text with English translation and commentary.

————. *Letters to Atticus,* trans. and ed. D. R. Shackleton Bailey. Harmondsworth: Penguin, 1978. English translation only.

————. *Letters to His Friends,* trans. and ed. D. R. Shackleton Bailey. Harmondsworth: Penguin, 1978. 2 vols. English translation only. The second volume includes *Letters to His Brother Quintus* and *Letters to Marcus Brutus.*

————. *Res Publica: Roman Politics and Society According to Cicero,* selected and trans. W. K. Lacey and B. W. J. G. Wilson. London: Oxford University Press, 1970.

————. *Works.* Loeb Classical Library. 28 vols. Latin texts and English translations by various scholars, with introductory essays.

Diogenes Laertius. *Lives of Eminent Philosophers,* trans. R. D. Hicks. Loeb Classical Library. 2 vols.

Lucretius. *On Nature,* trans. and ed. R. M. Geer. Indianapolis: Bobbs-Merrill, Library of Liberal Arts, 1965. Translation of *De Rerum Natura.*

Plato. *The Collected Dialogues, Including The Letters,* ed. Edith Hamilton and Huntington Cairns. Princeton, N.J.: Princeton University Press, 1963.

————. *Laws,* trans. and ed. T. J. Saunders. Harmondsworth: Penguin, 1975.

————. *Republic,* trans. and ed. F. M. Cornford. London: Oxford University Press, 1945.

————. *Statesman,* trans. J. B. Skemp, ed. Martin Ostwald. Indianapolis: Bobbs-Merrill, Library of Liberal Arts, 1957.

Plutarch. *The Parallel Lives,* trans. B. Perrin. Loeb Classical Library. 11 vols.

Polybius. *The Histories,* trans. W. R. Paton. Loeb Classical Library. 6 vols.

Sallust. *Works,* trans. J. C. Rolfe. Loeb Classical Library.

SECONDARY SOURCES

Aalders, G. J. D. *Political Thought in Hellenistic Times.* Amsterdam: Hakkert, 1975.

Achard, Guy. *Pratique, Rhétorique, et Idéologie Politique dans les Discours "Optimates" de Cicéron.* Leiden: Brill, 1981.

Adcock, F. E. *Roman Political Ideas and Practice.* Ann Arbor: University of Michigan Press, 1964.

Anderson, Perry. *Lineages of the Absolutist State.* London: New Left Books, 1974.

————. *Passages from Antiquity to Feudalism.* London: New Left Books, 1974.

Astin, A. E. *Scipio Aemelianus.* Oxford: Clarendon Press, 1967.

————. *Cato the Censor.* Oxford: Clarendon Press, 1978.

Badian, E. *Foreign Clientelae (264–70 B.C.).* Oxford: Clarendon Press, 1958.

————. *Roman Imperialism in the Late Republic.* 2d ed. Oxford: Blackwell, 1968.

————. *Publicans and Sinners: Private Enterprise in the Service of the Roman Republic, with a Critical Bibliography.* Rev. ed. Ithaca, N.Y.: Cornell University Press, 1983.

Balsdon, J. P. V. D. *"Auctoritas, Dignitas, Otium."* *Classical Quarterly* n.s. 10 (continuous 54) (1960): 43–50.

————. "Cicero the Man." Pp. 171–214 in *Cicero,* ed. T. A. Dorey. New York: Basic Books, 1965.

————. "Cicero." *Oxford Classical Dictionary.* Pp. 234–38 in 2d ed. Oxford: Clarendon Press, 1970.

————. *Life and Leisure in Ancient Rome.* 2d rev. ed. London: Bodley Head, 1974.

Beard, Mary, and Michael Crawford. *Rome in the Late Republic: Problems and Interpretations.* London: Duckworth, 1985.

Bolgar, R. R., ed. *The Classical Heritage and Its Beneficiaries.* Cambridge, England: Cambridge University Press, 1954.

————. *Classical Influences on Western Thought, A.D. 1650–1870.* Cambridge, England: Cambridge University Press, 1979.

Bonner, Stanley F. *Education in Ancient Rome: From the Elder*

Cato to the Younger Pliny. Berkeley and Los Angeles: University of California Press, 1977.

Brenner, Robert. "The Origins of Capitalist Development: A Critique of Neo-Smithian Marxism." *New Left Review* 104 (1977): 25–42.

————. *The Brenner Debate: Agrarian Class Structure and Economic Development in Pre-Industrial Europe,* ed. T. H. Aston and C. H. E. Philpin. Cambridge, England: Cambridge University Press, 1985.

Brunt, P. A. " 'Amicitia' in the Late Roman Republic." *Proceedings of the Cambridge Philological Society* n.s. 11 (o.s. 191) (1965): 1–20.

————. "The Roman Mob." *Past and Present* 35 (1966): 3–27.

————. *Italian Manpower, 225 B.C.–A.D. 14.* Oxford: Clarendon Press, 1971.

————. *Social Conflicts in the Roman Republic.* London: Chatto and Windus, 1971.

Buck, Robert J. *Agriculture and Agricultural Practice in Roman Law.* Wiesbaden: Steiner, 1983. *Historia* 45.

Cairns, Huntington. *Legal Philosophy from Plato to Hegel.* Baltimore: Johns Hopkins Press, 1949.

Carlyle, R. W. and A. J. Carlyle. *A History of Mediaeval Thought in the West.* Vol. 1. London: Blackwood, 1903.

Cauer, Friedrich. *Ciceros politisches Denken: Ein Versuch.* Berlin: Wiedmann, 1903.

Clarke, M. L. *Classical Education in Britain, 1500–1900.* Cambridge, England: Cambridge University Press, 1959.

Cochrane, Charles Norris. *Christianity and Classical Culture: A Study of Thought and Action from Augustus to Augustine.* Rev. ed. New York: Oxford University Press, 1944.

Colish, Marcia L. *The Stoic Tradition from Antiquity to the Early Middle Ages.* Vol. 1: *Stoicism in Classical Latin Literature.* Leiden: Brill, 1985.

Crawford, Michael. *The Roman Republic.* London: Fontana/ Collins, 1978.

Crook, J. A. *Law and Life of Rome.* Ithaca, N.Y.: Cornell University Press, 1967.

Cumming, Robert Denoon. *Human Nature and History: A*

Study of the Development of Liberal Political Thought.
Chicago: University of Chicago Press, 1969. 2 vols.

D'Arms, John H. *Commerce and Social Standing in Ancient Rome.* Cambridge, Mass.: Harvard University Press, 1981.

Daube, David. *Roman Law: Linguistic, Social and Philosophical Aspects.* Edinburgh: Edinburgh University Press, 1969.

Deane, Herbert A. *The Political and Social Ideas of St. Augustine.* New York: Columbia University Press, 1963.

————. "Classical and Christian Political Thought." *Political Theory* 1 (1973): 415–25.

Den Boer, W. *Private Morality in Greece and Rome: Some Historical Aspects.* Leiden: Brill, 1979.

Dorey, T. A., ed. *Cicero.* New York: Basic Books, 1965.

Douglas, A. E. "Cicero the Philosopher." Pp. 135–70 in *Cicero,* ed. T. A. Dorey. New York: Basic Books, 1965.

————. *Cicero.* Oxford: Clarendon Press, 1968.

Dover, K. J. *Greek Popular Morality in the Time of Plato and Aristotle.* Oxford: Blackwell, 1974.

Duncan-Jones, Richard. *The Economy of the Roman Empire: Quantitative Studies.* Corrected ed. Cambridge, England: Cambridge University Press, 1977.

Earl, Donald. *The Moral and Political Tradition of Rome.* Ithaca, N.Y.: Cornell University Press, 1967.

Edelstein, Ludwig. *The Meaning of Stoicism.* Cambridge, Mass.: Harvard University Press, 1966.

Fink, Z. S. *The Classical Republicans: An Essay in the Recovery of a Pattern of Thought in Seventeenth-Century England.* 2d ed. Evanston, Ill.: Northwestern University Press, 1962.

Finley, M. I. "Slavery." Vol. 14, pp. 307–13, in *The International Encyclopedia of the Social Sciences.* New York: Macmillan and The Free Press, 1968.

————. *The Ancient Economy.* Berkeley and Los Angeles: University of California Press, 1973.

————. *Ancient Slavery and Modern Ideology.* London: Chatto and Windus, 1980.

————. *Politics in the Ancient World.* Cambridge, England: Cambridge University Press, 1983.

Finley, M. I., ed. *Slavery in Classical Antiquity: Views and Controversies.* Cambridge, England: Heffer, 1960.

———. *Studies in Ancient Society.* London: Routledge and Kegan Paul, 1974.

———. *Studies in Roman Property.* Cambridge, England: Cambridge University Press, 1976.

Fried, Morton H. *The Evolution of Political Society: An Essay in Political Anthropology.* New York: Random House, 1967.

Frier, Bruce W. *Landlords and Tenants in Imperial Rome.* Princeton, N.J.: Princeton University Press, 1980.

———. *The Rise of the Roman Jurists: Studies in Cicero's "Pro Caecina."* Princeton, N.J.: Princeton University Press, 1985.

Fritz, Kurt von. *The Theory of the Mixed Constitution in Antiquity: A Critical Analysis of Polybius' Political Ideas.* New York: Columbia University Press, 1954.

Gay, Peter. *The Enlightenment: An Interpretation.* Vol. 1: *The Rise of Modern Paganism.* New York: Knopf, 1966.

Gelzer, Matthias. *Caesar: Politician and Statesman,* trans. Peter Needham. Oxford: Blackwell, 1969.

———. *Cicero: Ein biographischer Versuch.* Wiesbaden: Franz Steiner, 1969.

———. *The Roman Nobility,* trans. Robin Seager. Oxford: Blackwell, 1969.

Gruen, Erich S. *The Last Generation of the Roman Republic.* Berkeley and Los Angeles: University of California Press, 1974.

———. *The Hellenistic World and the Coming of Rome.* Berkeley and Los Angeles: University of California Press, 1984. 2 vols.

Hands, A. R. *Charities and Social Aid in Greece and Rome.* London: Thames and Hudson, 1968.

Highet, Gilbert. *The Classical Tradition: Greek and Roman Influences on Western Literature.* London: Oxford University Press, 1949.

Hopkins, Keith. *Conquerors and Slaves.* Vol. 1 of *Sociological Studies in Roman History.* Cambridge, England: Cambridge University Press, 1978.

How, W. W. "Cicero's Ideal in His *De Republica.*" *Journal of Roman Studies* 19 (1929): 24–42.

Jolowicz, H. F., and Barry Nicholas. *Historical Introduction to the Study of Roman Law.* 3d ed. Cambridge, England: Cambridge University Press, 1972.

Jones, J. W. *The Law and Legal Theory of the Greeks: An Introduction.* Oxford: Clarendon Press, 1956.

Jonkers, E. J. *Social and Economic Commentary on Cicero's "De Lege Agraria Orationes Tres."* Leiden: Brill, 1963.

Keyes, C. W. "Original Elements in Cicero's Ideal Constitution." *American Journal of Philology* 42 (1921): 309–23.

Kunkel, Wolfgang. *An Introduction to Roman Legal and Constitutional History,* trans. J. M. Kelly. 2d ed. Oxford: Clarendon Press, 1973.

Lacey, W. K. *Cicero and the End of the Roman Republic.* London: Hodder and Stoughton, 1978.

Lintott, Andrew. *Violence in Republican Rome.* Oxford: Clarendon Press, 1968.

———. *Violence, Civil Strife and Revolution in the Classical City, 750–330 B.C.* London: Croom Helm, 1982.

McIlwain, C. H. *The Growth of Political Thought in the West: From the Greeks to the End of the Middle Ages.* New York: Macmillan, 1932.

MacMullen, Ramsay. *Roman Social Relations, 50 B.C. to A.D. 284.* New Haven: Yale University Press, 1974.

Macpherson, C. B. *The Political Theory of Possessive Individualism: Hobbes to Locke.* Oxford: Clarendon Press, 1962.

Minyard, J. D. *Lucretius and the Late Republic: An Essay in Roman Intellectual History.* Leiden: Brill, 1985.

Mitchell, Thomas N. *Cicero: The Ascending Years.* New Haven: Yale University Press, 1979.

Morrall, John B. "Cicero as a Political Thinker." *History Today* 33 (1982): 33–37.

Morrow, Glenn R. *Plato's Cretan City: A Historical Interpretation of the "Laws."* Princeton, N.J.: Princeton University Press, 1960.

Murray, Robert J. "Cicero and the Gracchi." *Transactions and Proceedings of the American Philological Society* 97 (1966): 291–98.

Nicolet, Claude. *The World of the Citizen in Republican Rome,* trans. P. S. Falla. Berkeley and Los Angeles: University of California Press, 1980.

Nisbet, R. G. M. "The Speeches." Pp. 47–79 in *Cicero,* ed. T. A. Dorey. New York: Basic Books, 1965.

Ogilvie, R. M. *The Romans and Their Gods.* London: Chatto and Windus, 1969.

————. *Roman Literature and Society.* Sussex: Harvester; Totowa, N.J.: Barnes and Noble, 1980.

Rawson, Elizabeth. *Cicero: A Portrait.* London: Allen Lane, 1975.

————. "The Ciceronian Aristocracy and Its Properties." Pp. 85–102 in *Studies in Roman Property,* ed. M. I. Finley. Cambridge, England: Cambridge University Press, 1976.

————. *Intellectual Life in the Late Roman Republic.* London: Duckworth, 1985.

Sabine, George H. "Cicero." In vol. 3–4, p. 469, *Encyclopedia of the Social Sciences.* New York: Macmillan 1937. First published in 1930.

————. *A History of Political Theory.* 3d ed. New York: Holt, Rinehart, and Winston, 1961.

Ste. Croix, G. E. M. de. *The Class Struggle in the Ancient Greek World: From the Archaic Age to the Arab Conquests.* Ithaca, N.Y.: Cornell University Press, 1981.

Sandbach, F. H. *The Stoics.* London: Chatto and Windus, 1975.

Schumpeter, Joseph A. *History of Economic Analysis,* ed. E. B. Schumpeter. New York: Oxford University Press, 1954.

Scullard, H. H. *From the Gracchi to Nero: A History of Rome from 133 B.C. to A.D. 68.* 5th ed. London: Methuen, 1982.

Seager, Robin. "Cicero and the Word *Popularis.*" *Classical Quarterly* n.s. 22 (continuous 66) (1972): 328–38.

————. *Pompey: A Political Biography.* Oxford: Blackwell, 1979.

Seager, Robin, ed. *The Crisis of the Roman Republic.* Cambridge, England: Heffer, 1969.

Shackleton Bailey, D. R. *Cicero.* London: Duckworth, 1971.

Shaw, Brent D. "Bandits in the Roman Empire." *Past and Present* 105 (November 1984): 3–52.

Sherwin-White, A. N. *The Roman Citizenship.* 2d ed. Oxford: Clarendon Press, 1973.

Sibley, Mulford Q. *Political Ideas and Ideologies: A History of Political Thought.* New York: Harper and Row, 1970.

Skinner, Quentin. *The Foundations of Modern Political Thought.* Cambridge, England: Cambridge University Press, 1978. 2 vols.

Smith, R. E. *Cicero: The Statesman.* Cambridge, England: Cambridge University Press, 1966.

Snell, Bruno. *The Discovery of the Mind: The Greek Origins of European Thought,* trans. T. G. Rosenmeyer. New York: Harper Torchbooks, 1960.

Starr, Chester G. *The Economic and Social Growth of Early Greece, 800–500 B.C.* New York: Oxford University Press, 1977.

Stockton, David. *Cicero: A Political Biography.* London: Oxford University Press, 1971.

―――. *The Gracchi.* Oxford: Clarendon Press, 1979.

Syme, Ronald. *The Roman Revolution.* Oxford: Oxford University Press, 1960.

Taylor, L. R. *Party Politics in the Age of Caesar.* Berkeley and Los Angeles: University of California Press, 1949.

Treggiari, Susan. *Roman Freedmen During the Late Republic.* Oxford: Clarendon Press, 1969.

―――. "Sentiment and Property: Some Roman Attitudes." Pp. 53–85 in *Theories of Property: Aristotle to the Present,* ed. Anthony Parel and Thomas Flanagan. Waterloo, Ont.: Wilfrid Laurier University Press, 1979.

Trompf, G. W. *The Idea of Historical Recurrence in Western Thought: From Antiquity to the Reformation.* Berkeley and Los Angeles: University of California Press, 1979.

Vogt, Joseph. *Ancient Slavery and the Ideal of Man,* trans. Thomas Wiedemann. Oxford: Blackwell, 1974.

Walbank, F. W. *A Historical Commentary on Polybius,* vol. 1. Oxford: Clarendon Press, 1957.

―――. *Polybius.* Berkeley and Los Angeles: University of California Press, 1972.

Wardman, Alan. *Religion and Statecraft Among the Romans.* London: Granada, 1982.

Watson, Alan. *Roman Private Law Around 200 B.C.* Edinburgh: Edinburgh University Press, 1971.

Willoughby, W. W. *The Political Theories of the Ancient World.* New York: Macmillan, 1903.

Wirszubski, C. *Libertas as a Political Idea at Rome During the Late Republic and Early Principate.* Cambridge, England: Cambridge University Press, 1950.

————. "Cicero's *Cum Dignitate Otium:* A Reconsideration." *Journal of Roman Studies* 44 (1954): 1–13.

————. "*Audaces:* A Study in Political Phraseology." *Journal of Roman Studies* 51 (1961): 12–22.

Wiseman, T. P. *New Men in the Roman Senate, 139 B.C.– A.D. 14.* London: Oxford University Press, 1971.

Wolin, Sheldon S. *Politics and Vision: Continuity and Innovation in Western Political Thought.* Boston: Little, Brown, 1960.

Wood, Ellen Meiksins. "Agricultural Slavery in Classical Athens." *American Journal of Ancient History* 8 (1983): 1–47.

Wood, Ellen Meiksins, and Neal Wood. *Class Ideology and Ancient Political Theory: Socrates, Plato, and Aristotle in Social Context.* New York: Oxford University Press, 1978.

Wood, Neal. "The Social History of Political Theory." *Political Theory* 6 (1978): 345–67.

————. "Thomas Hobbes and the Crisis of the English Aristocracy." *History of Political Thought* 1 (1980): 437–52.

————. *The Politics of Locke's Philosophy: A Social Study of "An Essay Concerning Human Understanding."* Berkeley and Los Angeles: University of California Press, 1983.

————. "The Economic Dimension of Cicero's Political Thought: Property and State." *Canadian Journal of Political Science* 16 (1983): 739–56.

————. *John Locke and Agrarian Capitalism.* Berkeley and Los Angeles: University of California Press, 1984.

————. "African Peasant Terrorism and Augustine's Political Thought." Pp. 279–99 in *History from Below: Studies in Popular Protest and Popular Ideology in Honour of George Rudé,* ed. Frederick Krantz. Montreal: Concordia University, 1985.

————. "*Populares* and *Circumcelliones:* The Vocabulary of 'Fallen Man' in Cicero and St. Augustine." *History of Political Thought* 7 (1986): 33–51.

Yavetz, Z. "The Living Conditions of the Urban Plebs in Republican Rome." *Latomus* 17 (1958): 500–517.

Zielinski, T. *Cicero im Wandel der Jahrhunderte.* Leipzig: Teubner, 1908.

Index

Academy: New, 47–48, 58–61; Old, 47

Acting ability, of politician. See Politics, as theater

Acton, J. E. E. D., first baron, 160

Adams, John, 4

Aediles: curule, 24, 25, 26, 222n.16; plebeian, 24, 27, 48, 49

Aerarium (state treasury, public finance), 24

Ager publicus (public land), 34, 35, 119, 202–3

Agrarian reforms, 34, 35–37, 50, 190, 194, 202–4

Agriculture, 16, 21, 117–19. *See also* Agrarian reforms; Peasants

Agrippa, 44

Ahala, Gaius Servilius, 190

Alexander of Pherae, 155

Alexander the Great, 73

Americans: Cicero's influence on, 4; constitution, 159; slavery among, 19

Amicitia, 28, 182–83, 199, 255n.31; Cicero's use of, 184; generosity in, 78; in mixed constitution, 170, 171; trust in, 136

Anacyclosis theory of Polybius, 153–55

Anaximander, 153

Antiochus of Ascalon, 47, 67

Antonius, C., 49

Antonius, Marcus, 43, 44, 149

Antony, Marc, 31, 43, 54, 195

Apollonius of Alabanda (Molo of Rhodes), 46, 47

Aquinas, Thomas, 74

Aratus, 43

Arcesilaus, 59

Archias, Aulus Licinius, 43, 56

Areopagus, 148

Aristides, 152

Aristocracy, 16–17, 18, 22–23, 28–29, 36, 37–41, 208–12, 213; and gentlemanly ideals, 104; individualism of, 28, 32–33, 115, 210, 211, 213, 223n.24; and justice, 76–78; in mixed constitution, 22, 27, 154, 159, 160, 161, 163, 166, 170, 171, 174, 175; *optimates* among, 44, 62–63, 163, 189, 194–98, 203; *populares* among (see *Populares*); and private property, 96, 106; and religion, 28, 173, 174; and social inequality, 91, 93–96, 97–100, 104, 233n.10 (*see also* Proportionate equality); and social reform, 36, 37, 211–12; tribunes established by, 171; as type of state (*optimatium*), 144, 145, 146–48, 153, 154, 159 (*see also* Oligarchy). *See also* Decurions; Equestrians; Gentlemen; Natural aristocracy; Senators; Warrior class

Aristotle, 1, 5, 10, 98; aristocratic prescriptions of, 104; Cicero's education in, 46; and conservatism, 206; and constitutions, 22, 153, 160; and

275

Self-interest (*continued*)
and private property, 114, 142; state and, 142
Self-preservation, natural, 74, 105, 111
Senate, 22–24, 27–28, 198; and Catiline conspiracy, 188; Cicero in, 49, 51, 94; in mixed constitution, 22, 163, 165, 166, 169–70, 174, 198, 211; *optimates* and, 195–96; in *senatus populusque Romanus*, 25, 96, 125; Sulla's reforms of, 23, 30, 39, 169
Senators, 16, 22–23, 28, 31–32, 38–40, 154, 211–12; Caesar backed by, 37; Cicero's early influences by, 44–45; equestrian interests converging with, 31–32, 39–40, 196, 198–99, 210. *See also* Senate
Senatus populusque Romanus (*S.P.Q.R.*), 25, 96, 125
Seneca, 2
Sensory data, Academic skeptics and, 59
Separation of powers, 159
Serapio, P. Cornelius Scipio, 190
Serranus, C. Atilius, 118
Sertorius, Quintus, 30
Servius Tullius, 146, 164, 165, 167
Sestius, Publius, 52, 62
Shackleton Bailey, D. R., 255n.24
Sheridan, Richard Brinsley, 3
Sibley, Mulford Q., 8
Sicily, Cicero's political positions in, 49, 134, 201
Sidney, Algernon, 3
Skepticism, 47, 48, 58–61, 73, 82
Slaves, 19–22, 35, 37; Cicero's attitudes toward, 11, 211, 230n.33, 233n.10; uprisings of, 35, 37; wars by, 30, 35, 37
Smith, Adam, 3, 217n.9
Smith, S. B., 8–9, 10, 219n.21
Smyrna, Cicero in, 47, 64
Social classes, 16–22, 38, 167, 199, 221n.4; mixed constitution and, 161, 167–68, 170. *See also* Aristocracy; Inequality, social; Peasants; Urban plebeians
Social reform, 36–37, 211–12; grain doles, 36, 37, 202; land distribution, 34, 35–37, 50, 190, 194, 202–4
Social War, 15, 29, 39, 46

Societas generis humani, 79
Societas hominum, 138–39, 140, 245n.71. *See also* Commonwealth of reason
Society, 207, 245n.71; Ciceronian, 14–42; state distinguished from, 11, 120, 125, 136–42. *See also* Inequality, social; *Mos maiorum*; Social classes; Social reform
Socrates, 75, 94, 121, 157
Solon, 143, 160
Soul, psyche, human, 83, 84, 85–86, 87–88
Sparta: mixed constitution in, 145, 164; Polybius on, 23; respect for aged in, 152
Spartacus, 30, 35, 37
Speech, divine faculty of, 81, 82
S.P.Q.R. (*senatus populusque Romanus*), 25, 96, 125
State, 29, 65–66, 68, 120–42, 206; *civitas* vs. *res publica*, 126, 244n.50; definition of, 11, 74, 123–28, 137; government distinguished from, 11, 120, 124–25, 128, 132–36; and justice, 74, 112, 126–27, 129, 140; and private property, 11, 68, 105, 112, 120, 125–26, 129–32, 135, 140–41, 200, 206, 244n.49; purpose of, 128–32, 207; religion and, 172, 179; security of, 128–29, 188, 189–91, 193, 199; society distinguished from, 11, 120, 125, 136–42; types of, 143–58, 159–60 (*see also* Constitutionalism). *See also* Law, civil; Politics
Statesman, ideal, 44, 122, 177–79, 182, 193–94
Statutory law, 72, 229n.6. *See also* Law, civil
Stilo, Aelius, 46
Stoicism, 58, 60, 65; Antiochus and, 47; commonwealth of reason of, 138; and decorum, 236n.51; Diodotus teaching, 45; ethics of, 48, 68–69, 85; and gods, 71; and human nature, 79, 83, 85, 86, 88, 113; and ideal statesman, 178; and individualism, 85, 88, 114–15, 239n.37; on mixed constitutions, 160; and moral equality, 11, 90; and natural justice, 11, 75, 113, 138; and natural law,

Compositor: Auto-Graphics, Inc.
Text: 10/12 Bembo
Display: Bembo
Printer: Braun-Brumfield, Inc.
Binder: Braun-Brumfield, Inc.